When Governments Break the Law

When Governments Break the Law

*The Rule of Law and the Prosecution
of the Bush Administration*

EDITED BY

Austin Sarat and Nasser Hussain

NEW YORK UNIVERSITY PRESS
New York and London

NEW YORK AND LONDON
www.nyupress.org

Library of Congress Cataloging-in-Publication Data

When governments break the law : the rule of law and the prosecution of
the Bush administration / edited by Austin Sarat and Nasser Hussain.
p. cm.
Includes bibliographical references and index.
ISBN-13: 978-0-8147-4139-9 (cl : alk. paper)
ISBN-10: 0-8147-4139-8 (cl : alk. paper)
ISBN-13: 978-0-8147-3985-3 (pb : alk. paper)
ISBN-10: 0-8147-3985-7 (pb : alk. paper)
[etc.]
1. War on Terrorism, 2001–2009. 2. Rule of law. 3. Administrative responsibility.
4. International offenses. 5. United States—Politics and government—2001-2009.
6. Terrorism—Prevention—Law and legislation—United States. I. Sarat, Austin.
II. Hussain, Nasser, 1965-
KZ6795.T47W48   2010
340'.115—dc22   2010015386

New York University Press books are printed on acid-free paper,
and their binding materials are chosen for strength and durability.
We strive to use environmentally responsible suppliers and materials
to the greatest extent possible in publishing our books.

Manufactured in the United States of America
c   10 9 8 7 6 5 4 3 2 1
p   10 9 8 7 6 5 4 3 2 1

To my son Ben, with love and pride (A.S.)
To William (N.H.)

Contents

Acknowledgments

We gratefully acknowledge financial support from the Corliss Lamont Fund at Amherst College. We would like to thank Megan Estes and Samia Hesni for their help. We also want to thank our colleagues in Amherst's Department of Law, Jurisprudence, and Social Thought for helping to create such a congenial and stimulating intellectual environment. Last, we want to say publicly how much we value the chance to work with each other. This is our second book project, and we look forward to doing others in the future.

Introduction

Responding to Government Lawlessness:
What Does the Rule of Law Require?

NASSER HUSSAIN AND AUSTIN SARAT

Decency, security, and liberty alike demand that government officials shall be subjected to the same rules of conduct that are commands to the citizen. The government is the potent omnipresent teacher. For good or ill it teaches the whole people by its example. Crime is contagious. If the government becomes a lawbreaker, it breeds contempt for law; it invites every man to become a law unto himself; it invites anarchy.
> —Justice Louis Brandeis, *Olmstead v. United States,*
> 277 US 438, 485 (1928)

Accountability is the first step toward deterrence. With criminal offenses like this, it is necessary to send a clear message: No one is above the law, no matter their intentions. The security of any country can only exist within the rule of law. The war on terror is no exception.
> —Gonzalo Boyé, Spanish lawyer working to indict
> members of the Bush Administration,
> interview with *Mother Jones Magazine* (2009)

Today, as in the past, Americans pride themselves on their commitment to the rule of law.[1] This commitment is deeply rooted in America's history, or so the story goes, and it has been renewed from one generation to the next. From Tocqueville's observation that "the spirit of the laws which is produced in the schools and courts of justice, gradually permeates . . . into the bosom of society"[2] to the present, numerous commentators have said that America has the "principled character . . . of a Nation of people who aspire to live according to the rule of law."[3]

Invocations of the rule of law as a constitutive boundary separating this country from the rest of the world are pervasive.[4] Thus Ronald Cass, former dean of the Boston University Law School, observes that the commitment to the rule of law is "central to our national self-definition. . . . For most of the world . . . the nation most immediately associated with the rule of law—is the United States of America. The story of America . . . is uniquely the story of law."[5] The philosopher Michael Oakeshott suggests that "[t]he rule of law is the single greatest condition of our freedom, removing from us that great fear which has overshadowed so many communities, the fear of the power of our own government."[6] Similarly, former Secretary of Housing and Urban Development Henry Cisneros argues that "the fundamental identity of the U.S. is not an identity based on how people look, what language they learnt first or over how many generations they absorbed Anglo-Protestant values. Rather it is based upon acceptance of the rule of law."[7]

Recent controversies surrounding the war on terror and American intervention in Iraq and Afghanistan have brought rule of law rhetoric to a fevered pitch, with public officials and commentators uncritically linking it to America's boundary-marking values and arguments about America's distinctiveness. Typical was the statement of Jonathan Lippman, Chief Administrative Judge of the State of New York, who said, "The rule of law is what separates us from those who seek to defeat our democratic institutions and way of life through violence and terror."[8] Commenting on the scandal at Abu Ghraib, former Defense Secretary William Cohen argued, "The strength of this country is its insistence that we adhere to the rule of law."[9] A particularly bellicose version of such arguments took the following form: "The rule of law separates civilized societies from despotic societies. Unlike Iraq, the United States is a nation of laws, not men. . . . Yet if we blatantly violate the Constitution by pursuing an undeclared war, we violate the rule of law."[10]

Similar invocations of the rule of law have framed the ongoing debate about prosecuting Bush Administration officials with regard to domestic surveillance, authorizing the use of torture, and falsifying the case for going to war. Thus Elaine Scarry argues that, "If the country is to renew its commitment to the rule of law, that outcome will require reeducating ourselves about what the law is. The law aspires to symmetry across cases. . . . The international rules against war crimes and torture do not allow prosecution to be thought of as discretionary; they do not allow an escape provision based on electoral euphoria or on one's doubts about one's own stamina in fighting injustice. . . . So too the Convention against Torture requires that states 'submit' cases to the 'competent authorities for the purposes of prosecution.' This means . . . that where persons under color of law commit acts of torture in a country that is a party to the Torture Convention, the Convention requires prosecution."[11] Or, as the writer Glenn Greenwald puts it, "There is simply no way to (a) argue against investigation and prosecutions for Bush officials and simultaneously (b) claim with a straight face to believe in the rule of law, that no one is above the law, and that the U.S. should adhere to the same rules and values it attempts to impose on the rest of the world."[12]

More urgently, some worry that without legal consequences there will be no effective deterrence for the repetition of such acts in the future.[13] Michael Ratner, President of the Center for Constitutional Rights, insists that "only prosecutions can draw the clear, bright line that is necessary to insure that this will never happen again."[14] For Ratner and others,[15] putting the past behind us means leaving the historical record muddied, acquiescing in criminal wrongdoing, and turning the rule of law into an empty slogan.

Yet while President Obama has repeatedly emphasized his administration's commitment to transparency and the rule of law, nowhere has this resolve been so quickly and severely tested than with the issue of the possible prosecution of Bush Administration officials. Before his inauguration, Obama asserted his "belief that we need to look forward as opposed to looking backwards."[16] Since then, the president has seemed unenthusiastic about the prospect of launching an investigation into allegations of criminal wrongdoing by former President Bush, Vice President Cheney, Secretary Rumsfeld, members of the Office of Legal Counsel, and so on.[17]

Even some critics of the Bush Administration agree with Obama that we should avoid such confrontations, that the price of political division and of a bitter fight that could cripple Obama's ability to achieve his priorities is too high.[18] They also argue that the previous administration acted in the perilous context of a devastating attack and a new and confounding war and enemy.[19]

New York Times columnist Thomas Friedman's op-ed piece, "A Torturous Compromise" provides one example of this kind of argument.[20] Friedman observes that President Obama's decision to renounce torture, open up previous aspects of the program to public scrutiny, and yet reassure the lawyers and interrogators connected with the program of his intention not to pursue prosecutions is a justifiable compromise. This is because, according to Friedman, any prosecution down the chain, "taken to its logical end here would likely require bringing George W. Bush, Donald Rumsfeld and other senior officials to trial, which would rip our country apart." To proponents of prosecution, of course, that would be the point of proceeding; even so Friedman alerts us to the difficulty of fashioning a narrow inquiry, and to how complex and far-ranging such an effort could quickly become.

But Friedman's main objection to prosecutions involves what he sees as a ruthless and murderous enemy, "undeterred by normal means." Friedman here mixes familiar claims that emergencies require exceptions to the usual rules (an argument we will take up later) with a specific claim about the war on terror. "So, yes," he admits, "people among us who went over the line may go unpunished, because we still have enemies who respect no lines at all. In such an ugly war, you do your best."

The controversy surrounding the question of prosecution was vividly exemplified when Attorney General Eric Holder tasked a career prosecutor to investigate alleged CIA interrogation abuses, including episodes that resulted in prisoner deaths. Indeed Holder himself noted, "I fully realize that my decision to commence this preliminary review will be controversial." However, he claimed that "As Attorney General, my duty is to examine the facts and to follow the law. In this case, given all of the information currently available, it is clear to me that this review is the only responsible course of action for me to take."[21]

Measured or partisan, scholarly or journalistic, clearly the debate about accountability for the alleged crimes of the Bush Administration will continue for some time. [22] This book enters this debate not to advocate a single position on prosecution—our contributors take distinct positions for and against the proposition, offering revealing reasons and illuminating alternatives—but rather to use the debate as a prompt, as an invitation of sorts, to figure out what the commitment to a rule of law demands when governments break the law. The focus of our book, therefore, is not the substantive question of whether any Bush Administration officials, in fact, violated the law, but rather the procedural, legal, political, and cultural questions of what it would mean either to pursue criminal prosecutions or to refuse to do so. In short, by presuming that officials *could* be prosecuted, we ask, *should* they be prosecuted?[23] By phrasing the demands of a rule of law as a question we hope to highlight the capacious nature of that concept,[24] and the fact that the demands of a rule of law in the case of political crimes are not self-evident.[25]

In what follows we summarize the principal charges against the Bush Administration and review factors that illuminate the question of how we should respond when governments break the law. We take up the meaning of a rule of law, the role of emergency, the relation of a rule of law to international law, and finally the lessons of transitional justice.

The Charges

Numerous and varied charges have been leveled against the Bush Administration. While some are uncorroborated, many others have been corroborated and confirmed. They have been public for some time, yet important details, such as the vice president's possibly illegal concealment of a secret assassination program from Congress, have surfaced more recently.[26] For the sake of clarity we divide the charges into three categories: unauthorized domestic surveillance; misrepresenting to Congress and the American people the case for going to war in Iraq; and the use of torture. While we address each in turn, we will not provide a comprehensive summary of each charge, for to do so would take us beyond the scope of this essay and also duplicate much existing scholarly and journalistic literature. We briefly survey each charge, paying attention to the particular laws under which an indictment might be fashioned and the contingent circumstances in each case that would effect choosing to move forward or not. We base our summary, wherever possible, on investigative reports by various agencies of the U.S. government, from congressional committees to reports of inspectors general.

Unauthorized Domestic Surveillance

On December 16, 2005, the *New York Times* published a story about a decision by President Bush, following the attacks of 9/11, to ask the NSA to eavesdrop on Americans and others inside the United States, bypassing the existing procedure for obtaining warrants for such activity.[27] Those procedures, stipulated by the 1978 Foreign Intelligence Surveillance Act or FISA, "provide legislative authorization and regulation for all electronic surveillance conducted within the United States for foreign intelligence purposes."[28]

The Act requires that a special court issue a warrant for any surveillance of communications for foreign intelligence purposes, permitting only court-authorized surveillance of American citizens if they are shown to be agents of a foreign power. While the proceedings of the Court are classified, we know that the Court has issued warrants in nearly all instances in which they were requested. Nonetheless, as the *Times* reported, the Bush Administration decided to bypass FISA, citing gaps in the law and delays in the system. Since the publication of the initial story there have been numerous investigations, culminating in a single comprehensive report by the inspectors general of the Department of Defense, Department of Justice, the CIA, the National Security Agency, and the Office of the Director of National Intelligence.

The Report traces the inception of the program, initially referred to by the Bush Administration as the Terrorist Surveillance Program (TSP), but now simply called the President's Surveillance Program (PSP), to the months following 9/11. According to the Report, after 9/11 the NSA was pushed to produce more surveillance and information. NSA director Michael Hayden told the White House that "nothing more could be done within existing authorities" but that with additional authorization he could produce more information.[29] Soon after, the president gave the go-ahead for the NSA to initiate new (still highly classified) activities under a single Presidential Authorization, which was renewed every forty-five days based on "scary" memos produced by the CIA outlining the continuing terrorist threat and the need for additional surveillance. According to the Report, "[S]everal different intelligence activities were authorized in Presidential Authorizations, and the details of these activities changed over time."[30]

The program was given legal cover by a November 2, 2001 memorandum prepared by John Yoo in the Justice Department's Office of Legal Counsel, without the supervision or even knowledge of his immediate supervisor, Jay Bybee, a fact that left Bybee "surprised" and "a little disappointed."[31] The Report offers a sum and substance of the classified memo, in which Yoo argued that while FISA purported to be the exclusive mechanism for conducting surveillance for foreign intelligence, "such a reading of FISA would be an unconstitutional infringement on the President's Article II authorities."[32] Ignoring a section of FISA that explicitly deals with wartime situations and created a fifteen-day exemption for obtaining warrants, Yoo argued that FISA did not mention or concern the president's national security obligations as Commander-in-Chief.

Based on this memo alone, Attorney General Ashcroft certified the "legality" of the President's Surveillance Program. Yet the Report suggests that the need for the Justice Department's blessing was, in the words of Alberto Gonzales, who became attorney general after Ashcroft, "purely political," as it would provide value "prospectively" in the event of a future investigation.[33] Providing cover for a criminal act through a transparently false legal rationale does not, so the argument goes, immunize participants in that act. Indeed, some might argue that it evidences the kind of culpable intent necessary to prove criminal conspiracy.

While the inspectors general avoid calling either this threadbare legal justification, or the surveillance program itself, illegal, they make clear that many others certainly found them to be of questionable legality. Indeed, in March 2004 Yoo's successors at the OLC, Patrick Philbin and Jack Goldsmith (and Acting Attorney General Comey) refused to reauthorize the program based on Yoo's reasoning, forcing a showdown between the vice president's office and the Justice Department.[34] When the White House suggested that the program continue without DOJ authorization, a number of officials, including FBI Director Mueller, threatened to resign.

The dénouement to this story of warrantless wiretapping came in July 2008, when Congress (with a yes vote from then-Senator and presidential candidate Barack Obama) passed the FISA Amendment Act. The Act allows the attorney general in concert with the director of national intelligence to authorize surveillance programs for up to one year. The Act also allows for emergency surveillance without a warrant for seven days, after which, if a warrant is not granted, the government may still continue the surveillance during the appeals process and retain the information it gathers. Finally, the FISA Amendment Act retroactively immunizes from liability communications service providers who participated in the original program—a signal that even if the original program was illegal, there is little interest in prosecuting those involved.

This last fact has direct implications for our discussion of the demands of the rule of law. On the one hand, the rule of law does not prohibit Congress from retroactively immunizing such a program; on the other hand, to the extent that specific officials have *not* been immunized by Congress, the question remains: is proceeding with further investigations and prosecutions for violating FISA still in order?

The Case for War with Iraq

By now the broad outlines of the various misrepresentations in the case for war with Iraq are well known. By all accounts, the Bush Administration was fixated on Iraq even before 9/11, but that event provided new impetus for their desire to take action. Their case for war depended ultimately on two claims which, when put together, would paint a scenario of a devastating and imminent threat: the first was that Saddam Hussein had, or was acquiring, weapons of mass destruction, including nuclear weapons, and the second was that Hussein had contacts with al-Qaida to whom he would potentially hand over these weapons for use in new and catastrophic attacks. We now know, of course, that both these claims were false. What constitutes the crux of the debate now, and what would be the main focus of any future investigation or prosecution, is whether the administration made a mistake based on faulty intelligence or knowingly distorted or fabricated intelligence findings in order to support its own position.

Over time information supporting the conclusion that intelligence was distorted has been trickling out. For example, in 2006 Michael Isikoff and David Corn published *Hubris*, an exhaustive account of one of the central claims in the lead-up to the Iraq war: the alleged sale by Niger of yellowcake uranium (a key ingredient in the making of nuclear weapons) to Saddam Hussein.[35] Their book details how the claim was based on a file of documents acquired in 2002 by an operative in Italy. When Simon Dodge of the State Department reviewed the documents, he quickly declared them to be a hoax. That was not, however, the end of the story. As Isikoff and Corn explain it, partly by accident but also somewhat willfully (again the blurring of distortion and outright deception), the White House uncritically used the documents, enabling President Bush to say in his 2003 State of the Union address that Iraq was in the process of acquiring uranium to build nuclear weapons.

There have been many other accounts of this kind, but surely the most systematic and comprehensive is the Senate Intelligence Committee's June 2008 "Report on Whether Public Statements Regarding Iraq By U.S. Government Officials Were Substantiated By Intelligence Information."[36] The result of a multiyear investigation, it chronicles a consistent gap between the Bush Administration's statements on Iraq and the then-existing intelligence. Thus, on the question of Iraq's acquisition of nuclear materials and capabilities, the Report describes several policy speeches by the president and vice president in which they made unequivocal claims that Iraq had restarted its nuclear program. In one speech in Cincinnati on October 7, 2002, President Bush claimed that Iraq had purchased aluminum tubes needed for the construction of centrifuges, and was "moving ever closer to developing a nuclear weapon."[37] This was, in fact, a clear distortion of the intelligence estimates. The Report notes that there was a split in the intelligence community (principally it seems between the State Department's Bureau of Intelligence and Research and the CIA) over not just the particular purpose of the tubes, but also the general conclusion that Iraq had restarted its nuclear program. Some of this disagreement was recorded in the October 2002 National Intelligence Estimate. Yet none of it made it into any of the administration's speeches. The Report goes on for dozens of pages with similar exercises, the cumulative effect of which is to reveal a consistent pattern of distortion and deception around the two main arguments that shaped the push for war: Iraq's acquisition of WMDs and its association with al-Qaida.

What, however, is the crime here? The president lying to Congress is certainly a deeply corrosive element in any constitutional democracy; it is, however, an impeachable offense, not a crime, for which the Constitution lays down detailed and specific procedures. However, the attorney and author Vincent Bugliosi argues that the crime with which President Bush could and, in his view, should, be charged is conspiracy to commit murder. Bugliosi proposes that jurisdiction for such prosecution might be lodged in any state from which at least one serviceman has died.[38]

The Minority Report, written by the Republicans on the Senate Intelligence Committee, raises some equally disturbing questions about Congress's own lapses and rush to judgment, lapses which in the view of some commentators would doom any effort to prosecute Bush Administration officials.[39] Thus, staying with the same example of the October 2002 NIE and claims made around that time about Iraq's nuclear ambitions, the Republicans point out that numerous Democratic senators with access to the NIE, including senators Clinton, Schumer, Edwards, and Kerry, made equally forceful warnings about Iraq's nuclear program in October 2002. In short, the Minority Report accuses the Democrats of "seeking cover."[40]

Of course, this may just be partisan bickering, but we believe that it is important for two reasons. First, it points to a complete absence of any bipartisan support for an investigation or prosecution for misrepresentations in the run-up to the war. Second, and we think more importantly, the partisan flavor of the Minority Report reminds us of the important fact that Congress was a willing partner in the Bush Administration's war effort. Individual senators may now claim that they were misled, but they did little to initiate any of their own investigations or to make any effort to slow down the rush to war.

The war efforts of modern governments are large scale and involve multiple political actors, complicating the legal case against the president alone. The trial at Nuremberg certainly highlights this fact, even as it involved a case of criminal conspiracy for crimes against peace by the leaders of the German Reich. While there may be a seductive simplicity in focusing responsibility on President Bush—such as Bugliosi's call for indicting the president for conspiracy to commit murder—that approach raises legitimate questions. Thus in a response to Bugliosi, Professor Carl Boggs asks, "[W]hy limit criminal indictments to Bush alone when the trail of culpability is so lengthy?"[41]

Torture

Of all the charges against the Bush Administration, the charge of torture has gained the most traction, bringing inchoate moral, legal, and political objections into sharp focus. In some ways this is not surprising. Descriptions of torture and abuse, and even more so perhaps photographs, such as the pictures from Abu Ghraib, provoke deep moral revulsion.[42] Moreover, as Scarry noted, torture is a domestic and international crime, for which there are no exceptions for wartime or for national security. The Convention against Torture and Other Cruel, Inhuman or Degrading Treatment or Punishment stipulates that no exceptional circumstances whatsoever may be invoked as a justification for torture (Article 2); creates a universal jurisdiction by treating offenses "as if they had been committed not only in the place in which they occurred but also in the territories of states required to establish their jurisdiction" (Article 8); and demands that states incorporate the Convention into their domestic criminal law (Article 4).[43] In accordance with the demands of Article 4, the United States prohibits torture in domestic law.[44]

Given what we already know about practices such as waterboarding, there is also a pragmatic dimension to the focus on torture. Attorney Scott Horton accurately notes, "In weighing the enormity of the administration's transgressions against the realistic prospect of justice, it is possible to determine not only the crime that calls most clearly for prosecution but also the crime that is most likely to be successfully prosecuted. In both cases, that crime is torture."[45]

There is by now a large literature on the use of torture or "enhanced interrogations," including a substantial investigative report by the Senate's Armed Services Committee.[46] After 9/11, a number of administration officials believed that preventing another attack depended upon gathering information from "high value" detainees. This conclusion would not by itself have led to the interrogation practices we now know so much about but for the fact that the president had declared that the Geneva Conventions did not apply to the detainees, coupled with Vice President Cheney and Secretary of Defense Donald Rumsfeld's belief, in stark disagreement with veteran FBI interrogators, that only a "gloves off" approach would produce needed information.[47] In fact, even before the president's decision not to apply Geneva to the detainees, the Department of Defense General Counsel's office had approached the Joint Personal Recovery Agency (JPRA), which is responsible for overseeing the SERE (Survival Evasion Resistance and Escape) training program for captured U.S. servicemen. In effect, what JPRA produced was a "reverse engineering" of SERE's tactics, which included sleep deprivation, stress positions, exposure to extreme temperatures, and waterboarding.

Just as questionable as the provenance of the new interrogation tactics used on detainees was the legal reasoning produced to justify them. Once the decision was made to "enhance" interrogations, lawyers at the Department of Defense and the Office of Legal Counsel in the Department of Justice went to work. The main policy memo, innocuously titled "Counter Resistance Techniques," was drafted by William Haynes, General Counsel to Donald Rumsfeld, and signed by the latter on December 2, 2002.[48]

Even before that memo, however, a series of memos were written by members of the Office of Legal Counsel. In particular, Jay Bybee's August 2002 memo manipulates the definition of torture beyond recognition.[49] Bybee argues that only something akin to "organ failure" would violate the injunction against severe physical pain; severe mental pain, he argues, should not be read as meaning mental suffering imposed at the moment but "significant psychological harm of significant duration, e.g. lasting for months or even years."[50] Even more explicit legal cover came later with John Yoo's March 14, 2003 memo arguing that criminal laws such as the federal torture statute would not apply to military interrogations.[51]

The role of the OLC lawyers and their legal memoranda represents a particularly vexing aspect of the debate on prosecutions.[52] While many other legal experts, including lawyers who came later to the Office of Legal Counsel, repudiated the reasoning of these opinions, it is still a large step from regarding these memos as examples of egregious legal thought (perhaps even warranting professional sanctions such as disbarment) to treating them as evidence of complicity in war crimes.[53]

The British lawyer Phillipe Sands takes up these questions in his book *Torture Team*, a careful reconstruction of the trail from the memos of Yoo and Bybee to the interrogation procedures drafted by Haynes and signed by Rumsfeld.[54] Mindful of the difficulty of trying to assign criminal guilt to professional lawyers, Sands notes that there is only one real precedent for such an action—the Altsttoter case (also known as the Justices case) at Nuremberg that found "legal advisors who prepare legal advice that is so erroneous as to give rise to an international crime are themselves subject to the rules of international criminality."[55] Sands's ultimate conclusion is that the OLC lawyers bear "direct responsibility" for policies that led to violations of the Geneva Convention.

Read together, various official reports offer a seemingly exhaustive catalog of questionable practices and possible legal violations throughout the Bush Administration. The sheer scope of these reports—the Senate reports on the case for war and on interrogation are multiyear, multivolume efforts—makes clear that legal violations were neither isolated nor confined to a couple of individuals. As Scott Horton puts it, "[T]he administration did more than commit crimes. It waged war against the law itself."[56]

Horton's argument leads to the sobering realization that the case for prosecutions will have to be made with care, for the "very breadth and audacity of the administration's activities would make the process so complex as to defy systems of justice far less fragmented than our own."[57] Horton advocates a two-part solution, beginning with an independent investigation, followed by prosecutions. Moreover, he warns that any effort to fashion a narrow prosecution by focusing on a deputy in the Office of Legal Counsel or a few CIA operatives will be both legally difficult and normatively suspect.

With regard to those who call for investigations instead of prosecutions,[58] the scope of these reports seems already to have fulfilled that need. There is already sufficient knowledge, some would argue, for a prosecutor to be appointed, and calling for further investigations could only be seen as a way to delay and deflect. On the other hand, these reports equally make clear that the record is not complete, or at least not as complete as it would be with a commission set up with full subpoena powers. The Inspector General's Report on the President's Surveillance Program notes that key players, such as John Yoo, then White House Chief of Staff, Andrew Card, and Cheney's legal counsel and Chief of Staff, David Addington, refused requests for interviews.[59] Thus, even a cursory review of the charges reveals that the decision to prosecute or not is not an easy one, and requires a fuller consideration of the claims of law and justice, peace and security, memory and accountability. It is to these considerations that we now turn.

Does the Rule of Law Require Prosecution?

References to the rule of law point toward a set of related concepts summarized in the idea that, as Ronald Cass puts it, "[S]omething other than the mere will of the individual deputized to exercise government powers must have primacy."[60] Cass identifies several core ideas that compose the rule of law. The first, "fidelity to rules," is that "rules tell officials how, to what ends, and within what limits they may exercise power,"[61] or that "government in all its actions is bound by rules fixed and announced beforehand," such that the rule of law makes possible a "principled predictability" in the actions of government.[62] Where rules govern, they must emanate from "valid authority"[63] and impose meaningful constraints on officials.[64]

Friedrich Hayek, an Austrian and British economist and philosopher, argues that the rule of law should not be confused with any specific content of law but is only meant to convey the more narrow sense of rules "applicable to all manner of persons."[65] Similarly, Justice Antonin Scalia says that the rule of law is a "law of rules."[66] For others, however, the rule of law is more than a collection of rules; it embodies an expansive normative vision that also includes ideals of individual freedom and of government without arbitrary discretion.[67]

One of the earliest and most enduring modern expositions of a rule of law was provided by the nineteenth-century English constitutionalist, Albert Venn Dicey. His monumental *Introduction to the Study of the Law of the Constitution* focused on a couple of key features. First, that "everyman was subject to ordinary law administered by ordinary tribunals," and second, that law rather than individual discretion reigned supreme in guiding official decisions.[68] In Dicey's hands, the rule of law appears as both an institutional structure and a normative vision.

As the concept has gained global currency, this dual emphasis has only been strengthened. In "The Rule of Law and Its Virtues," Joseph Raz points to a 1959 statement by the International Congress of Jurists declaring that the purpose of a rule of law "is to create and maintain the conditions which will uphold the dignity of man as an individual."[69] Raz goes on to assert that given the multiple meanings associated with the rule of law, "we have now reached the stage in which no purist can claim truth on his side."[70]

The concept of a rule of law is a capacious one, made up of multiple and sometimes even conflicting norms and values. Even when faced with the more quotidian operations of the criminal justice system, the law cannot avoid interest balancing.[71] While the rule of law requires adherence to legal norms, officials must sometimes contend with competing norms, such as balancing fairness with finality;[72] while the rule of law favors fixed rules over discretion, nonetheless discretion pervades the system, from prosecutors deciding on indictments to judges deciding on punishments;[73] finally, for any system to function, it will have to embrace the reality of less than full enforcement.[74]

Focusing specifically on the question of prosecution for ordinary crimes, the recognition of discretion is not new. Then-Attorney General Robert Jackson might have been exaggerating when he said, in 1940, that the "prosecutor has more power over life, liberty, and reputation than any other person in America,"[75] but he was certainly correct in observing, simply and matter-of-factly, that "[h]is discretion is tremendous."[76] In the more than sixty years since Jackson spoke these words to a group of federal prosecutors, little has changed.[77]

Today it is widely recognized in both the academic literature and the mainstream media that prosecutors have substantial discretion. Some suggest that prosecutors are granted "considerable latitude in devising and executing . . . [their] own enforcement strategies" out of respect for the separation of powers.[78] For others, discretion is a part of the prosecutor's responsibility to "seek justice."[79] Still others see discretion as a necessary consequence of legal imprecision: "Gaps in rules" create the need for someone to exercise discretionary power.[80] Finally, some argue that prosecutorial discretion is a dangerously tyrannical power that must be contained. For this group, discretion is a threat to justice, fairness, and the rule of law.[81]

And, of course, the issue of discretion and the impulse to engage in interest balancing become even more urgent and controversial in periods of political uncertainty and in cases of political crimes. While prosecutions of "normal crimes" can serve a range of purposes from retribution to deterrence, prosecutions for political crimes may involve a different calculus. There the importance of accounting for the past, how the alleged crime came about, and what could be done to prevent its recurrence, may take precedence over individual retribution.

On the Logic of Emergency

All theories of a rule of law acknowledge the periodic need during times of emergency for rights and rules to be suspended and for the powers of the government to be correspondingly enlarged. The maxim *salus populi suprema lex* (the safety of the people is the supreme law) has been a constant guiding principle in moments of crisis and danger. From Locke's *Second Treatise* where he defines executive prerogative as the "power to act according to discretion, for the publick good, without the prescription of law and sometimes even against it," to the so-called "derogation" provisions of the various United Nations covenants on human rights,[82] allowance for such moments is found in all conceptions of lawful and legitimate rule.

While the need for emergency powers is universally acknowledged, the questions of who shall exercise these powers, under what conditions of review, and through what procedures, remain deeply vexing ones. Both the need for such powers and their inherently dangerous and corrosive potential were succinctly caught in C.L. Rossiter's 1948 study of comparative emergency powers in France, Germany, Britain, and the United States, with the trenchant and, by Rossiter's own admission, "disturbing" title, *Constitutional Dictatorship*.[83]

Rossiter discusses a range of possible procedures for invoking emergency powers, from the express provisions for suspension in the French "state of siege" to the more implicit assumptions of power according to necessity that guide the Anglo-American common law tradition. With regard to the United States, while Article 1, Section 9 of the Constitution permits the suspension of habeas corpus by Congress when "in Cases of Rebellion or Invasion the public Safety may require it," in fact, emergency rule has almost always meant increased powers for the president. This is, as Rossiter explains, made possible not only because in most countries the response to an emergency is fundamentally the province of the executive, but also more specifically because of "the broad and flexible grants of power to the President found in the Constitution."[84] Thus, under the so-called "plenary Article II powers" theory, so often invoked by the Bush Administration, the president's position as Commander in Chief entails the grant of large and unspecific powers considered necessary to fulfill those functions.

And history has only confirmed this constitutional design. Regardless of one's position on the mythology surrounding Lincoln, there is no denying the breathtaking sweep of executive powers he assumed and exercised during the Civil War. From enlarging the army and navy to drawing money from the treasury and suspending habeas corpus, Lincoln undertook a series of actions expressly reserved for the legislative branch in the Constitution. He simply disregarded Chief Justice Taney's decision denying the president's claimed authority to suspend habeas corpus in the circuit court case of *Ex parte Merryman*. After its return, Congress, faced with a fait accompli, could only register its retroactive approval of the proclamations and orders of the president.[85]

Presidential powers have amplified since the start of the twentieth century.[86] The Cold War and the growth of what Harold Koh calls the "national security constitution" contributed to the "imperial presidency."[87] From C. Wright Mills's 1950s classic, *The Power Elite*[88] to the present, scholars have noted that presidential power has grown exponentially in the movement from World War II to the Cold War to the war on terror.[89] And in times of crisis, especially of threats from abroad, presidential popularity spikes as the public rallies round the flag.[90]

There have, of course, been countervailing forces at work as well. In the now famous 1952 case of *Youngstown Co. v. Sawyer* (commonly referred to as the Steel Seizure case), the Supreme Court limited President Truman's power to seize private property under the guise of war needs.[91] Justice Jackson's concurring opinion is still used as the benchmark for understanding presidential powers and the role of Congress. Jackson refused to draw any sharp boundary between congressional and presidential powers.[92] Instead, he offered three categories in order of legitimacy. The first category, in which presidential power was strongest, was when the president acted in concert with either the expressed or implied will of Congress; the second was made up of cases in which Congress was silent; and the final category, where the president's power was at its "lowest ebb," was when the president acted in defiance of congressional will.

Attorney General Holder has often invoked this tripartite scheme, asserting, for example, that in the case of wire tapping, Congress's passage of the FISA Amendment Act allows the president to act from a position of strength.[93] Some conservatives, however, have criticized the invocation of Jackson, noting that not only does the opinion oversimplify the problem, but even Jackson understood that the "lowest ebb" was not an illegality.[94] Throughout this debate, however, what is clear is that in the American rule of law, emergency powers are flexible at best and amorphous at worst. As a result, any effort to criminalize presidential actions with regard to an emergency situation will be a difficult one.

This does not mean, of course, that presidents have unlimited powers in emergency situations, that, as Richard Nixon once remarked (and Vice President Cheney recently reaffirmed), "when the President does it, that means it is not illegal."[95] In the aftermath of 9/11, the Supreme Court has on numerous occasions pushed back, holding in *Hamdi v. Rumsfeld* that the president does not have the right to hold a citizen indefinitely as an enemy combatant;[96] granting in *Boumediene v. Bush*, the right of habeas corpus to alien detainees;[97] and striking down in *Hamdan v. Rumsfeld*, the president's military commission scheme which was initially constructed without congressional authorization.[98] One could conceivably argue that these cases themselves provide evidence of a functioning rule of law, requiring no further congressional or criminal sanctions. Yet it is important to keep in mind that there have been no cases involving the most contentious accusations of torture and abuse. This leaves open the question of whether there is a way to accommodate the clearest excesses of the administration under the logic of emergency.

As we have already noted, international law recognizes no national security exception to Common Article 3 of the Geneva Conventions or to the Torture Convention. That still leaves open the question of domestic law on not just detainee abuse but also on unauthorized surveillance. If illegalities occurred in order to avert imminent harm, Congress can always grant immunity from prosecution and/or the president can use his pardon power.

This is one option Oren Gross believes might be used to reconcile the demands of the rule of law and the exigencies of an emergency. Gross calls his model "the extra-legal measure" model, one in which due recognition is given to the sometimes overwhelming demands of safety while the bright line of inviolable rules is left intact.[99] He imagines a scenario where public officials and functionaries break the law but then plead the defense of necessity either directly to the public or to a court of law. While Gross offers an ingenious solution to reconciling the existence of rules and the demands of necessity, it is important to note that a theory such as his depends upon an *admission* of the violation of rules and only then the further defense of *mitigation*. The situation with the Bush Administration is, however, entirely to the contrary: the administration claimed that no rules were broken, that what was done was both necessary *and* legally correct.

On the Claims and Requirements of International Law

While classic rule of law theories focus on the domestic structure of legality, at least since the end of World War II, a state's robust commitment to the rule of law includes its respect for international law, for multilateral institutions, and for human rights, concretely codified in treaty obligations. The interplay between domestic and international law is a dynamic one, with norms sometimes coinciding and sometimes colliding. The United States has, for example, accommodated international differences over the death penalty by stipulating a Reservation to the International Convention on Civil and Political Rights, whereby "the United States reserves the right, subject to its Constitutional constraints, to impose capital punishment on any person (other than a pregnant woman) duly convicted under existing or future laws permitting the imposition of capital punishment, including such punishment for crimes committed by persons below eighteen years of age."[100] An even more pertinent example is the United States's reservation to its ratification of the torture convention:

> The Senate's advice and consent is subject to the following reservations:
> (1) That the United States considers itself bound by the obligation under Article 16 to prevent "cruel, inhuman or degrading treatment or punishment," only insofar as the term "cruel, inhuman or degrading treatment or punishment" means the cruel, unusual and inhumane treatment or punishment prohibited by the Fifth, Eighth, and/or Fourteenth Amendments to the Constitution of the United States.[101]

Some claim that such reservations do not in and of themselves pose a challenge to the rule of law. As Jeremy Waldron notes, in the case of "a state indicating that it prefers to be bound by the human rights constraints contained in its own constitution rather than by those contained in an international instrument—there is nothing incompatible with the rule of law in that."[102] One may argue that Waldron moves too quickly over norm discrepancies and their consequences, but his main argument is that there is a large difference between arguing over whether domestic or international law has priority in placing constraints on state power and arguing that in the international realm the state should *be free from constraint* altogether. Skeptics of the role of international law tend to confuse the first argument with the second.

Skepticism about the binding quality of international law on the domestic rule of law sometimes makes reference to so-called "American exceptionalism." According to Michael Ignatieff, the argument about American exceptionalism takes three specific forms: exemptions, whereby the United States either utilizes reservations to treaties or refuses to participate in institutions such as the International Criminal Court; double standards, whereby other countries are held accountable in a way that the United States itself is not; and finally, the denial of jurisdiction to human rights laws within U.S. domestic laws.[103] Given a robust domestic culture of rights and even a history of liberal internationalism (one thinks of Woodrow Wilson's Fourteen Points), Ignatieff stresses that for the United States, "what needs explaining is the paradox of being simultaneously a leader and an outlier."[104]

Most explanations of American exceptionalism tend to focus on institutional and political factors. The iconic, if not mythic, status of the Constitution, coupled with a strong tradition of judicial review, produce a suspicion of outside influences. Moreover, just as a matter of institutional design, ratification of treaties requires a two-thirds vote in the Senate, a higher hurdle than in other democracies.[105] Finally, the rise to prominence of conservatism in the last few decades means that a program of liberal internationalism may have little "sustained electoral appeal among the American public."[106] For better or worse, the U.S. attitude toward international law and institutions has been, as Ignatieff correctly notes, "tied to the fortunes of American liberalism, and these fortunes have not fared well in the last thirty years."[107] What this means is that any decision to participate in or cooperate with an international investigation or tribunal in dealing with the alleged crimes of the Bush Administration will face significant domestic political opposition.

There is also, of course, a realist explanation for American exceptionalism, or indeed the posture of any major power, which in effect argues that it is not in its interest to submit to substantial international, legal constraints. It makes more sense for "middling" powers such as France or Canada to pursue a vigorous international regime, because as Igantieff explains, "for middling powers the cost of their own compliance with human rights and humanitarian law instruments is offset by the advantages they believe they will derive from international law regimes that constrain larger powers. For the U.S. the calculus is reversed."[108]

Today, given the ongoing fight against transnational terrorism, where strong allies and international cooperation are indispensable, the realist calculus may be shifting. This much has repeatedly been asserted by the Obama Administration, most recently in the decision to close Guantánamo, partly in order to restore U.S. credibility and standing in the world. But without some measure of accountability for crimes, particularly torture, such overtures may be insufficient.

Scott Horton notes that if "U.S. courts and prosecutors will not address the matter . . . foreign courts appear only too happy to step in."[109] For Horton and others, the international dimension to the domestic obligation to pursue accountability, combines pragmatic and normative concerns. Ruti Teitel suggests that foreign complaints "grounded in so-called universal jurisdiction would hardly have a leg to stand on were there credible investigations underway here. . . . [W]e risk foreign lawyers and judges (through processes already underway in Europe) supplanting a process of truth telling that, given our own political transition, we Americans owe ourselves."[110] Many of our European allies have indicated a willingness to move forward with their own criminal investigations and prosecutions in the absence of any domestic effort. If we are going to take a more expansive view of the rule of law, one that responds to arguments about security, then we have to take seriously claims about international credibility as an argument for prosecutions.

Truth Commissions and the Lessons of Transitional Justice

For some time now scholars and advocates have debated how to respond to government lawbreaking in the context of transitions from authoritarian to democratic regimes. Teitel offers the following succinct definition: "[T]ransitional justice can be defined as the conception of justice associated with periods of political change, characterized by legal responses to confront the wrongdoing of repressive predecessor regimes."[111] Drawing on historical examples from South Africa to Chile, the field of transitional jurisprudence considers the proper role of amnesty and reconciliation versus prosecution and explores alternatives to prosecution, from truth commissions to programs of lustration.[112]

Can the theory of transitional justice be helpful in thinking about the alleged crimes of the Bush Administration? To the extent that the theory considers the range of questions and trade-offs embedded in fashioning a response to a previous regime's wrongdoing, the answer would seem to be yes. But to the extent that transitional justice involves a move from an authoritarian to a democratic regime in a period where normal political accountability and transition have broken down, its utility seems less obvious.

Some would claim that because the United States is not a transitional regime, the considerations and compromises that are struck due to the precariousness of an emerging democracy have little relevance here. This is a criticism that we take seriously: since 2002–03, the period in which many of the more serious charges occurred, there have been two presidential elections, with the last one explicitly contested on an agenda of change in policy. In a mature functioning political system such as the United States, elections and stable transitions are mechanisms that provide for accountability.[113]

In this regard, the election of President Obama and his subsequent efforts forcefully to realign national security issues with domestic and international law may be taken as a repudiation of the Bush Administration and a vindication of the rule of law. Here the democratic institutions of government remain fully functioning. Thus Kenneth Anderson dismisses calls for a truth commission and points out: "If Congress wants to hold hearings, it is always free to hold hearings. . . . If Congress were serious about criminalizing waterboarding and other interrogation tactics, all it has to do is draft a specific law."[114] Because many of the excesses of the Bush Administration have been, or can be, publicly disavowed and discontinued, the case for accountability and prosecutions—the preoccupations of transitional justice—becomes less pressing.

Or does it? There are those who argue that, absent prosecution, the government's return to fuller compliance with national and international laws has the effect of reducing criminal wrongdoing to mere "policy differences." This is precisely what Elaine Scarry has argued. In her view, a lasting injury to the rule of law would occur if we "trivialize into a matter of personal preference any future President's adherence to the law. Will we become a country in which the rule of law is just another policy preference?"[115]

Despite these concerns, some members of Congress, such as Senator Patrick Leahy, have called for a South African-style truth commission, making the idea of drawing on transitional jurisprudence less quixotic than it may first appear. Many scholars consider truth commissions as not just a second-best alternative to criminal trials but as possessing independent normative and practical value. Priscilla Hayner, a proponent of truth commissions, reminds us that the purpose of trials is not to expose the truth in some large, contextual, and systematic way but only to verify that the facts meet a specific legal standard of credibility.[116] Martha Minow argues that "only if we acknowledge that prosecutions are slow, partial, and preoccupied with the either/or simplifications of the adversary process can we recognize the independent value of commissions investigating the larger patterns of atrocity and the complex lines of responsibility and complicity."[117] Moreover, as Horton reminds us, perhaps it is the nomenclature of truth commissions that throws people off, for the United States has a long and somewhat successful history with commissions of inquiry, from the Warren Commission established in 1963 to investigate the assassination of President Kennedy to the more recent bipartisan and independent 9/11 Commission. [118]

The genealogy of transitional justice stretches back to the Nuremberg trials, the first sustained and successful efforts to prosecute leaders of a sovereign government for war crimes. Nuremberg and the series of so-called "successor" trials set the bar for criminal accountability. But the postwar prosecutions gave way to a so-called second "realist" phase of transitional justice, marked by the appearance of truth commissions and debates about the proper role of amnesty in securing peace and reconciliation.[119] As a result, some worry that in instances of transition "justice is all too frequently bartered away for political settlements."[120] While acknowledging a role for truth commissions and the importance of repairing a divided polity, M. Cherif Bassiouni insists, "[T]ruth commissions, however, should not be deemed a substitute for prosecution for the four *jus cogens* crimes of genocide, crimes against humanity, war crimes and torture."[121]

It is worth remembering that truth commissions need not be linked with amnesty and bars to prosecution. While it is true that South Africa set up an exchange of "amnesty for truth," in other situations prosecutions and truth commissions operated in tandem, and the discoveries of the truth commission have sometimes led to a call for the revocation of amnesties and a reopening of investigations.[122] Horton notes that while we have examples of truth commissions eclipsing prosecutions, "in other cases, however, the commission's fact-finding process gradually built a public consensus that prosecutorial action was needed. In Peru and Chile, prosecutions occurred even after comprehensive pardons had been granted, as the courts relied on international-law concepts to disregard those pardons."[123] The final contours of any given transitional solution will depend on the objectives that need to be achieved. These may range from reconciling a divided polity and providing justice to victims to creating a complete account of what transpired and deterring future misconduct. As the United States contends with the excesses of the previous administration, the latter two objectives would be paramount. By raising the question of the wisdom of prosecutions as against amnesty and truth commissions, transitional jurisprudence forces us to pin down the values prosecutions provide, and whether some of these goals could be achieved through alternative means.

Another invaluable dimension to the debates within transitional jurisprudence involves the question of whom to prosecute. This question is a difficult one because of the immensely complicated nature of legal and moral culpability when governments break the law. Unlike individual crimes for personal enrichment, the person closest to the execution of torture may be the least culpable while the leaders and officials further away may be the most culpable. Larry May argues that political crimes are a special type precisely because they are crimes of policy and overall design.[124] Even as a legal matter, May points out, while the so-called minor players may carry out acts that are themselves morally or legally proscribed, the overall crime is the policy itself. In that regard, we may say the person enacting the policy may have a "guilty mind" in relation to the particular act, but we cannot assume that they have a "guilty mind" in relation to the larger crime of the policy.[125] And yet in many cases, leaders and policymakers are the more difficult targets of prosecution and, as a result, accountability settles on relatively minor players.

These considerations have special relevance for our discussion of accountability for the Bush Administration. To date, the only people court-martialed for the scandal of Abu Ghraib have been soldiers under the rank of staff sergeant; no officers have been held accountable, much less policy makers at the Pentagon.[126] This same concern now attaches to Attorney General Holder's decision to appoint a special prosecutor but only to investigate a very narrow category of persons who may have overstepped the guidelines for enhanced interrogations, leaving out the lawyers, politicians, and policymakers who were the undeniable architects of the policy. No doubt, Holder was deeply mindful and genuinely torn between the political considerations of the White House and the demands of justice.

But for some critics who have called for investigations and prosecutions, this investigation amounts to "something close to the worst of both worlds."[127] Glenn Greenwald argues that not only does such a narrow focus unfairly scapegoat the lowest officers but it actually presumes that the legally suspect guidelines offered by Yoo and company *were settled law at the time*.[128] It is possible that as events unfold and the possibility of prosecutions becomes more imminent, there will be renewed calls for a truth commission with sub-poena and immunity-granting powers as a possible middle-ground solution. What is clear is that these debates greatly benefit by being considered within larger theoretical and historical contexts. Doing so is the task of this book.

The work collected here considers how we should respond to the alleged crimes of the Bush Administration. Some of our contributors make the case for prosecution, argue that the rule of law requires it, and explore different jurisdictional and procedural devices through which prosecution might occur. Others oppose prosecution and explore different avenues for holding Bush, Cheney, and Rumsfeld accountable and for preserving the memory of a "lawless" period in recent American history.

In the first chapter, Claire Finkelstein argues that the rule of law can only be vindicated by a criminal prosecution of Bush Administration officials. For her the rule of law requires that what the government does must be congruent with what the government says. Deception and the secrecy which accompanies it are incompatible with the rule of law's requirement of public reason.

Finkelstein notes that in the case of torture, what the Bush Administration said was at great variance from what it did. She argues that the United States benefits significantly from being viewed by other nations as a leader in human rights: it makes it easier to secure the cooperation of those nations, and also gives us a secure position from which to insist on the humane treatment of our own POWs when captured by enemy forces. Other nations benefit similarly from the commitment to human rights in a variety of ways, and so it might be said that there are mutual gains to be had from the coordinated restraint of personal maximizing on the part of nation-states in favor of adherence to international norms of human rights.

Unfortunately, she argues, for the Bush Administration it was not the actual adherence to such norms that provided access to the benefits of international cooperation, but the *appearance* of adhering to such norms. And so it is not entirely surprising that while President Bush consistently and expressly rejected torture, lawyers for the Office of Legal Counsel issued a crucial memorandum seeking to defend extreme interrogation methods that had been used up to that point on terror suspects in Guantánamo Bay and in American prisons in Iraq.

At least one of the techniques authorized by the Justice Department, Finkelstein notes, namely, the infamous technique of "waterboarding," had already been adjudged to violate the Convention against Torture and was found by the international community more generally to provide a basis for prosecutions for war crimes at several points in the twentieth century. In addition to the highly questionable interpretation of the term "torture" in the Bybee memo, evidence continues to mount that the extreme interrogation methods that the memo sought to defend were not the only forms of harsh treatment to which detainees in Guantánamo and in Iraq were subjected. If this turns out to be the case, the Bybee memo seeking to justify waterboarding and other such practices as falling short of torture will, in Finkelstein's view, present a particular puzzle: how should we understand the relationship among, first, the Bush Administration's public rhetoric condemning torture; second, its private internal efforts to justify its own use of harsh interrogation methods to itself; and third, its actual practices, whose brutality appears to outstrip anything that government lawyers were themselves prepared to justify? And what bearing would this relationship have on whether officials who authorized such techniques should be subject to prosecution?

If it is really the case, Finkelstein argues, that such lawyers advocated and sought to justify the use of such techniques by making legal arguments they *knew* to be invalid, and hence knowingly advocated the commission of crimes under federal and international law, they ought to be prosecuted as accomplices. They would possess the mens rea for accomplice liability—purposely assisting in the commission of an offense—and also the actus reus—soliciting or encouraging the commission of such offenses. That is the correct *legal analysis* of the situation. The moral analysis would suggest as well that their position would be significantly worsened by the revelation that their attempts at legal argumentation were disingenuous, for by making false legal arguments, they show themselves to be *intentional free riders* on the international agreements of mutual benefit to which we paid such courteous lip service. And finally, from the standpoint of professional ethics, for a lawyer to render a legal opinion he *knows* to have little support from statutory and precedential sources would be a serious violation of professional ethics—a fact that arguably bolsters the call for criminal prosecution.

On the other hand, Finkelstein notes, in addressing the question of prosecution, we must also consider the possibility that what was actually coloring the thoughts of lawyers from the Office of Legal Counsel was that they thought there was a strong *justification* available for the violation of law in such cases, a justification that motivated them, but that they dared not fully articulate in honest terms. The idea that former Bush officials believed that the United States's interrogation practices were *illegal but nevertheless justified,* is one that is only now slowly making its way into Republican defenses of the Bush Administration's policies. Yet it is this argument that provides the strongest defense such officials might have against prosecution, and hence the argument that most stands in need of examination. In her chapter Finkelstein examines the logic of justification in detail.

Taking the logic of self-defense and of necessity seriously, and imagining the defense that lawyers from the Office of Legal Counsel might make to any attempted prosecution, this chapter asks whether in democratic states, members of the reigning executive branch have a moral basis for regarding legal restrictions designed to defend personal rights as dispensable on grounds either of assertion of public right, or of the supremacy of public utility over individual rights. And if not, can and should they be prosecuted for the violation of federal and international norms in this connection?

Finally, to return briefly to President Bush's statements condemning torture, Finkelstein observes, we might now be in a position to understand why the president would have been keen to make such statements, despite the fact that he was fully aware that the United States was making extensive use of techniques that had previously been prosecuted as torture and that provided a strong basis for thinking it violated the terms of the Convention. Since the United States was in effect clandestinely turning its back on its own normative commitment to other nations, it was crucial to the Bush Administration to deny its own status as free riding on basic social contracts with other nations. For the extreme disadvantages of free riding on human rights agreements would not make themselves felt if the free riding could be conducted in secret—or so the Bush Administration thought. Whether or not such secret free riding is destabilizing of cooperative agreements in the international arena, once it becomes known we impair our own advantages from cooperation if we do not discipline the agents who endorsed and advocated the free riding in the first place. As a result, Finkelstein concludes that President Obama's firm statements that no one from the former administration would be prosecuted for condoning torture, and his later decision not to seek prosecution for the authors of the policies themselves, impairs the rule of law and the attempt by the United States to secure international cooperation in the war on terror.

In the next chapter Daniel Herwitz argues that certain abusive treatments of prisoners at Guantánamo may arguably be considered crimes against humanity. Not to deploy human rights instruments in the face of such abuses is to bury the crime and normalize the state of exception through which the United States arrogates unbridled power unto itself. While the deployment of American as well as international human rights instruments against the Bush

Administration might well have the ill-effect of further entrenching Bush-style unilateral positions, the cost of not deploying human rights instruments is to confirm a "state of exception" as "business as usual" and to erode faith in the rule of law. This is what Hannah Arendt called the banality of evil, serving to bury crimes under a tide of pragmatism, weakness, and fear.

Even if human rights instruments cannot achieve their goals, even if a Cheney will not show up in the Hague, it is important for international courts to make the gesture of saying: "This/he too must be judged, for this/him too a case must be mounted." Herwitz argues that the culture of human rights demands such a gesture.

What then are the most appropriate human rights instruments to deploy in the face of U.S. alleged abuse in Guantánamo? Herwitz argues that a South African-style truth and reconciliation commission is not appropriate for reasons which come from the soul of that enterprise. Formed out of an agreement between warring factions (the National Party of South Africa and the African National Congress), the TRC centered around victim testimony, giving dignity to victim families who were given voice. Central to the TRC was "qualified amnesty" which occasioned "full confession" by perpetrators seeking it, while also allowing for the TRC to formulate itself as a religious enterprise aiming in a moment of political transition for a culture of reconciliation. The TRC served, Herwitz notes, the specific demands of transitional justice.

To restage such an event, or transpose its terms to the United States, first, the victims and families would have to be given similar voice, making the event clearly international; second, there is no agreement between international parties at war which could be imagined to serve as the starting point of the procedure; and third, it is therefore unclear who would be reconciled to whom.

More appropriate, Herwitz argues, would be a Senate/Congressional Commission of Inquiry into Guantánamo, along the lines of that used in the "Iran Contras" scandal. Nonetheless he does not think that this is going to take place. Equally unlikely and equally necessary would be a trial in the World Court. While alleged U.S. perpetrators would not show up and no trial would ensue, the gesture would be one of world solidarity, preserving the dignity and uniformity of the court as a human rights instrument at a contemporary moment when the authority and dignity of international law and the entire edifice of humanitarianism are in danger of collapse.

Agreeing on the importance of prosecuting members of the Bush Administration, Lisa Hajjar explores another avenue for doing so in her chapter.

The right not to be tortured, Hajjar notes, is universal and non-derogable: it applies to all people everywhere under all circumstances. The practice of torture, a gross crime under international law, attaches universal jurisdiction: perpetrators and abettors can be prosecuted in foreign or international courts if they are not prosecuted by their own state or the state with jurisdiction where torture occurred.

Hajjar's chapter offers a brief account of the state of universal jurisdiction for torture and other gross crimes, followed by a consideration of the current state of investigations in Europe (mainly Spain) of alleged U.S. torturers. The second part of the chapter addresses the politics of legal accountability. Specifically, Hajjar considers first, the political implications of either prosecuting or not prosecuting the authors of the U.S. torture policy at home; second, the implications internationally if there is de facto impunity domestically as a result of no prosecutions; and third, the contested legitimacy of foreign prosecutions of officials on the basis of universal jurisdiction. Woven through this discussion is a consideration of domestic discourse and debates about torture, terror, and the law, and the international implications (diplomatic/political, legal, and security-related) of superpower immunity for prosecutable crimes. Hajjar concludes by arguing for the superiority of universal jurisdiction as a basis for prosecutions of torture as opposed to either domestic or international jurisdiction.

The next three chapters each present the case against prosecution. Unlike Finkelstein, Stephen Holmes sets out to show the various ways in which the rule of law offers protection for government officials who violate the law. For Holmes the reality is that the rule of law is not an effective constraint on official misconduct. Moreover, he believes that pursuing a prosecution would have the perverse effect of allowing Bush Administration officials to claim that they have been legally exonerated. Instead, we should acknowledge the way law serves power and pursue other avenues of redress.

As important as "the rule of law" is to the legal order, it is, Paul Horwitz contends, unlikely to take us very far in answering the question of whether it is advisable to pursue criminal prosecutions of former Bush Administration officials for their actions in the war on terror—or, to the extent that they continue any of the same policies, whether to pursue prosecutions of current Obama Administration officials. A more careful examination of the question will be needed. In pursuing that question, then, Horwitz says, we ought not to ask what the "rule of law" demands as such, but what the congeries of values and practices found within the broader term "rule of law" demand in any particular society with respect to any particular question.

To that end, Horwitz contends, it may be useful to think about what the rule of law demands with respect to the actions of government officials in societies with different forms of legal order and at different degrees of stability and development. Building on the role of "truth and reconciliation commissions," international war crimes proceedings such as the Nuremberg trials, and other methods of addressing alleged national and international crimes, Horwitz suggests that there are reasons to think that the "rule of law" may not require the same actions in different states.

The rule of law in a properly functioning society, after all, includes not only judicial but also political processes. In transitional regimes, it may be necessary for pragmatic and political reasons to provide for formal proceedings such as war crimes tribunals and truth and reconciliation commissions if the state is to command adequate popular consent as it moves forward. Similar proceedings may be unnecessary in stable and well-developed democratic states like the United States, in which the political process itself, and the process of changing political leadership, commands widespread consent and obedience. Indeed, criminal prosecutions and other uses of the judicial process may be counterproductive, adding a destabilizing element to otherwise properly functioning states.

In Horwitz's view while there are compelling reasons to conclude that, no matter what the rule of law might require with respect to states at other stages and levels of development, it will rarely require criminal prosecution of the relevant decision makers in a political system such as the United States. He concludes that we should think long and hard before following that path.

Stephen Vladeck's chapter invites us to think about how we should respond to the alleged crimes of the Bush Administration by revisiting a previous instance of government abuse of its power in the United States. Any accounting of the most serious human rights abuses committed by the U.S. government during the twentieth century, he says, must necessarily begin with the forcible relocation of over 100,000 Japanese and Japanese-American citizens to "internment camps" during World War II. Over time, the "moral judgments of history" to which Justice Jackson famously referred in his dissent in *Korematsu v. United States*, have been rather unkind, and condemnation of the camps has become all but universal—culminating in Congress's decision in 1988 to formally apologize for the camps on behalf of the U.S. government, with over $1.6 billion in reparations subsequently appropriated for the internees and their heirs. And *Korematsu* itself, the 1944 Supreme Court decision in which the Court indirectly but unequivocally upheld the constitutionality of the camps, has been so soundly discredited that it has effectively become an "anti-precedent," that is, a decision so reviled that it is cited only to prove the incorrectness of the rule for which it purportedly stands.

Yet no one, Vladeck reminds us, was ever held personally liable for the policies leading to internment. No government official was prosecuted; no government lawyer was disbarred—even though the Justice Department affirmatively misled the courts as to the gravity of the military threat posed by Japan. Indeed, the conventional narrative is that the gravest harm to the "rule of law" resulting from internment was not caused by the camps themselves, nor by the failure to investigate those responsible for creating them, but by the Supreme Court's legal rationalization thereof in *Korematsu*. As Justice Jackson put it, "A military commander may overstep the bounds of constitutionality, and it is an incident. But if we review and approve, that passing incident becomes the doctrine of the Constitution. There it has a generative power of its own, and all that it creates will be in its own image." Thus, and tellingly, the prevailing historical memory of internment was, Vladeck notes, created over time without the benefit of criminal prosecutions, truth commissions, or any other systematic effort to identify the role played by individual government officers in the policies behind the camps.

Vladeck's chapter shows how the creation of internment's historical memory might inform contemporary debates over whether senior Bush Administration officials should be investigated and/or prosecuted for their role in the torture of detainees held as part of the "war on terrorism." In particular, in retracing the development of a critical narrative of the internment camps, Vladeck explores the relationship between individual accountability and concerns over the "rule of law."

The historiography of internment suggests that abuses by the U.S. government can successfully be documented—and their justifications categorically debunked—without individual accountability. This chapter asks whether that assumption holds up under closer scrutiny, or whether the same Justice Jackson might have been closer to the mark in his closing statement at Nuremberg, where, after invoking the specter of *Richard III*, he concluded with the observation that, "If you were to say of these men that they are not guilty, it would be as true to say that there has been no war, there are no slain, there has been no crime."

Taken together the work collected in this book illuminates the complexity that necessarily attaches to the question of how we should respond when governments break the law and when those violations occur in a systematic fashion in the context of an ongoing "war on terror." While some of our contributors worry about the effect on rule of law values of a decision not to prosecute, others do not think that the rule of law is very meaningful as a guide for action. How we should respond depends not just on our adherence to the rule of law but also on our respect for the transnational normative and legal order, on the ability of our political system to enforce real accountability, on our confidence in the ability of devices like investigative or truth commissions to flush out the truth of what the government did, and on the lessons we glean about how, in the absence of any particular response, history will render its judgments.

NOTES

1. See William F. Buckley Jr., "Strange Uses of Tolerance," *San Diego Union-Tribune*, January 27, 1985, C2.

2. Alexis de Tocqueville, *Democracy in America, vol. 1* (New York: Knopf, 1945), 278.

3. See *Planned Parenthood v. Casey*, 505 U.S. 833, 868 (1992).

4. Samuel Huntington, *The Clash of Civilizations and the Remaking of World Order* (New York: Simon & Schuster, 1996), 311.

5. Ronald Cass, *The Rule of Law in America* (Baltimore: Johns Hopkins University Press, 2001), xii.

6. Michael Oakeshott, *Rationalism in Politics and Other Essays* (Indianapolis: Liberty Press, 1991), 389.

7. Henry Cisneros, "Extra Spice for American Culture," *Financial Times of London* (May 24, 2004), 17. See also Marci Hamilton, "The Rule of Law: Even as We Try to Export the Ideal of Justice by Law, Not Whim, Some in America Resist That Very Ideal" (October 23, 2003),

8. See Jonathan Lippman, "Preserving Safety and Access to the Courts," *New York Law Journal* 83 (April 30, 2004): 9.

9. Ann Parks, "Former Secretary of Defense Shares Views on War, Business, and the Rule of Law," *Daily Record* (May 17, 2004). See also Law Tribune Advisory Board, "Are We Still the Land of the Free?" *Connecticut Law Tribune* (April 12, 2004), 19.

10. Ron Paul, "War in Iraq, War on the Rule of Law?" *Texas Straight Talk*, August 26, 2002, (accessed May 27, 2005). See also "Our Opinions: Ignoring Detainees Rights Weakens U.S. Principles," *Atlanta Journal Constitution* (May 18, 2004), 10A; and John Hutson, "Rule of Law: Guantánamo Offers U.S.a Chance to Showcase Ideal of Due Process," *Recorder* (January 16, 2004), 4.

11. Elaine Scarry, "Presidential Crimes: Moving On Is Not an Option," *Boston Review* (September/October 2008), http://bostonreview.net/BR33.5/scarry.php

12. Glenn Greenwald, "Binding U.S. Law Requires Prosecutions for Those Who Authorize Torture," *Salon.com* (Sunday, January 18, 2009), http://www.salon.com/opinion/greenwald/2009/01/18/prosecutions/

13. See Jeremy Waldron, "Torture and Positive Law: Jurisprudence for the White House," 105 *Columbia Law Review* (2005): 1681.

14. Michael Ratner, "We Need a Special Counsel," http://roomfordebate.blogs.nytimes.com/2009/03/02/a-truth-commission-for-the-bush-era/

15. Jordon J. Paust, "Above the Law: Unlawful, Executive Authorizations Regarding Detainee Treatment, Secret Renditions, Domestic Spying, and Claims to Unchecked Executive Power," *Utah Law Review* (2007), 348. See also Scott Horton, "We have a duty to posterity, and that is to bear witness to these events. We must document them carefully. We must act to avoid the destruction of valuable evidence—and recognize, as we have already seen, that it is in the character of those who commit crimes to destroy the evidence of their misdeeds. In this way we lay the path for the justice which will in good time be meted out to those who betrayed a nation's trust. For I believe, like the Puritans, in the certainty that justice will triumph and that wrongdoers will be held to account, though I am not so foolish as to think that this will happen soon." See "Torture, Secrecy and the Bush Administration," http://velvelonnationalaffairs.blogspot.com/2007/04/remarks-on-torture-and-secrecy-by.html

16. David Johnston and Charlie Savage, "Obama Reluctant to Look into Bush Programs," *New York Times* (January 11, 2009), http://www.nytimes.com/2009/01/12/us/politics/12inquire.html

17. Despite Obama's statements, news reports suggest that Attorney General Eric Holder is considering prosecution in at least some limited context. See David Johnson, "For Holder, Inquiry on Interrogation Poses Tough Choice," *New York Times* (July 21, 2009), http://www.nytimes.com/2009/07/22/us/22holder.html

18. See "Advice to a Democratic President: Don't Prosecute Bush Officials for War Crimes," *redblueamerica*, http://redblueamerica.com/blog/2008-04-10/advice-a-democratic-president-dont-prosecute-bush-officials-war-crimes-2496. See also, "Prosecute Bush . . . Forget about Healthcare," *Barack Oblogger* (April 23, 2009), http://www.barack-oblogger.com/2009/04/prosecute-bush-forget-about-healthcare.html

19. For an example of this argument, see David Margolis, "Memorandum of Decision Regarding the Objections to the Findings of Professional Misconduct in the Office of Professional Responsibility's Report of Investigation into the Office of Legal Counsel's Memoranda Concerning Issues Related to the Central Intelligence Agency's Use of 'Enhanced Interrogation Techniques' on Suspected Terrorists," January 5, 2010, Washington, D.C.: U.S. Department of Justice.

20. Thomas L. Friedman, "A Torturous Compromise," *New York Times* (April 28, 2009), http://www.nytimes.com/2009/04/29/opinion/29friedman.html

21. Carrie Johnson, "Prosecutor to Probe CIA Interrogations Attorney General Parts with White House in Approving Preliminary Investigation," *Washington Post* (August 25, 2009), found at http://www.washingtonpost.com/wp-dyn/content/article/2009/08/24/AR2009082401743.html

22. See, for example, Office of Professional Responsibility Report, "Investigation into the Office of Legal Counsel's Memoranda Concerning Issues Related to the Central Intelligence Agency's Use of 'Enhanced Interrogation Techniques' on Suspected Terrorists," July 29, 2009, Washington, D.C.: U.S. Department of Justice.

23. We understand that this premise will be unacceptable to two types of readers. The first, such as John Yoo, who believed and continue to believe that no violations of the law occurred, will obviously find any discussion of whether prosecutions are a good idea to be entirely moot.

The second—we call them rule absolutists—believe that if one can presume that a violation of the law occurred then there is almost nothing further to be done and said—that any violation requires legal vindication. See, for example, Mike Farmer, "Why We Must Prosecute Bush and His Administration for War Crimes," *Online Journal* (December 16, 2008), http://onlinejournal.com/artman/publish/article_4135.shtml.

Farmer quotes Robert Jackson at Nuremberg, "Let me make clear that while this law is first applied against German aggressors, the law includes, and if it is to serve a useful purpose it must condemn aggression by any other nations, including those which sit here now in judgment."

Or, as Larry Cox puts it, "If the US fails to prosecute those responsible for torture, we can take our place alongside countries we have long criticized for privileging politics over justice and accountability by letting criminals go free." "Obama Must Prosecute Bush-Era Torture Enablers," *Christian Science Monitor* (June 15, 2009), http://www.csmonitor.com/2009/0615/p09s01-coop.html

For a criticism of this kind of absolutism, see Abraham Goldstein and Joseph Goldstein, *Crime, Law and Society* (New York: Free Press), 1987, 151. As they put it, "Full enforcement . . . is not a realistic expectation." See also Joseph Stigler, "The Optimum Enforcement of Laws," *Journal of Political Economy,*, Vol. 78, No. 3 (May–June 1970): 526–36.

24. Joseph Raz, "The Rule of Law and Its Virtue," *Law Quarterly Review* 93 (1977): 196; see Ian Shapiro, *The Rule of Law*. Nomos XXXVI (New York: NYU Press, 1994); Guillermo O'Donnell, "Why the Rule of Law Matters," 15 *Journal of Democracy* (2004): 32–46.

25. See Jeffrey Ian Ross, *The Dynamics of Political Crime* (New York: Sage, 2002).

26. See Pamela Hess, "Cheney Told CIA to Hide Program from Congress, *Huffington Post* (July 11, 2009), http://www.huffingtonpost.com/2009/07/11/cheney-told-cia-to-hide-p_n_230093.html

27. James Risen and Eric Lichtblau, "Bush Lets U.S. Spy on Callers without Courts," *New York Times* (December 16, 2005).

28. The legislative history and scope of FISA can be found in the OIG of the Department of Defense, Department of Justice, Central Intelligence Agency, National Security Agency, and Office of the Director of National Intelligence, Unclassified Report on the President's Surveillance Program (July 10, 2009). Report No. 2009-0013-AS.

29. Ibid., 5.

30. Ibid., 1.

31. Ibid., 14.

32. Ibid., 11.

33. Ibid., 7.

34. Jack Goldstein, *The Terror Presidency* (New York: W. W. Norton, 2007).

35. Michael Isikoff and David Corn, *Hubris: The Inside Story of Spin, Scandal, and the Selling of the Iraq War* (New York: Crown Books, 2006).

36. U.S. Senate, Select Committee on Intelligence, "Report on Whether Public Statements Regarding Iraq By U.S. Government Officials Were Substantiated By Intelligence Information Together with Additional and Minority Views" (S. Rpt. 110 -) 2008.

37. Ibid, 9.

38. See Vincent Bugliosi, "The Prosecution of George W. Bush for Murder," *Huffington Post* (May 19, 2008), http://www.huffingtonpost.com/vincent-bugliosi/the-prosecution-of-george_b_102427.html

39. See, for example, Eric Posner, "Does Holder's 'Waterboarding Is Torture" Comment Implicitly Commit Him to Prosecuting Bush Administration Officials?" *Volokh Conspiracy* (January 17, 2009), found at http://Volokh.com/posts/1232221565.shtml

Posner notes, "One can easily imagine the defense strategy, which will start by calling to the stand various Democratic senators and representatives who . . . did not publicly object . . . at the time."

40. U.S. Senate, Select Committee on Intelligence, "Report on . . . Public Statements Regarding Iraq" (S. Rpt. 110 -) 2008, 102.

41. Carl Boggs, "Prosecuting Bush, Counterpunch" (October 17/20, 2008). Available at www.counterpunch.org/boggs10172008.html

42. See Anne Norton, "On the Uses of Dogs: Abu Ghraib, Guantánamo, and the American Soul" in *Performances of Violence*, eds. Austin Sarat, Carleen Basler, and Thomas Dumm (Amherst: University of Massachusetts Press, forthcoming, 2010).

43. Convention against Torture and Other Cruel, Inhuman or Degrading Treatment or Punishment. Available at www.hrweb.org/legal/cat.html

44. USC, 113, S2340. www.law.cornell.edu/uscode/18/usc_sec-18_00002340

45. Scott Horton, "Justice after Bush: Prosecuting an Outlaw Administration," *Harpers* (2008), 1. www.harpers.org/archive/2008/12/0082303.

46. U. S. Senate, Committee on Armed Services, "Inquiry into the Treatment of Detainees in U.S. Custody" (S. Rpt. 110 -) 2008. See also Mark Danner, *Torture and Truth: America, Abu Ghraib, and the War on Terror* (New York: New York Review of Books, 2004). Also see Karen J. Greenberg and Joshua L. Dratel, eds., *The Torture Papers: The Road to Abu Ghraib* (New York: Cambridge University Press, 2005).

47. Jane Meyer, *The Dark Side: The Inside Story of How the War on Terror Turned into a War on American Ideals* (New York: Doubleday, 2008).

48. Greenberg and Dratel, eds., *The Torture Papers*, Memo 21, 237.

49. Greenberg and Dratel, eds., *The Torture Papers*, Memo 14, 172.

50. Senate Armed Services Committee, "Inquiry into the Treatment of Detainees," xv. For the full text of the memo, see Greenberg and Dratel, eds., *The Torture Papers*, Memo 14, 172.

51. Ibid., xxii.

52. See Office of Professional Responsibility Report, "Investigation into the Office of Legal Counsel's Memoranda Concerning Issues Related to the Central Intelligence Agency's Use of 'Enhanced Interrogation Techniques' on Suspected Terrorists," July 29, 2009, Washington, D.C.: U.S. Department of Justice. Also see Katherine Eban, *"Torture Memos Link Lawyers and Psychologists,"* Vanity Fair (April 17, 2009), http://www.vanityfair.com/online/politics/2009/04/torture-memos-link-lawyers-and-psychologists.html As Eban puts it, "Taken as a whole, the memos point up how much damage two sets of professionals with fancy-sounding degrees can accomplish when they join forces. Under the cloak of law and science, the Bush Administration lawyers and the SERE psychologists managed to evade the Geneva Conventions, subvert U.S. law, and sanction the torture of detainees."

53. Ruth Wedgwood and R. James Woolsey, "Law and Torture," *Wall Street Journal Online* (June 28, 2004). http://spirit.tau.ac.il/government/Wedgwood_article2.pdf

54. Phillipe Sands, *Torture Team: Rumsfeld's Memo and the Betrayal of American Values* (New York: Palgrave Macmillan, 2008).

55. Ibid., 184.

56. Horton, "Justice after Bush," 1.

57. Ibid.

58. See David Cole, "First, Find Out What Happened, *New York Times* (March 2, 2009). http://roomfordebate.blogs.nytimes.com/2009/03/02/a-truth-commossion/

59. Unclassified Report on the President's Surveillance Program, 11.

60. Cass, *The Rule of Law in America*, 3. See also Richard Fallon, "'The Rule of Law' as a Concept in Constitutional Discourse," 97 *Columbia Law Review* (1997): 1.

61. Cass, *The Rule of Law in America*, 4.

62. Ibid., 7.

63. Ibid., 12.

64. Ibid., 17.

65. Friedrich A. Hayek, *The Constitution of Liberty* (Chicago: Gateway, 1972), 164–65.

66. Antonin Scalia, "The Rule of Law as a Law of Rules," 55 *University of Chicago Law Review* (Fall 1989): 1175–88.

67. See Lon Fuller, *The Morality of Law* (New Haven: Yale University Press, 1964).

68. A.V. Dicey, *Introduction to the Study of the Law of the Constitution*, 5th ed. (1855; reprint, London: Macmillan, 1897), 179–87.

69. Joseph Raz, "The Rule of Law and Its Virtues," in *The Authority of Law: Essays on Law and Morality* (Oxford: Clarendon Press, 1979), 210–11.

70. Ibid., 211.

71. For a useful discussion and criticism of interest balancing, see Denise Meyerson, "Why Courts Should Not Balance Rights against the Public Interest," 31 *Melbourne University Law Review* (2007): 801–30.

72. See *Herrera v. Collins*, 506 U.S. (1993), 390.

73. Kenneth Culp Davis, *Discretionary Justice: A Preliminary Inquiry* (Baton Rouge: Louisiana State University Press, 1963).

74. Goldstein and Goldstein, *Crime, Law, and Society.*

75. Robert H. Jackson, "The Federal Prosecutor," 24 *American Judicial Society* (1940): 18.

76. Ibid.

77. Recently many states have acted to limit prosecutorial discretion in domestic violence cases. See Daniel A. Ford and Susan Breall, *Violence against Women: Synthesis of Research for Prosecutors* (Washington, D.C.: National Institute for Justice, 2000), 7. In addition, in both the federal and state systems, some chief prosecutors have devised official policies governing charging decisions. See Marc Miller and Ronald Wright, *Criminal Procedures: Cases, Statutes, and Executive Materials*, 2nd ed. (New York: Aspen Publishers, 2003), 803.

78. See Andrew B. Loewenstein, "Judicial Review and the Limits of Prosecutorial Discretion," 38 *American Criminal Law Review* (2001): 351, 357.

79. See Amie N. Ely, "Prosecutorial Discretion as an Ethical Necessity: The Ashcroft Memorandum's Curtailment of the Prosecutor's Duty to 'Seek Justice,'" 90 *Cornell Law Review* (2004): 237.

80. See Laurie L. Levenson, "Working Outside the Rules: The Undefined Responsibilities of Federal Prosecutors," 26 *Fordham Urban Law Journal* (1999): 553, 557.

81. See Angela J. Davis, "The American Prosecutor: Independence, Power, and the Threat of Tyranny," 86 *Iowa Law Review* (2001): 393; and James Vorenberg, "Decent Restraint of Prosecutorial Power," 94 *Harvard Law Review* (1981): 1521.

82. John Locke, *Two Treatises of Government*, Peter Laslett, ed. (1690; reprint, Cambridge: Cambridge University Press, 1988), 375. Article 4 of the United Nations International Convention on Civil and Political Rights permits countries to derogate from some of its stipulations during a public emergency. See www2.ohchr.org/english/law/ccpr.htm

83. Clinton L. Rossiter, *Constitutional Dictatorship: Crisis Government in Modern Democracies* (Princeton: Princeton University Press, 1948).

84. Ibid., 217–18.

85. See ibid., 226–30.

86. Richard Neustadt, *Presidential Power: The Politics of Leadership from FDR to Carter* (New York: John Wiley, 1980).

87. Harold Koh, *The National Security Constitution: Sharing Power after the Iran- Contra Affair* (New Haven: Yale University Press, 1990).

88. C. Wright Mills, *The Power Elite* (New York: Oxford University Press, 1956).

89. See Frederick A. O. Schwarz Jr. and Aziz Z. Huq, *Unchecked and Unbalanced: Presidential Power in a Time of Terror* (New York: New Press, 2008). Also Joseph Marguiles, *Guantánamo and the Abuse of Presidential Power* (New York: Simon & Schuster, 2007).

90. See John R. Oneal and Anna Lillian Bryan, "The Rally 'Round the Flag Effect in U.S. Foreign Policy Crises, 1950–1985,'" 17 *Political Behavior* (1995): 379–401.

91. *Youngstown Sheet & Tube Co. v. Sawyer*, 343 U.S. 579 (1952).

92. Ibid., 647.

93. See, for example, Eric Holder, "Remarks as Prepared for Delivery by Attorney General Eric Holder at West Point's Center for the Rule of Law Grand Opening Conference," West Point, New York (April 15, 2009),
http://www.usdoj.gov/ag/speeches/2009/ag-speech-090415.html

94. Andrew C. McCarthy, "Holder Should Heed Justice Jackson's Words," *National Review Online* (May 8, 2009), http://article.nationalreview.com/?q=MjIxOGJlYTdjOTTc0YThiNzM5OTYyODc3ZWYxMjA3MmE=#

95. For Nixon's famous remark during an interview with David Frost in May 1977, see www.youtube.com/watch?v=ejvyDn1TPr8. For Vice President Cheney's reiteration, see www.huffingtonpost.com/.../cheney-if-president-does_n_152663.html

96. *Hamdi v. Rumsfeld*, 542 U.S. 507 (2004).

97. *Boumediene v. Bush*, 553 U.S. ___ (2008).

98. *Hamdan v. Rumsfeld*, 548 U.S. 557 (2006).

99. Oren Gross, "Chaos and Rules: Should Responses to Violent Crises Always Be Constitutional?" 112 *Yale Law Journal* (March 2003): 1011.

100. "U.S. Reservations, Declarations, and Understandings, International Covenant on Civil and Political Rights," 138 *Cong. Rec.* S4781-01 (daily ed., April 2, 1992). Available at http://www1.umn.edu/humanrts/usdocs/civilres.html. See *Roger v. Simmons*, 543 U.S. 551 (2009).

101. "U.S. Reservations, Declarations, and Understandings, Convention against Torture and Other Cruel, Inhuman or Degrading Treatment or Punishment," *Cong. Rec.* S17486-01 (daily ed., October 27, 1990). Available at http://www1.umn.edu/humanrts/usdocs/tortres.html

102. Jeremy Waldron, "Is the Rule of Law an Essentially Contested Concept?" 21 *Law and Philosophy* (2002): 22.

103. Michael Ignatieff, ed., *American Exceptionalism and Human Rights* (Princeton: PrincetonUniversity Press, 2005), 3.

104. Ibid., 2.

105. Ibid., 17.

106. Ibid., 25.

107. Ibid.

108. Ibid., 12.

109. Scott Horton, "The Bush Six to Be Indicted," *Daily Beast* (April 14, 2009).

110. Ruti Teitel, "Bringing Transitional Justice Home," *Findlaw* (December 16, 2008). http://writ.news.findlaw.com/commentary/20081216_teitel.html

111. Ruti Teitel, "Transitional Justice Genealogy," 16 *Harvard Human Rights Journal* (2003): 69.

112. See Martha Minow, *Between Vengeance and Forgiveness: Facing History after Genocide and Mass Violence* (Boston: Beacon Press, 1998); for a theoretical and country study account, see Neil Kritz, *Transitional Justice*, 3 vols.; for truth commissions and their role, see Priscilla Hayner, *Unspeakable Truths: Facing the Challenge of Truth Commissions* (New York: Routledge, 2002).

113. Jack Beerman, "Presidential Power in Transitions," 83 *Boston University Law* Review (2003): 947.

114. Kenneth Anderson. "A Cycle of Political Payback: A Truth Commission for the Bush Era," *New York Times* (March 2, 2009). http://roomfordebate.blogs.nytimes.com/2009/03/02/a-truth-commission-for-the-bush-era/

115. Scarry, "Presidential Crimes," 2.

116. Hayner, *Unspeakable Truths*, 100.

117. Minow, *Between Vengeance and Forgiveness*, 87.

118. Horton, "Justice after Bush," 7.

119. See Ruti Teitel, *Transitional Justice Genealogy*.

120. M. Cherif Bassiouni, "Searching for Peace and Achieving Justice: The Need for Accountability," *Law and Contemporary Problems* 59, no. 4 (Autumn 1996): 9–28, 11.

121. Ibid., 20.

122. For the legislation setting up the truth commission and its amnesty granting powers, see Promotion of National Unity and Reconciliation Act, 1995, Act 34 of 1995, Preamble (S. Afr). For a very useful collection of essays debating amnesty versus prosecutions, see Charles Villa-Vicencio and Wilhelm Verwoerd, eds., *Looking Back, Reaching Forward: Reflections on the Truth and Reconciliation Commission of South Africa* (London: Zed Books, 2000).

123. Horton, "Justice after Bush," 7.

124. Larry May, *Crimes against Humanity: A Normative Account* (New York: Cambridge University Press, 2005).

125. Ibid., 126–27.

126. "Prosecutions and Convictions. A Look at Accountability to Date for Abuses at Abu Ghraib and in the Broader 'War on Terror,'" *Salon.com* (2006). www.salon.com/news/abu_ghraib/2006/03/14/prosecutions_convictions/

127. Glenn Greenwald, "Eric Holder Announces Investigation Based on Abu Ghraib model," *Salon.com* (August 24, 2009). www.salon.com/opinion/greenwald/2009/08/24/holder/index.html

128. For a thorough review of the adequacy of the legal analysis provided by Yoo, see Office of Professional Responsibility Report, "Investigation into the Office of Legal Counsel's Memoranda Concerning Issues Related to the Central Intelligence Agency's Use of 'Enhanced Interrogation Techniques' on Suspected Terrorists," July 29, 2009, Washington, D.C.: U.S. Department of Justice.

1

Vindicating the Rule of Law

Prosecuting Free Riders on Human Rights

CLAIRE FINKELSTEIN

I

On June 26, 2003, the United Nations celebrated "International Day in Support of Victims of Torture." To mark the day, President Bush issued a statement in which he said:

> The United States is committed to the world-wide elimination of torture and we are leading this fight by example. I call on all governments to join with the United States and the community of law-abiding nations in prohibiting, investigating, and prosecuting all acts of torture and in undertaking to prevent other cruel and unusual punishment. I call on all nations to speak out against torture in all its forms and to make ending torture an essential part of their diplomacy.[1]

The irony of these remarks is pointed in the face of subsequent revelations that high-ranking members of the Bush Administration, with the assistance of attorneys at the Office of Legal Counsel (OLC), developed and implemented a system of torture to assist in the interrogation of suspected terrorists. In the early days of the new administration, when the public knew nothing of the inner workings of the war on terror, official rhetoric could afford to be morally highhanded with only minimal embarrassment. Another typical example was Bush's January 22, 2005 call for a worldwide end to tyranny and oppression: "All who live in tyranny and hopelessness can know: the United States will not ignore your oppression, or excuse your oppressors. When you stand for your liberty, we will stand with you."[2] The executive branch's public discourse was at this time a daring act of brinksmanship with the threat that its own disregard for human rights would be revealed.

After the full extent of the administration's commitment to torture had come to light, the motivation for continuing unabashedly to make such remarks became even more puzzling. To take a prosaic example from this period, on the eve of the Olympic Games in Beijing (August 2008) President Bush attacked China's record on human rights: "The United States believes the people of China deserve the fundamental liberty that is the natural right of all human beings. . . . So America stands in firm opposition to China's detention of political dissidents, human rights advocates, and religious activists."[3] Did the president fail to notice that our record on human rights might actually appear to be worse than Beijing's?

Among the many ironies of the Bush Administration's clandestine commitment to torture was its enthusiastic adoption of the interrogation practice known as "waterboarding." The OLC's August 1, 2002 memorandum, mostly written by John Yoo but signed by Jay Bybee (hereafter the "Bybee memorandum") argues that waterboarding is insufficiently painful for it to count as torture. But high on the list of ironic twists is the fact that Americans had themselves decried waterboarding as torture when the Japanese used it against American and British POWs during World War II.[4] After the war, the International Military Tribunal went so far as to prosecute Japanese interrogators for its use, and the Americans followed suit, with the result that some defendants were put to death; others were awarded long prison sentences.[5] Given, then, that there was a prior American interpretation of the term "torture" that included waterboarding among its ranks, it is especially disturbing that the Bybee memorandum resorts entirely to its own definition of torture, without so much as a nod in the direction of the only American precedent on point.

To date, no one in the former administration has been held responsible for the Bush Administration's torture policy. In connection with the release of several of the previously classified OLC memoranda, President Obama announced that there would be no prosecutions of investigators who relied on the memos in their decision to use so-called "enhanced interrogation techniques" (or EITs). Stating that "this is a time for reflection, not retribution," Obama went on to reveal the pragmatic foundations of his rejection of prosecution, saying that "nothing will be gained by spending our time and energy laying blame for the past."[6] Although his remarks deliberately left open the possibility of criminal prosecution for more senior members of the Bush Administration, the likelihood of pursuing criminal sanctions against any member of the former administration is exceedingly low. Evidence for this lies not only in President Obama's clear anti-prosecutorial remarks, but also in a pair of reports recently released by the Justice Department.

The first report, issued by the Justice Department's Office of Professional Responsibility, concludes that "former Deputy AGG John Yoo committed intentional professional misconduct when he violated his duty to exercise independent legal judgment and render thorough, objective, and candid legal advice."[7] The report came to the same conclusion about the conduct of James Bybee, except that Bybee was found to have acted "in reckless disregard" of his professional duties rather than with "intentional professional misconduct."[8] Although little mention was made of criminal prosecution, such a recommendation would in any event have been beyond the scope of the OPR, which is charged only to comment on the professional ethics of the lawyers' conduct. Had the OPR report been allowed to stand, however, it might have lent credence to those who believed criminal prosecution an appropriate response. That report, however, was overridden by another memorandum released the same day, namely that written by Assistant Attorney General David Margolis.[9] Margolis rejected the conclusions of the OPR and restricted himself to saying that Yoo and Bybee exercised "poor judgment."[10] This sequence of events is regrettable. Among other things, it is regrettable that the only complete factual investigation into the role of the OLC attorneys was so summarily cast aside. In addition, by overriding the OPR report, Margolis' report drove the final nails in the coffin of potential disciplinary proceedings for violations of professional ethics. And although there will be efforts to revive the question of criminal prosecution, the Margolis report has also for all practical purposes foreclosed the possibility that such prosecutions will ever take place.

Rather than focusing on the pragmatic preoccupations that have shaped the current administration's stance toward those responsible for the torture policy, this essay is motivated by deeper philosophical concerns relating to the status of the rule of law.[11] In particular, the current project is prompted by the thought that the further the public reason of a government journeys from its actual administrative functioning, the greater the reach of executive power, and, as an associated phenomenon, the more enfeebled the rule of law. This is not an incidental feature of the relationship between public discourse and executive power, but a reflection of a fundamental aspect of the rule of law, namely that a necessary, though not sufficient, condition for a society to be governed by strong rule of law values is a simultaneous commitment in that society to the public nature of the rules and principles that structure its legal system.[12] There are, in short, three elements that form an indissoluble triad in a society governed by law: first, the public reason of the regime along with the values that reason expresses, second, the actual administrative functioning of the regime and the rules and principles by which such functioning is guided, and third, the robustness of the rule of law in the society governed by that regime. My concern is that when the first and second of these elements come apart, the third element, the rule of law, may be permanently and irrevocably impaired.

The dependence of the rule of law on the relative transparency of governmental reasoning, although intuitively plausible, is in fact rather difficult to fully explain. A complete account of the connection is beyond the scope of this essay, but such an account would ultimately have to do with the fundamentally public character of legal rules, combined with a clear understanding of the role that legal rules play in maintaining democratic processes. When a government publicly declares its fidelity to one set of rules while covertly following another, it is effectively rejecting the very idea of governance by rules. Where democratic governance is concerned, there is no such thing as private rule by law. The hypocrisy of the Bush Administration's stance on human rights was an early sign of its diminished executive fidelity to the rule of law.

Consistent with the aims of the present volume, I shall not discuss the possible legal structure of a prosecution of those responsible for the torture policy in all its details, but will instead make the assumption, for purposes of argument, that at least a prima facie case of accomplice liability against certain individuals for encouraging CIA interrogators to commit torture exists. My primary focus instead will be on questions that might be raised beyond the level of the prima facie case, namely matters that concern both the wisdom and the ultimately legal solidity of the case for prosecution. For several reasons, I focus on former Department of Justice lawyers, rather than higher-ranking officials like Donald Rumsfeld, Richard Addington, or Dick Cheney, to whom the torture trail might lead. There are several reasons for this.

First, ordinary, if flawed, legal arguments played a pivotal role in advancing the interrogation policies of the administration: OLC lawyers did far more than simply rule on the legality of an existing program; they helped to craft that program by putting in place sweeping reinterpretations of familiar and well-theorized legal concepts—concepts such as executive power, torture, and defenses like necessity and self-defense. Second, it is an important, but largely unresolved, question whether government lawyers should be subject to prosecution for illegal practices their advice helps to establish or sustain. Addressing this question is a thorny, though crucial task, for the way we handle the current controversy will set a precedent for the treatment of government lawyers called on to give benediction to an administration's illegal activities for years to come. Third, government lawyers who endorse and help to foster illegal policies of the executive branch play a singular role in damaging the rule of law, especially when such assistance depends on an illicit expansion of executive privilege: although disregarding legal norms will always damage the rule of law to *some* extent, the damage is of an entirely different order when illegal policies are wrapped in the mantle of legal legitimacy. If legal argumentation itself becomes distorted, the law will no longer provide a constraint against the erosion of legal values through the press of ideology. Prosecution is a particularly forceful way to seek to vindicate the rule of law in such cases. Correcting the excesses of specious legal analysis through the legal process itself reasserts the legitimacy of the internal logic of law. This effect is unlikely to be attained if the attempt to vindicate the rule of law focuses on the political process alone.[13] Criminal prosecution would thus appear to be an indispensable tool of democratic governance, one that can be crucial for restoring society's commitment to core democrati c values.

The idea of using criminal prosecution as a response to prior governmental misconduct has always been controversial, both in the domestic context and in the transitional justice literature.[14] Those who disfavor prosecution in the domestic context do so for the most part *not* because they think the torture policy morally and legally valid, but because they see prosecution as both doomed to failure and unwise from the standpoint of our political and military objectives. Rather than seeking to balance the pragmatic, philosophical, and political considerations that might factor into any actual decision about prosecution, however, my aim in this essay will be to point out the theoretical merits of what one might call the "prosecution model" for vindicating the rule of law, a task made especially important by the upper hand gained by practical and political objections to prosecution under the Obama Administration. In limiting my inquiry in this way, I am asking whether we ought, in the first instance, to regard the prosecution of government lawyers for giving illegal advice as a defensible and potentially effective way to redeem the rule of law in the face of severe injuries it may have sustained.[15]

Part II explores, inter alia, the requirement that lawmaking is fundamentally public, meaning that the reasoning that stands behind the allocation of rights and duties under the law should be available to all. After articulating the basic argument in favor of a societal "publicity condition" with respect to legal rules, I take such a condition for granted as a necessary feature of a society organized with adequate respect for the rule of law. I then suggest that the gap between the publicly announced commitment to democracy and human rights, on the one hand, and the actual policies used to govern, on the other, is objectionable, among other things, because it constitutes a form of free riding.[16]

Part III applies the above framework to the acts of the OLC lawyers. It suggests that the creation of the gap between publicly articulated rules and private reasoning is a clear violation of the publicity condition, particularly in its call for the significant expansion of executive powers argued for in the Bybee memorandum. It is this aspect of the private reasoning of OLC attorneys that poses the most serious threat to the rule of law, and the part that most stands in need of public correction. In the first half of Part III, I apply this argument to establish the case for liability not only for authorized instances of torture, but for anticipated unauthorized uses of torture during interrogation as well. I thus suggest that it is not unreasonable to hold the OLC lawyers responsible for both the interrogation techniques they actually endorsed, but also for the escalation of a culture of violence that foreseeably grew out of such authorization. In the remainder of Part III, I explore a possible rebuttal of the argument that the call for expanded executive authority establishes a violation of the rule of law, namely that lawyers from the OLC may be exonerated for distorting the law in defense of torture by the fact that they held a *good faith* belief that they were rendering valid legal opinions. Since the impermissibility of torture is something that every one can be expected to know without the benefit of instruction or additional notice, I argue that good faith reasoning should not provide a defense.

Part IV turns to another avenue of defense for the OLC lawyers, namely one that denies the culpability of the interrogators, with respect to whom the lawyers would be accomplices. There are several theories under which the principals might claim a defense: they can be thought of as having a legal justification for their use of torture, an excuse for having done so, or an immunity to prosecution. This Part argues that defenses and immunities for the principals ought not to apply, and it criticizes the Bybee memorandum's efforts to establish such a defense.

Part V concludes with some further remarks about the relation between free riding and vindicating the rule of law.

II

On August 1, 2002, the Office of Legal Counsel issued a crucial memorandum seeking to defend "enhanced interrogation techniques," or "EITs," methods whose use had already begun in "black sites" in Iraq and elsewhere. There were twelve such methods, only eleven of which have been declassified. The known methods are the "attention grasp," "walling," "facial hold," "facial or insult slap," "cramped confinement," "insects," "wall standing," "stress positions," "sleep deprivation," "use of diapers" (and concomitant denials of access to toilet facilities), and "waterboarding."[17] The central argument of the Bybee memorandum was that for an act to qualify as "torture" under the federal torture statute (*18 U.S.C. § § 2340–2340A*), it must constitute an "extreme act," one that inflicts pain "equivalent in intensity to the pain accompanying serious physical injury, such as organ failure, impairment of bodily function, or even death." Alternatively, it must inflict mental pain resulting in "significant psychological harm of significant duration, e.g. lasting for months or even years."[18] The Bybee memorandum went on to conclude that the techniques generally employed in connection with the interrogation of detainees would not meet this standard, though it made no attempt actually to identify the subjective quality of the pain of "organ failure," "impairment of bodily function," or "death." Furthermore, there was also no attempt made to respond to the historical irony of this conclusion, and little argument was offered to justify the narrow definition of the term "torture" in the federal statute. Nor was any attempt made to establish what the degree of pain or psychological pressure was for a person undergoing the most severe of the known EITs, namely, waterboarding.

The debate about the narrow definition of torture in the Bybee memorandum has raged on since the memo first saw the light of day. This point has drawn more fire in the popular press than any other part of the memorandum. While garnering less attention, however, there are other parts of the memorandum that are of still greater concern, such as the view of executive authority the memorandum defends. Finally, there is a strange and poorly argued discussion of a possible necessity defense or self-defense claim for the interrogators who used the government-endorsed techniques. Whatever the concerns about the specific positions taken, however, the aspect of the memorandum that has drawn the greatest ire from legal professionals has been the lack of fidelity to established sources of law. With regard to the quality of its legal scholarship, the Bybee memorandum has been nearly universally condemned by the American legal profession as reflecting inaccurate and unprofessional argumentation and research. The condemnation comes not only from partisan sources. Yoo's former colleague at the OLC, for example, Jack Goldsmith, ultimately repudiated the memos Yoo authored, calling the work "flawed in so many important respects," "too simplistic and potentially erroneous," and "mak[ing] overly broad and unnecessary claims about possible defenses to various federal crimes . . . without considering, as we must, the specific circumstances of particular cases."[19]

Of greatest interest for our purposes is the analysis the memorandum offers of the proper place of executive authority in a constitutional system. Yoo's arguments for expanded executive powers is a long-standing feature of his constitutional law scholarship, both before and after he worked at the Office of Legal Counsel. His central claim is that the commander-in-chief power in times of war is virtually unlimited, and that the president must have the power to decide on the scope of his own authority. Indeed, the Bybee memorandum portrays the president's powers during times of war as so extensive that even a federal statute that contravened executive prerogative in this context would itself have to be considered unconstitutional.

> Even if an interrogation method arguably were to violate Section 2340A, the statute would be unconstitutional if it impermissibly encroached on the President's constitutional power to conduct a military campaign. . . .
> *Any effort to apply Section 2340A in a manner that interferes with the President's direction of such core war matters as the detention and interrogation of enemy combatants . . . would be unconstitutional.*[20]

The conception of unlimited sovereignty makes a frontal assault on two mainstays of Anglo-American constitutional jurisprudence: first, the Enlightenment idea that the sovereign is himself a creature of the laws, and second, the foundational idea that executive power must be balanced against or constrained by other branches of government. Ironically, the Bybee memorandum's conception of executive privilege is so strong that it effectively makes the attempt to narrow the definition of "torture" in the first part of the memo otiose, for as the above quotation suggests, even if the authorized interrogation techniques *do* contravene the statute, that would only indicate that the statute is unconstitutional if construed as limiting the wartime powers of an executive branch convinced of the wisdom of using such techniques! Yoo has recently defended his own commitment to this interpretation of executive authority in several interviews. In an interview with an investigator from the Office of Professional Responsibility (OPR), for example, he was asked whether the president's wartime powers could include ordering an entire village of civilians to be exterminated. Yoo's response was that such an order "would fall within the commander-in-chief's power over tactical decisions."[21]

The appeal to the unlimited nature of the commander-in-chief powers is the intellectual heart of the OLC memos. It is also the doctrinal commitment that poses the deepest threat to the rule of law. The argument from executive privilege creates an exception to the rule of law so great that, as Yoo effectively explains, no statute or other source of law could constrain executive authority on this theory. And the constitutional argument for these expanded privileges that lurks in the background makes the "vesting" powers of the executive branch so significant that ordinary constitutional constraints, such as the bill of rights, do not provide much limitation either.[22]

A mystery lies in the fact that though clandestine, these arguments were written as though for public consumption, and at least one of their authors, John Yoo, has been willing to endorse their logic publicly in books and in public interviews. Yet the formal legal analysis in which the administration appears to have invested so much was intended to be classified, and it was, on the whole, an object of shame, not pride. Thus although they are the kinds of arguments one would normally prepare to convince a disbelieving judge or jury, the documents were actually intended to be buried forever in internal, classified memoranda, documents designed to remain as secret as the conduct they were meant to justify. What, then, could the possible benefit be of developing elaborate legal arguments, whose only purpose is to provide a legal justification to a close circle of presidential advisors who presumably never themselves felt the need to establish a justification for the relevant EITs in the first place? Since the use of legal argumentation appears to be as nakedly political as the commitment to the torture policy, it is not clear what the Bush Administration saw itself as gaining by wrapping its illegal policies in legal trappings.

A number of political philosophers over time have articulated objections to private lawmaking, the best known of these being the point expressed by John Rawls' famous "publicity condition." As Rawls first articulates this condition in *A Theory of Justice*, it is a requirement that the basic institutions of a democratic society function according to a set of *public rules*. Moreover, the public availability of such rules is a requirement that Rawls builds into the definition of an institution in a "well-ordered society."[23] He writes:

In saying that an institution, and therefore the basic structure of society, is a public system of rules, I mean then that everyone engaged in it knows what he *would* know if these rules and his participation in the activity they define were the result of an agreement. A person taking part in an institution knows what the rules demand of him and of the others. He also knows that the others know this and that they know that he knows this, and so on. . . . The principles of justice are to apply to social arrangements understood to be public in this sense.[24]

In other words, Rawls' two principles of justice, which parties in an "original position" of choice would select to govern their society, apply strictly to institutions that are organized according to rules that are public in the foregoing sense.

As Rawls describes it, there are two aspects to such publicity. First, it must be the case that each individual affected by the relevant institution has the knowledge that he *would* have "if the rules and his participation in the activity they define were the result of an agreement."[25] Second, such knowledge has a regressive aspect: each person participating in an institution knows the rules of that institution and his and others' obligations under the rules, and he knows that others know the rules, and that they know that he knows this, and so on. The second aspect of the publicity condition is the legal analogue to the game theoretic assumption known as the "common knowledge of rationality."[26]

There is a countervailing strain of thought about publicity in political theory, however, and this is the rather darker, Machiavellian idea that the efficacy of government depends on the maintenance of a certain respectful distance between those with the right to rule and those over whom they rule. A number of political and legal philosophers, starting as early as Plato's famous description of government and its relation to the general public in the *Republic,* have endorsed a separation between public governmental reason and the operative principles of political rule.[27] Just such a separation appears to have been at work in the elaborate attempt to justify, in private terms, what could never have been accepted as a piece of legitimate legal analysis if held up to the light of public scrutiny.

Interestingly, none of the philosophers who maintain that rules of government should be clandestine has suggested that observing a separation between the rules governing institutions and the public knowledge of such rules would *enhance* a society's commitment to the rule of law. Instead, their idea is the utilitarian thought that administrative control and efficiency are increased if the public can be kept in the dark about the policies their government is actually pursuing. For these purposes, the rule of law proves an inconvenience. The more one is able to leave the public in a state of ignorance with respect to one's actual policies, the less interference one can expect, and hence the more effectively government is able to implement its real priorities. But the rule of law requires more than administrative efficiency; it requires a deep societal commitment to a shared set of ideals and principles. These function not as figureheads on governments organized around wholly disassociated premises, but as a normative basis for a shared standard, both within and outside a given society. The rule of law, for this reason, should function as an impediment to the widening of the gap between public reason and private administrative function.

From a contractarian point of view, violation of the publicity condition in democratic governance presents a grave breach of the rational foundations of cooperative arrangements. This is so in two respects. First, domestically, the extensive use of clandestine executive governance forecloses the possibility of public debate over the conditions of political rule, and impedes individual citizens from engaging in an assessment of whether their grant of authority to a sovereign entity satisfies the original conditions that made such grant rational. Secrecy thus deprives citizens of an opportunity to evaluate the rationality of their own deference to authority, and hence to the continuing rationality of their adherence to the terms of the contract. The existence and form of government must be continuously justified to individual subjects in terms of advantages to their own welfare, the contractarian asserts. But a government conducting its business in secret fails to provide the necessary justification, because the lack of information makes it impossible for the citizen to assess where this interest lies. It therefore takes advantage of the political fidelity of citizens, without having had to prove that it is worthy of such fidelity. The rational response on the part of the citizen can only be to reject the authority that governs in this way.

Second, internationally the gap between public rhetoric and private lawmaking produces immense distrust in the broader world community, especially when the humanitarian commitments to which lip service is paid serve as a disguise for extensive violations of basic human rights. Insofar as any nation professes adherence to universal humanitarian norms and thereby enhances its credibility in international arrangements, it acquires an illegitimate advantage over other nations by the making of false promises. Once those promises have been shown to be false, the violating nation establishes itself as a free rider relative to other nations. The rational response on the part of the international community can only be expulsion from the community of nations.

This is a point that Thomas Hobbes recognized over four centuries ago:

> [H]e which declares he thinks it reason to deceive those that help him can in reason expect no other means of safety than what can be had from his own single power. He, therefore, that breaketh his covenant, and consequently declareth that he thinks he may with reason do so, cannot be received into any society that unite themselves for peace and defence but by the error of them that receive him.[28]

For a rational contractarian like Hobbes, the foregoing represents the most essential reason to take domestic action against free riders: rendering false legal arguments is like engaging in political rule with a "Ring of Gyges." It creates power for the ruler that cannot be questioned or confronted. Given that the foundation of political authority is a social contract for the mutual benefit of all members of society, anyone who intentionally free rides on the trust of social cooperators does so at his peril. If discovered, he is to be sharply rejected from the community, and this means rejected from the basic terms of social cooperation.

A nation that treats other nations with which it has entered into agreements of mutual benefit as though they were mere tools for its own domestic aims thus violates the terms of cooperation in the community of nations. If the United States manifests disregard for the basic agreements regarding international human rights to which it had formerly pledged its allegiance, then other nations having exercised self-restraint have been disadvantaged by their own cooperation. In order to avoid a total collapse into a general state of war, the cooperating nations must expel the free rider. And with regard to the latter, they have no choice but to reject the agreement and all other possible terms of cooperation.

Domestically, then, the argument that establishes a governing regime as a free rider is that found in the exaggerated claims about the supremacy of executive power over democratic processes. Internationally, the argument lies in the suggestion of the supremacy of domestic over international law and the disregard for international agreements that would restrict that superiority. The Bybee memorandum makes both types of arguments, and suggests on the one hand that the counterweight to domestic executive authority—the rules of democratic governance, on the one hand, and the rules and customs of international comity, on the other—are normatively powerless and should be disregarded. But such reasoning is manifestly false: free riding on agreements regarding the democratic foundations of government, as well as those pertaining to universal human rights, is damaging in the extreme to the rule of law. Large-scale agreement can survive if there is only a small number of people who fail to conform, as long as their nonparticipation is either sufficiently covert, or else sufficiently isolated from the behavior of others that it will fail to generalize. Under such conditions, the defection will not significantly weaken the agreement. But as the above quotation from Hobbes suggests, where defection is *known* to exist, no matter how minor, the overt rejection of fidelity to the social contract provides the basis for excluding the free rider from the terms of cooperation.

A question arises whether *all* defections must be punished. Would such a rule not be overly demanding, not to mention unrealistic? Sometimes, arguably, it is less destabilizing to ignore a small defection than to punish everyone to the full degree authorized by law. And might that not turn out to be the case where government actors are concerned, in particular government lawyers who were merely being careless in the legal advice they offered?

There is, I think, a real answer to this question, one that is implicit in many passages in Hobbes, and that seems to be foundational to Kantian ethics as well. The problem with tolerating free riders, Hobbes notes, is that it suggests that we embrace their behavior, and it signals to others that we would be committed to the same from them.[29] For this reason, Hobbes suggests, it must be an integral part of the original terms of the agreement that free riding on its benefits cannot be tolerated. The absurdity of entering into an agreement for mutual benefit and failing to stick to that agreement, Hobbes would say, is tantamount to declaring at the outset that although we mutually pledge our cooperation toward one another, there will be no requirement that anyone actually adhere to the conditions of the agreement. Such reasoning would be internally contradictory, and cannot be either rationally or politically maintained.

III

Let us suppose that at least one of the techniques endorsed in the Bybee memorandum, most likely waterboarding, constitutes torture under 18 U.S.C. § § 2340–2340A. And let us also suppose that that the appeals to expanded executive authority to override the authority of the federal statute are not legally well-founded. What would be the case for prosecuting the lawyers from the OLC for torture under the statute? The most straightforward way to make the legal case is that the lawyers are accomplices to the federal crime of torture, where the principals are the interrogators who actually employed it. The argument most often made against this position, however, is that the OLC lawyers cannot be prosecuted for sanctioning the EITs endorsed in the August 1 memorandum, because they truly believed that such methods were permissible under the federal torture statute, for all of the foregoing reasons. The defense most often raised on their behalf is that the arguments for the legality of the EITs were offered in good faith, a point we will address below.

However, evidence continues to mount that the EITs the memo sought to defend were not the only forms of harsh treatment to which detainees in Guantánamo, Abu Ghraib, and at other "black sites" were subjected. Beyond the officially sanctioned *torture light* that the administration was willing to cast its moral weight behind, there was also an unofficial use of more extreme methods. Although the number is disputed, it seems clear that a not insignificant number of detainees died under torture, and despite the fact that officials all the way up the chain of command were aware of the potential consequences of the use of these harsher methods, they continued to condone them or at least to look the other way, despite the fact that many outstripped the officially sanctioned techniques identified in the Bybee memorandum.[30]

Whether the interrogation techniques actually employed fall within or without those that were officially sanctioned, there is an argument against prosecution. On the one hand, the lawyers cannot be liable for the interrogators' use of the officially sanctioned techniques, because their endorsement of such techniques, whether or not legally correct, was made in good faith, and so constitutes an excuse for any violation of the prohibition on the use of torture. On the other hand, there are the harsher, unofficial interrogation techniques that spread from the official ones. These *would* presumably fit the definition of torture under § 2340, even by the lawyers' lights. But these can also not count against the lawyers of the OLC, it is said, because they were ultra vires with respect to the techniques the memos actually authorized. Thus either the interrogator adhered to the list of techniques authorized by the OLC memos, in which case neither the principal nor the lawyer authorizing the conduct could be prosecuted for torture, given that they acted in good faith adherence to the law, or the interrogator's behavior exceeded the OLC limits, in which case he *could* be guilty of torture, but on his own account. Either way, The OLC lawyers escape criminal liability for officially endorsing acts of torture as legally permissible.

There are, however, arguments against this apparent catch-22. Once interrogators become convinced that a detainee possesses useful information, the violence can easily spread from the officially approved methods to harsher, informally sanctioned methods. Arguably, in authorizing torture on a more restricted scale knowing it would have a tendency to increase, OLC lawyers may also be ripe for prosecution for foreseen or foreseeable uses of torture that were not specifically authorized in OLC memoranda. Similar to the expansion of liability to co-conspirators under a foreseeability theory, the extension of OLC responsibility for torture seems a natural line to take in light of the known, or easily knowable consequences of placing the bodily integrity of prisoners in the hands of individual interrogators. To confer such a broad grant of physical and psychological power on CIA agents and other clandestine interrogators, who have little to no accountability to publicly articulated rules, is to take a grave risk that there will be abuse.

The opposite process is also possible, and can also be anticipated under certain circumstances. If the social contract makes clear the fate of free riders, and parties to the agreement are consistent in their responses to such individuals, the degree of compliance with the agreement will increase, since more people will be willing to self-constrain in order to reap the benefits of cooperation. They will do so with ever-increasing confidence that they will in fact achieve those benefits if they incur the cost of the agreement. The point is clear in both the domestic and the international contexts in any instance in which large numbers of individuals must regulate an agreement without the help of a central enforcement agency. And in both the domestic and international contexts, there is a serious difficulty with enforcement; in the domestic context, the lack of enforcement stems from the fact that the central enforcer has turned against democratic principles, and in the international context, there simply is no enforcer, and the result is more or less the same.

If, for example, nearly all citizens voluntarily pay their income tax, there is a tendency for the norm of paying taxes to strengthen, and the number of taxpayers has a tendency to increase.[31] Similarly, if there is sufficiently high compliance with ticket requirements on public transportation in countries where an honor system is in place, the degree of compliance with the ticket rules will tend to strengthen further, until it is nearly universal.[32] Presumably individuals in such a society benefit most if everyone observes the tax and transportation requirements, even if the cost of such rules requires them to sacrifice some well-being as compared with the world in which they free ride on the compliance of others. But assuming this latter option is ruled out by the terms of the agreement (and by a rationality condition, such as common knowledge that would make such cheating readily discoverable), we have reason to treat free riding on the efforts of others as infeasible, and so to regard our highest good as realized in the context of cooperation. Against this background, it will turn out that if most people voluntarily pay for their subway tickets in an honor code system, that will tend to increase the number of people who voluntarily pay taxes. Conversely, if there is sufficient public flouting of tax obligations and ticket requirements, the degree of compliance with such rules will tend to spiral downward, until there is very little social compliance with the rule.

Arguably, a similar "tipping" phenomenon was at work in Iraq, and was particularly on display in the abuses that occurred at Abu Ghraib. Since the rates of compliance with international human rights norms were intentionally reduced by official sanction of enhanced interrogation, the general level of compliance with such norms began to spiral downward, until there was widespread rejection of humanitarian norms on all sides. The result was significantly decreased rates of compliance with basic human rights norms, which in turn made compliance risky, and drove the rates of cooperation further down. Of course the objects of this treatment will respond in kind, since although they do not personally and specifically have a contract with their captors that commits them to extending and receiving humane treatment, any implicit agreements regarding civilized exchange are quickly shed, and captor and captive will further descend into that Hobbesian state of war. There are, then, significant dangers of noncompliance with fundamental norms and principles of governance, and significant benefits to be had from cooperation with such norms. Indeed, in some cases compliance can safely be extended to those who have failed to comply, and the possibility of upward improvement can be increased even by unilateral action.

Since the federal torture statute (18 U.S.C. § § 2340–2340A) is primarily a codification of an international instrument—the United Nations Convention against Torture (CAT)—we encounter both the domestic and the international examples of intentional free riding in one and the same conduct, namely, lack of compliance with the legal norms governing the use of torture. In the international context, it makes sense for us to return to first principles and ask whether treaties such as CAT would be regarded by the nations who sign and ratify it as sufficiently attractive to garner their own agreement were they to know at the time of signing that at least one of the major signatories to the Convention would free ride on the other members of the Convention and refuse to adhere to its terms when inconvenient to do so. In other words, if we assume that nation-states are roughly rational, self-interested entities with "nonaltruistic preferences," would they agree to contract with other nations if they knew that those states secretly disavowed the treaties they signed? The answer, of course, is *no*. Contracting with other nations on matters with important domestic implications makes sense only on the condition that the other party can be assumed to be collaborative. And if it is rational to free ride, because the chances of detection, are sufficiently low, then adherence to international agreements cannot be anticipated and relied upon without a system of sanctions for violators in place.

The same might be said of prosecution under federal law. In democratic governments, we can think of the force of law as stemming from the fact that good law reflects that set of agreements that rational agents with largely self-interested preferences would adopt in order to further their own welfare. Such agreements are not rational merely because they consist in mutual forbearance from the infliction of evil on one another, but because they allow mistrustful agents to capture the gains of cooperation with others. In effect, if free riders on agreements of mutual advantage are not disciplined, the rational basis for entering into such contracts in the first place would be undermined.

The OLC lawyers recommended to the president that members of al-Qaida and the Taliban be treated as so-called "enemy combatants," rather than domestic criminals, and hence as falling outside the scope of possible collaborative agreements. This was often defended with a quasi-contractarian argument. As Yoo has repeatedly suggested, Al-Qaida doesn't follow the Geneva Conventions, so why should we? This argument comes close to making a sensible contractarian argument, but in the end it misses its mark. The obligation to follow international human rights norms is not owed primarily to the individuals such norms were meant to protect. The obligation is owed instead to our fellow citizens, with whom we have pledged to maintain a government of limited powers, and other nation-states with whom agreements regarding basic human rights have been made. All other individuals or states are mere *third-party beneficiaries* of such agreements. But when an agreement is violated and an individual's rights ignored, the relevant contractual duty that has been breached is one that is owed to all other individuals, or nations, and not uniquely to the one whose violation of the agreement was anticipated. In that sense, the public rhetoric that the United States is committed to human rights does not, and should not, save it from incurring the wrath of those other nation-states who are willing to abide by such commitments in deed as well as in word.[33]

Assuming that the conduct of those engaging in enhanced interrogation techniques did indeed violate both international law and federal statutes, and that the OLC lawyers who sanctified such techniques can fairly be thought of as accomplices to that conduct,[34] one would think prosecuting those involved—both at the higher and lower levels—would be a natural way to proceed. In the trials at Nuremberg, both types of actors were prosecuted. But in this case, there are some compelling arguments on the other side. With regard to those who acted on military or CIA orders, it is hard to deny the normative force of their claim to exoneration based on the fact that they were merely implementing a policy decided on by others. And with respect to the government lawyers, they were merely functioning in the way that lawyers usually do, namely, giving their opinions as to the legality of a government initiative. Surely they cannot be prosecuted for *that*, one might suppose. Are they not hired for this very purpose, namely, to articulate the background law to the best of their abilities and to present their true opinions of the legal imperatives under the circumstances? Moreover, there is little precedent for prosecuting lawyers who were acting in a purely advisory role.[35] This is entirely different, it is said, from prosecuting an actual accessory, since the lawyers supposedly do not themselves wish to encourage the conduct on whose legality they are advising, and are not seeking to encourage it. At worst, the conduct appears to be a violation of a rule of professional ethics, such as Model Rule 1.2(d), which forbids a lawyer from assisting a client in conduct known to be criminal or fraudulent.[36]

The two obstacles to prosecution—the "just following orders" defense and the defense of the supposedly neutral, disengaged lawyer, merely stating his honest opinion—together present a significant threat to the rule of law, given that their combined effect is to exonerate anyone involved in either creating or implementing the torture policies. There are two reasons why that combination of immunities is particularly deleterious to the rule of law: first, it abandons a crucial opportunity to repudiate the incursions into the rule of law by condemning conduct that was previously endorsed and accepted. President Obama had the idea of just such a public repudiation when he declared in his inaugural address that "the United States does not torture."[37] This statement suggested to many that President Obama was prepared to reject the Bush-era policies as forcefully as possible, but the backing away from prosecution for torture has belied their hopes.

Second, failure to prosecute damages the rule of law by constituting an implicit endorsement of the conduct of the previous administration, however illegal or wrongful it may have been. What it condones is admittedly complicated, for turning one's back on wrongdoing need not always constitute an endorsement of the wrongful conduct. What the failure to prosecute signifies is an acceptance of the expanded conception of executive power the Bybee memorandum advances. If I am correct, the strongest reason to prosecute the Office of Legal Counsel lawyers who wrote and signed the "torture memos" is to publicly repudiate the conception of executive privilege on which their conclusions in part depended. This aim, combined with the need to affirm, through deeds, the United States' commitment to human rights at more than a merely rhetorical level, provide two powerful reasons to prosecute Justice Department attorneys for aiding and abetting torture through memos that endorse it.

The next question is whether a good faith belief on the part of the lawyers, if indeed that claim can be maintained, should constitute a defense to the suggestion that they can be prosecuted as accomplices to torture. To allow the good faith defense amounts to the suggestion that the lawyers cannot be accessories to torture unless they actually believed that what they were advocating was in fact torture. This argument, however, is highly questionable.

First, why should accessorial liability for torture in this case require that lawyers endorsing the torture policies have believed that the advice they were giving was false? It has never been a requirement, after all, that a criminal defendant believe he was guilty of a crime in order to be guilty of that crime. Roughly speaking, he need only believe that he has engaged in the relevant conduct, not that he know its legal status.[38] This is the familiar point in criminal law that *ignorance of the law is no excuse.*[39] So arguably, if the lawyers gave grossly false advice about the legal status of the torture policies, they might still be prosecuted as accessories to torture (or, alternatively, as conspirators), even if they did in fact make an honest mistake about the proper interpretation of federal and international law. The requirement that a lawyer be aware of the illegal nature of his client's conduct is an appropriate requirement for the relevant professional ethics prohibition on assisting a client with a course of action known to be illegal. But it makes little sense for ordinary accessorial liability.

Second, is a point of fact: if the lawyers from the OLC really *did* believe their own legal rhetoric: if, as Yoo maintains, the torture policy was both legal and wisely adopted, why *did* the Bush Administration go to such lengths to keep its interrogation policies secret? That is, given that they had constructed an extensive network of legal arguments to support the legality of the policy, and that this network purported to justify the policy in overt, publicly consumable form, why not just declare the policy publicly, along with the elaborate legal construction designed to support the policy from a legal standpoint? Why not just come clean and draw out the implications publicly from the position that was taken to justify the relevant methods of interrogation, namely, that members of al-Qaida and the Taliban are "unlawful enemy combatants," rather than either prisoners of war or criminal suspects, and as such are not in fact entitled to the respect for human rights for which the president expressed such admiration in his 2003 speech at the United Nations? Although the appeal to the concept of an "unlawful combatant" was made public, the true implications of that label remained hidden for many years, namely, that as such, the administration believed that individuals so designated had acted in a way that forfeited even the most basic human rights. And insofar as they fall outside the ambit of civilized society, and hence outside the domain of rules such as those governing prisoners of war under the Geneva Conventions, they fall outside the bounds of all moral restraint. Thus, the puzzle is once again the combination of public rhetoric with private content: why did the Bush administration pour great effort into providing a *legal* justification for a policy it never intended to present publicly? Or, to turn the question once again the other way around, given that it *thought* it had a valid legal justification for the policy, why did it not reveal the nature of the policy and the legal justifications for it alongside?

A likely answer is that the OLC lawyers actually knew that the legal arguments they were making to support those techniques had little legal foundation. Indeed, this will probably be clear to anyone who bothered to read the August 1st memorandum, and would have been clear to members of the inner cabinet who presumably commandeered the memo, without caring much about the legal reasoning it contained. In other words, this was a way of distracting attention from the fact that the administration's own lawyers had, by 2002, taken the official, but secret, position that neither domestic nor international law can hold sway over domestic executive authority, and that therefore in times of war, there are no legitimate restrictions on the power of the Commander-in-Chief. The administration was walking a very fine line: it needed the sweeping arguments of domestic executive supremacy in order to convince itself that it possessed adequate grounds for ignoring the various sources of law and political authority that rejected its approach to the war on terror, at the same time that it sought to insulate the use of its own arguments from public scrutiny. For this latter purpose, the more strongly the United States could appear to respect international human rights, the more isolated its secret but powerful arguments for rejecting those rights in particular contexts could be made to seem. The Bush Administration thus ironically sought to bolster its own policies *rejecting* human rights law by appearing to accept them in other, less controversial contexts, such as in the example of the Beijing Olympic Games.

What is the evidence for the suggestion of bad faith, and how can we make such an assertion based on so little actual knowledge of mental state? First and foremost, there is the quality of the arguments themselves: many of the legal claims offered in support of these techniques were transparently lacking in legal credentials. Arguments pertaining to the interpretation of the relevant federal statutes contain little to none of the usual citations to legislative intent, inference regarding intent drawn from a careful interpretation of the statutes themselves, evidence regarding the contemporaneous understanding of the language of the statutes when they were drafted, and so on. Instead, what we find is short phrases and isolated terms analyzed without benefit of context or common understandings, no evidence whatsoever that might bear on legislative intent, and specious arguments of a quasi-textualist nature designed to bolster highly ideologically driven interpretations of the relevant sources of law. This point was made repeatedly, and in careful detail, in the OPR memorandum.

By advancing legal arguments of any sort, whether true or false, precise or careless, well supported or utterly invented, the president's legal advisors were able to appear as though they were arguing for the legitimacy of certain methods of interrogation in good faith. And insofar as the legal advisors appeared to be arguing in good faith, those in the administration who had designed the relevant interrogation methods and fervently believed them to be of crucial utility in the war against terror could also seek cover by relying on those opinions. In this way we had legitimation through division of labor: those who design and implement intelligence policies are not themselves directly responsible for knowing the legal status of their conduct; they are permitted to design such policies on the basis of utilitarian considerations alone. And those who pronounced on the legality of these policies neither directly drafted them nor sought to encourage them. The true authors of the policy are not responsible, because they cannot be held to making correct judgments about the legality of their conduct, and those whose job it is to pass on the legality of the policy are also not responsible, because they are merely rendering an honestly held opinion, a stance whose supposed passivity guarantees its own immunity.

IV

I have thus far made a case for prosecuting former lawyers from the OLC for violations of federal law based on the suggestion that vindication of the rule of law requires the explicit and visible rejection of free riders on democratic principles. This argument, however, has something in the nature of a consequentialist flavor to it, given that it takes into account the *effects* of prosecution as an argument that counts in favor of it. Any such argument in the case of criminal prosecution will be dangerous, in that it lacks the individualized component that retributivist intuitions seem to require. In this regard, it will be crucial to consider several further defenses that the lawyers might have based on the individual responsibility of the principals to whom their liability would be attached as accessories in an actual prosecution. And it is these factors that most focus our attention on the question of individual justice and responsibility.

First, might the lawyers from the Office of Legal Counsel share a possible *justification* defense of the principals for advising others in the administration about the legality of manifestly illegal conduct? This is indeed an argument the Bybee memorandum itself makes with regard to individual interrogators applying Justice Department guidelines. The suggestion is that individual interrogators might be able to claim a necessity defense to the charge of torture, once all other arguments have failed. The defense would be based on a kind of collective or societal self-defense claim: just as an individual whose life is at risk may sometimes engage in illegal actions in order to prevent or preempt harm to himself, so society might engage in such acts when the threat to itself is sufficiently grave and sufficiently imminent.[40] The idea that former Bush officials believed that U. S. interrogation practices were *illegal but nevertheless justified,* is one that is only now slowly making its way into Republican defenses of the Bush Administration's policies.

The major obstacle to claiming a necessity defense in this context, however, is that necessity cannot strictly speaking be demonstrated because the pressure to torture one particular individual is never as severe as the legal philosophers who pose the truly wrenching torture hypotheticals would purport to suggest. The use of torture at Abu Ghraib did not fit the "ticking time bomb" scenario, not least because the vast majority of detainees had little to no information to offer.[41] The more likely claim in this domain would be self-defense, and the 2002 memo indeed makes an argument in this direction as well. But it is weak and unconvincing: self-defense was never meant to apply to society's welfare. It applies to individual actors who once again find themselves in a situation in which they must act immediately if they are to avert a threat to their lives or bodily integrity. And it is once again safe to say that in the vast majority of cases of enhanced interrogation, no such immediate need will manifest itself.

Lawyers in the Bush Administration, however, were so convinced that the survival of the country depended on the acquisition of information about terror plans in the making, and that such plans could not be gleaned from ordinary methods of interrogation, that they believed that they had a justification for doing what the law does not allow, and this belief was presumably replicated on the level of individual interrogators. Should we not allow that *if* they were indeed acting in good faith in a second sense, namely they believed their use of torture was justified and would be legally excused, that they might benefit from a defense like *mistake?* Even if they incorrectly assessed the applicability of the concept of justification to their case, then, should not the honest, but mistaken, assessment of the need to use defensive force result in some sort of excuse (that is, mistaken justification), as long as they were reasonable in believing in the need for justification? Notice that this is not the kind of *mistake of law* defense we discussed above, which I denied should have significant import as a defense for Bush interrogators and lawyers. Rather, it is *mistake about the availability of a justification defense,* which is different from the lack of knowledge of illegality. Normally, however, we do not allow criminal defendants to convert what should be a justification defense into a kind of excuse. For if a justification applies to a prima facie offense, it would override the culpability that attaches to a defendant's fulfillment of a prohibitory norm. But the same cannot be said when a defendant makes a mistake about a justification. In that case, there can be no override; there can only be a denial of the mens rea conditions that could serve to establish culpability in the first place. Since, as I argued above, knowledge of the illegality of the conduct promoted is not necessary to be guilty of a crime, there is no mens rea requirement that attaches to the illegality condition, and hence no way to generate a "mistake" defense regarding the belief that one's conduct was justified.

If the concept of justification really does play the role I have suggested it does in the thinking of principals and accessories about the use of torture, we can now make sense of why President Bush had the sangfroid to make the statement he did about America's adherence to the Convention on Torture in June 2003. It is not *really* that he and lawyers at the Office of Legal

Counsel believed that waterboarding was not torture; they knew full well it was. Rather, they saw the months and years following September 11, 2001 as a protracted condition of siege, one in which ordinary legal rules could be *justifiably* dispensed with on grounds of either justification (self-defense) or for social welfare (necessity). This explains a great deal about the mind-set of Yoo and Bybee in fashioning these policies. The lawyers of the OLC presumably thought they were engaged in developing highly necessary concessions to emergency planning. One must not be afraid to get one's hands dirty when survival itself depends on it.

Finally, we should consider a third type of mistake of law defense, and this is when there has been inadequate notice. Although they were aware of a risk that the enhanced interrogation techniques might turn out to be illegal, they were *not* on notice that such lapses could actually result in prosecution. That is, because human rights abuses of this sort are sufficiently widespread, and the prosecution of those who merely offer legal advice to sanctify this conduct sufficiently rare, they had every reason to suppose that the world would look the other way when suspected terrorists were tortured in the name of national security.[42] This argument, however, once again seems to me to fail in light of the post–World War II prosecutions we ourselves conducted against Japanese soldiers who used the waterboarding technique on captured enemies. The same might be said more generally of the most significant of the novelties of the Bush Administration's approach to detainees, namely, the decision to treat them as "unlawful combatants." Since this decision itself had little precedent and was highly tendentious, legally speaking, the OLC lawyers should have been aware of a risk that they might have made a legal mistake in making use of this category, given that it stripped individuals of rights they might traditionally have had.

What I have been implicitly suggesting in this and the preceding section is that the key to the legal cover for both lawyers from the Office of Legal Counsel and for individuals acting to implement their opinions can be located in the idea that each individual acts pursuant to a specific and delimited role: a presidential legal advisor has an obligation to give advice on the legality of executive conduct to the very best of his ability, taking into account the available sources and experts who can correctly inform him of the legal status of such conduct. From a moral point of view, then, making a mistake about the governing law is not necessarily criticizable, as long as one's errors are made in the absence of any legal knowledge to the contrary, and based on a thorough review of all the legal sources that might have a bearing on the matter. The utility of the appeal to human rights and other democratic values is that such rhetoric, offered at the same time that such values are being systematically ignored, provides an apparent basis for exonerating the individuals who were implementing the administration's most cherished, illegal policies of the time. If the administration as a whole could be understood to prize the very values its policies are intent on ignoring, a presumption might be raised that lawyers interpreting international and domestic legal constraints will do so in a way that respects them. At the very least, the administration can be presumed to be acting on the basis of a set of honestly held views about the legal permissibility of the policies it sought to defend. And since the misperception that government lawyers may be punishable for bad faith interpretations of law but not for good faith ones appears to be an abiding view, it is not hard to see why the rhetoric appealing to human rights and rejecting the use of torture would be appealing.

V

The United States benefits significantly from being viewed by other nations as a leader in human rights: it makes it easier to secure the cooperation of those nations, and also gives us a secure position from which to insist on the humane treatment of our own POWs when captured by enemy forces. Other nations benefit similarly from the commitment to human rights in a variety of ways, and so, we might say, there are mutual gains to be had from the coordinated restraint of personal maximizing on the part of nation-states in favor of adherence to international norms of human rights. Unfortunately, as President Bush was also aware, it is not the actual adherence to such norms that provides access to the benefits of international cooperation, but the *appearance* of adhering to such norms. If the United States is, indeed, free riding on the commitment to international agreements regarding human rights, by paying lip service to its dictates while ignoring its contents, what response should the international community have? Should it expel the United States from human rights agreements, on the ground that it does not contribute to the mutual benefit for which others sacrifice? As we saw above, such an argument was raised by John Yoo in his defense of treating the Taliban and al-Qaida members as unlawful combatants instead of as prisoners of war, which would have afforded them POW status under the Geneva Conventions. He argued that this categorization was morally permissible on the grounds that they themselves do not follow the Geneva Conventions. As Yoo correctly points out, they deliberately target civilian populations, use civilian populations for cover, do not accord prisoner of war status to their own hostages, and so on. In contractarian terms, Yoo might say that given that the Taliban and al-Qaida have exempted themselves from the human rights conventions in their treatment of others, the United States have no reason to afford *them* any of the benefits of self-restraint in war when they have clearly manifested their ill-intentions towards us.

But we have also seen that this argument is weak in several respects. First, contravention of the federal torture statute does not hang on whether the victims of torture are protected by the Geneva Conventions. Second, expulsion from the terms of the social contract does not entail that anything goes, morally speaking. As we saw above, our primary duty to respect the terms of the humanitarian social contract is owed not to those who *violate* the contract, but to those who adhere to it. And it is reasonable to suppose that the terms of the contract include conditions regarding treatment of those who are not members of the contract. Assuming the contract is one established for purposes of mutual advantage, then, animals, the insane, the severely disabled, and children would not be among its members. But the conditions of the contract provide for their care and establish rights on their behalf, and the respect of those rights is a basic condition of the contract established with others. Thus, in some cases nonmembers of the contract may be the beneficiaries of our duties to one another under the social contract. We therefore have duties to respect the most basic humanitarian rights of members of al-Qaida and the Taliban, which entails that any use of force against them must be *justified* in ways that do not contravene the basic terms of social cooperation.

Although we have not entered into the details of a possible theory of prosecution, the most compelling way to spell out the theory of liability for torture for the OLC lawyers is via the doctrine of accomplice liability. Liability here can be established by a rather straightforward legal analysis: the OLC lawyers possess the mens rea for accomplice liability to torture—namely, purposely assisting in the commission of torture—and also the actus reus—soliciting or encouraging the commission of such offenses. And we saw that with regard to *this* argument, it is not clear why it would make a difference to their positions whether they knew or did not know that the legal advice they were giving was in all likelihood false, since mistake of law does not traditionally constitute a defense. Alternatively, one could proceed via conspiracy analysis: the OLC lawyers conspired with one another and with others in the administration to violate the federal torture law, as well as basic treaties of international law. Proceeding by way of conspiracy law, as we have seen, would give us a basis for finding liability for acts of torture *not* authorized by the OLC memos, on the grounds that such ultra vires acts could be reasonably foreseen from the authorization of illegal acts of torture as part of official policy.

I have argued that legally speaking, it does not matter whether the lawyers were acting in good faith when they counseled the legal permissibility of certain forms of torture. We must distinguish legal from moral analysis, however. Where *moral* evaluation of the lawyers' conduct is concerned, their position would surely be worsened by the revelation that their attempts at legal argumentation were disingenuous. There are at least several reasons for this. First, it is a grave breach of professional ethics for a lawyer to render legal opinions merely for the sake of achieving a certain political result, and especially so if he does not actually believe in the correctness of the legal opinions he is presenting. Rendering advice on the basis of a hoped-for result, without regard to the underlying sources of law, is a matter of grave moral and professional misconduct. It also constitutes a serious violation of the publicity condition, since it presupposes the legitimacy of a "private" basis for lawmaking, namely the instrumental features of legal reasoning as related to some pragmatic end. And thus if an agent's moral status matters to the advisability of prosecuting him, and if failing to prosecute immoral agents contributes to a disregard for the rule of law, the fact that the OLC lawyers probably intentionally ignored contravening sources of legal and moral authority against their positions would contribute significantly to the case for resorting to prosecution.

Finally, by making false legal arguments with the aim of justifying the denial of basic human rights, the OLC lawyers have shown themselves to be *intentional free riders* on both domestic and international agreements of mutual benefit that enhance personal security and welfare. The domestic agreements are those that establish the proper role of lawyers and the forms of reasoning that are socially available to them. And the international agreements are those establishing the foundations of human rights law, and that assign legal reasoning about domestic priorities a subordinate place in their relation to the welfare of the whole.

In light of these arguments, let us return briefly to President Bush's heartfelt statement condemning torture and pledging to prosecute its practitioners. We might now be in a position to understand why the president would have been keen to make such a statement, despite the fact that he was fully aware that the United States was making extensive use of techniques that had previously been prosecuted as torture, and that provided a strong basis for thinking it violated the terms of the Convention. Since the executive branch of the United States was clandestinely turning its back on its own normative commitments to the domestic democratic order, as well as to other nations, it was crucial to the administration to be able to vindicate its own status and to reject its image as a free rider on moral and legal constraint. For the extreme disadvantages of free riding on democratic principles like the separation of powers and limited government would not make themselves felt if the free riding could be conducted in the absence of public awareness. Once we are understood to be free riders—whether free riders on internal democratic processes or free riders on international adherence to human rights conventions—we impair our own ability to reap the benefits of cooperation if we do not discipline the agents who endorsed and advocated the free riding in the first place. This, finally, is the reason why Obama's firm stance that no one would be prosecuted for following the advice of lawyers who advocated torture is so problematic, and why the Justice Department's more recent backpedaling on the condemnation of the OLC lawyers for professional misconduct leaves our persuasiveness with regard to domestic and international arguments in favor of self-constraint impaired.

I have argued that violations of the rule of law that stem from the distortion of fundamental legal concepts ought to be vindicated through the legal process itself, as this is the most effective way to publicize, and thus to deter, shameless government freeriders. The argument for this appeal to public vindication is *contractarian*: because the commitment to the rule of law in a democracy depends on the perceived mutual advantages of living under the curtailment of legal rules, the public repudiation of illegal conduct through legal processes is crucial for vindicating the rule of law. Contractarian political theory thus gives us a basis for using legal proceedings to reject the legitimacy of domestic and international free riding on the self-imposed constraints of others. The argument for bringing to justice those who have contributed most to the infringement of the rule of law through their attempt to replace public reason with clandestine executive rule would then be that we do most to strengthen the rule of law when we use law itself to assert its own supremacy, because it is through law that rational self-constraint asserts itself. Law thus constrains not only the society it purports to govern, but its own operation as a protector of governance by law. Such self-restraint is rational, because it is voluntarily chosen by members of society who can perceive it as contributing to their mutual benefit.

1. President George W. Bush, speaking for United Nations International Day in Support of Victims of Torture, on June 26, 2003.

2. Second Inaugural Address. Periodic obeisances to the notion of freedom were also a regular part of Bush's argument for invading Iraq, since the war on Iraq was routinely justified on humanitarian grounds after the threat that Saddam Hussein had weapons of mass destruction had been revealed as false.

3. Remarks delivered in Bangkok in early August 2008.

4. Some scholars have attempted to distinguish the waterboarding conducted by the Japanese during the war from the waterboarding carried out by American soldiers and the CIA in the war on terror with regard to the label torture, claiming that the Japanese use of this technique was much more brutal than our own. See Remarks by Michael Lewis, *Federalist Society Debate* (with Claire Finkelstein), University of Pennsylvania Law School, November 19, 2009.

5. The British executed Japanese interrogators for the use of waterboarding, and the United States tried Japanese interrogators and sentenced some to twenty-five years of hard labor. Evan Wallach, "Drop by Drop: Forgetting the History of Water Torture in U.S. Courts," *Columbia Journal of Transnational Law* 45 (2007): 472, 482–94. As Eric Holder admitted in his confirmation hearings for Attorney General: "If you look at the history of . . . [waterboarding] used by the Khmer Rouge, used in the inquisition, used by the Japanese and prosecuted by us as war crimes, we prosecuted our own soldiers in Vietnam, I agree with you, Mr. Chairman, waterboarding is torture." Eric Holder, testifying before the U.S. Senate Committee on the Judiciary, January 15, 2009.

6. "In releasing these memos, it is our intention to assure those who carried out their duties relying in good faith upon legal advice from the Department of Justice that they will not be subject to prosecution." Statement by President Obama on Release of OLC Memos, April 16, 2009.

7. Office of Professional Responsibility Report, "Investigation into the Office of Legal Counsel's Memoranda concerning Issues related to the Central Intelligence Agency's Use of 'Enhanced Interrogation Techniques' on Suspected Terrorists," July 29, 2009, Washington, D.C.: U.S. Department of Justice, 260.

8. Ibid.

9. Memorandum to the Attorney General from David Margolis, Associate Deputy Attorney General (Jan. 5, 2010), http://media.washingtonpost.com/wp-srv/nation/pdf/MargolisMemo_021910.pdf.

10. Ibid.

11. Although not pragmatic, my focus is also not the usual philosopher's hypothetical about whether it would *ever* be permissible to torture one person to save an entire city from the ravages of a ticking time bomb—an example about which reasonable minds can surely differ. See Michael Moore, "Torture and the Balance of Evils," in *Placing Blame: A General Theory of Criminal Law* (Oxford: Oxford University Press, 1989).

12. See John Rawls, *Political Liberalism* (New York: Columbia University Press, 1993), 213–54.

13. It is for this reason that I reject the suggestion of two of the authors in this volume, Steve Vladeck and Paul Horwitz, to the effect that prosecution is often unnecessary and

generally dispreferred as a way of vindicating the rule of law. Both authors suggest that intervention by the political process is preferable to prosecution as a way of vindicating the rule of law, hence that prosecution should be considered only as a last resort. If my suggestion is correct, prosecution should be a first, rather than a last, resort.

14. See, e.g., Ruti G. Teitel, *Transitional Justice* (New York: Oxford University Press, 2000).

15. It is with personal sadness and regret that I pose this question about the OLC lawyers, insofar as one of them, John Yoo, was both a law school classmate of mine, and for several years a close colleague and friend at the University of California, at Berkeley. There we occupied adjacent offices and spent much time sharing views about the experience of being junior faculty members at a new institution. It is difficult to imagine the affable, pleasant, and engaging colleague that John was in the role in the Bush Administration he subsequently came to occupy.

16. A good example of this last point might be the relations of the United States to the work of an organization like the Red Cross. Insofar as we rhetorically support Red Cross efforts to supply needy populations with food, clothing, and medicine, we are relieved of the responsibility to do so ourselves, especially when the condition of such populations is in part a product of our own conduct. Furthermore, when our governmental administration verbally endorses the aims of such organizations and aligns itself sufficiently vocally with the rescue efforts such NGOs make, the international perception of Western, democratic aid tends to rub off substantially on the United States, and we receive implicit credit for work done by others. One example would be the contrast between the retrospective perceived large U.S. government response to the tsunami in the Indian Ocean in 2004 and the actual response of the Bush Administration. Initially, the Bush Administration only committed $15 million in aid, which over the next several months grew to $950 million, following criticism. Alan Cowell, "Asia's Deadly Waves: Bush and Other Leaders Quick to Offer Condolences and Aid," *New York Times*, December 27, 2004, World section, http://query.nytimes.com/gst/fullpage.html?res=9C02E7DA1F30F934 A15751C1A9629C8B63&sec=&spon=&pagewanted=1; BBC News, "Bush Aims to Boost U.S. Tsunami Aid," *BBC News*, Americas section, http://news.bbc.co.uk/2/hi/americas/4252171.stm. By the end of 2005, however, American NGOs and American citizens donated nearly $1.9 billion. Center on Philanthropy at Indiana University, *U.S. Organizations Providing Tsunami Relief*, Report, December 23, 2005, http://www.philanthropy.iupui.edu/Research/Giving/tsunami_relief_giving_12-23-05.pdf.

17. Jay S. Bybee to John A. Rizzo, memorandum, 1 August 2002.

18. In addition, the August 1, 2002 memo required that the infliction of mental pain or suffering could amount to torture under § 2340 only if it resulted from "one of the predicate acts listed in the statute," which included centrally threats of imminent death or threats of infliction of the kind of pain that would amount to physical torture. Bybee memo, 1.

19. Jack Goldsmith, *The Terror Presidency: Law and Judgment inside the Bush Administration* (New York: W. W. Norton, 2007).

20. Bybee memo, Part V (emphasis added).

21. John Yoo, interview by Michael Krasny, *Forum with Michael Krasny*, KQED Public Radio, February 22, 2010, http://www.kqed.org/epArchive/R201002220900.

22. *See* John Yoo, *The Powers of War and Peace: The Constitution and Foreign Affairs after 9/11* (Chicago: Chicago University Press, 2005).

23. John Rawls, *A Theory of Justice* (Cambridge, Mass.: Harvard University Press, 1971), 33.

24. Ibid., 55–56.

25. Ibid.

26. Ken Binmore, *Game Theory: A Very Short Introduction* (New York: Oxford University Press, 2007), 43.

27. Plato, *The Republic*, 3.389b; Machiavelli, *The Prince*, chap. 18; Meir Dan-Cohen, "Decisions Rules and Conduct Rules: On Acoustic Separation in Criminal Law," *Harvard Law Review* 97 (1983): 625; Paul Robinson and John Darley, "The Utility of Desert," *Northwestern University Law Review* 91 (1997): 477–88.

28. Hobbes, *Leviathan,* Book I, Chapter XV, ¶ 5.

29. See Hobbes' reply to the Fool. Ibid., ¶¶ 3-4.

30. Human Rights First's report, *Command's Responsibility*, based on its study of autopsy reports and interviews with military personnel, witnesses, and physicians, found that between August 2002 and February 2006 nearly a hundred detainees had died "while in the hands of U.S. officials in the global 'war on terror.'"

31. Thomas C. Schelling, *Micromotives and Macrobehavior* (New York: W. W. Norton, 1978), 101–10.

32. For other common examples of tipping phenomena, see Malcolm Gladwell, *The Tipping Point* (New York: Little, Brown, 2000).

33. But see Alan Dershowitz, "Tortured Reasoning," in Sanford Levinson, ed., *Torture: A Collection* (New York: Oxford University Press, 2004), arguing that *none* of the nations that has agreed to abide by conventions imposing human rights norms in fact strictly rejects torture when deemed necessary for national security.

34. See Christopher Kutz, "Causeless Complicity," *Criminal Law and Philosophy* 1 (2007): 289–305. The accomplice liability analysis is somewhat complicated, but one can articulate it in a straightforward way: the attorneys encouraged and solicited torture by writing the memos they did. And that means that they have the mens rea for the offense (intentional encouragement of violation of the prohibition on torture), they have a relevant actus reus, namely, the overt act consistent with the mens rea of encouragement, and they have no particular defense. *Model Penal Code*, § 2.06.

35. Nevertheless, there are some well-known instances of individuals being prosecuted for their advisory role. For example, Joachim von Ribbentrop, the Foreign Policy Advisor to Hitler, wrote a memorandum justifying instances of Nazi aggression and was later prosecuted for war crimes. Ellia Ciammaichella, "A Legal Advisor's Responsibility to the International Community: When Is Legal Advice a War Crime?" *Valparaiso University Law Review* 41 (2004): 1146.

36. A lawyer shall not counsel a client to engage, or assist a client, in conduct that the lawyer knows is criminal or fraudulent, but a lawyer may discuss the legal consequences of any proposed course of conduct with a client and may counsel or assist a client to make a good faith effort to determine the validity, scope, meaning, or application of the law. Model Rule 1.2(d).

37. President-elect Barack Obama, remarks in press conference announcing his Intelligence Team, on January 9, 2009. He went on to indicate that the United States would abide by the Geneva Conventions.

38. To be more precise, in the usual case he had to know he was engaged in the relevant conduct, or be aware of a risk that he was engaged in that conduct. In occasional cases, he

can be convicted merely because he *should* have been aware that he was running a risk of engaging in the relevant conduct. That is, he must either have been aware of his conduct, have been reckless with respect to engaging in it, and occasionally have been negligent with respect to that conduct (or result, to be strictly correct). But knowledge of the illegality of that conduct is virtually never required.

39. There are two important exceptions to this principle: first, mistake of law *is* an excuse when the relevant prohibitory norm makes the lack of knowledge of the law itself an element of the offense, to which mens rea then applies. Even where the mens rea for the crime is *intent,* rather than knowledge, this is usually not the case. Second, knowledge of the illegality of one's conduct must be demonstrated when it is fair to assume that the defendant did not have adequate *notice* of the illegality of his conduct, as can often be the case with so-called "regulatory" offenses. See *Model Penal Code,* § 2.04.

40. See Kutz, "Causeless Complicity"; Moore, "Torture and the Balance of Evils," in *Placing Blame*; and Philip Montague, *Punishment as Societal Self-Defense* (Chicago: University of Chicago Press, 1995).

41. See interview with General Janet Karpinsky, former military commander of the Abu Ghraib prison, in the film *Ghosts of Abu Ghraib,* who estimates that over 90 percent of those rounded up for purposes of divulging information had no information to offer, and that most were arrested indiscriminately.

42. Some support for this thought lies in the creation of the Japanese detention camps during World War II. See Stephen I. Vladeck, "Justice Jackson, the Memory of Internment, and the Rule of Law after the Bush Administration," in this volume.

2

Guantánamo in the Province of The Hague?

DANIEL HERWITZ

I

Certain abusive treatments of prisoners at Guantánamo may arguably be considered crimes against humanity. Not to deploy human rights instruments in the face of such abuses would be to bury the crime and normalize what I shall call in this essay the state of exception through which the United States arrogates unbridled power unto itself. The hard question is: What would be the appropriate human rights instruments to deploy in the face of U.S. alleged abuse in Guantánamo?

Within the United States a number of options have been activated, with varying degrees of success. These include a Senate Armed Services Committee Full Report, May 2009 hearings by Senator Sheldon Whitehouse of the Senate Judiciary Committee featuring testimony by Philip Zelikow, a former member of Condelezza Rice's State Department team who argued for observance of Geneva Convention Protocols while employed by Rice, and individual suits launched by former detainees at Guantánamo and elsewhere. One example is the case against former U.S. Attorney General John Ashcroft by Abdullah al-Kidd. Al-Kidd is a U.S. citizen and former University of Idaho student who was detained at the Dulles International Airport in Washington because the government thought he possessed crucial information in a computer-terror case against another University of Idaho student, Sami Omar Al-Hussayen, accused (later acquitted) of using his computer abilities to launch terrorism. The case against Ashcroft was upheld by the Federal Appeals Court in early September 2009.

Some progress has been made toward self-correction of the system of incarceration created by the United States at Guantánamo and also in Afghanistan in the wake of 9/11. The Supreme Court of the United States granted legal rights to prisoners at Guantánamo in April 2009. The Obama

Administration has expanded Detainee Review at Bagram, the military prison outside Kabul where prisoners have been held without charge for up to six years. The new Pentagon guidelines assign military-appointed representatives to each of the roughly 600 detainees at the American-run prison. Unlike Guantánamo these representatives need not be lawyers but they can "gather witnesses and evidence, including classified material, on behalf of the detainees to challenge their detention," according to a front-page article in the *New York Times* (September 13, 2009). Improvements at Bagram have followed "obligatory congressional review," according to the same article. The physical site of the prison is being closed and a newer one will replace it at another site. More significantly the United States will now register detentions with the Red Cross.

What the effect of these new review procedures will be remains to be seen. Various human rights groups are skeptical, arguing this is change on paper to make the United States appear more cosmetically acceptable to the gaze of the world which has been so negatively focused on inherited Bush Administration policies. Moreover, in weighing the demands of human rights against those of global security the Obama Administration has in other situations opted to retain Bush Administration policies, as for example in its opposition to a ruling by federal district judge John Bates (April 2009) that inmates at the Bagram Military Prison outside Kabul have similar rights to prisoners at Guantánamo. Finally, President Obama has vowed to close Guantánamo but this is proving more difficult than he expected.

The dilemma of international policy made between the demands of human rights and global security has brought the culture of humanitarianism a step toward the breaking point. Humanitarianism consists of a loosely linked system of universal declarations, laws, International Court of Justice, activities by nongovernmental organizations, media reportage, foreign aid, international boycott, and in extreme cases, military entry into sovereign states in the name of right rather than spoilage, theft, or conquest.[1] The Bush Administration's unilateral intervention in Iraq, which happened at a zipping rate of zero to sixty after 9/11 has done significant damage to humanitarianism, since in the eyes of many parts of the world the second Iraq war was about conquest, control, and claim over oil thinly veiled by a cheap patina of humanitarianism, a patina all the more distrusted on account of the long history of U.S. interventions in Greece, Latin America, Iran, even Granada since World War II. Granada was the comic book version, a twenty-four-hour conflagration story-boarded in the Hollywood version so that every soldier could end up unscathed with a Medal of Honor and President Reagan could have another speech opportunity. The others have been considerably less comic. So, combined unilateral invasion, largely viewed as Dirty Harry politics for financial gain, together with miserable treatment of detainees causes the culture of humanitarianism to receive another major, possibly lethal blow. Europe has been so appalled by the Bush Administration that President Obama received the 2009 Nobel Peace Prize simply for getting the Republicans out of office and setting forth new terms of dialogue. Many in Europe consider this prize a demand rather than a pat on the back, a way of saying, make good on your fine words. Many also believe Europe is now powerless to influence the United States in all but symbolic ways: hence the importance of prize-giving.

All the more reason for swift *international* response that sends the instruments of human rights spinning into action to again prove their worth by deploying them against the world's (current) major power. But therein resides the problem. One does not want to further weaken these instruments by deploying them in a way that confirms their powerlessness. On the other hand there may be important *symbolic* capital to be gained by a demonstrable gesture wherein one of the international human rights instruments is deployed against former Bush Administration officials (Cheney, for example). Even if a Cheney were not successfully brought up and prosecuted before the International Court of Justice in the Hague (and which country would submit the charge against him, anyway?), just imagine the front-page story in every European and Middle Eastern newspaper, the blogs on the Internet, the news announcers on TV networks across the globe: Cheney et al. charged! Symbolic capital, gained though global media circuitry, can be huge, even if its half life is very short. Can such symbolic capital shift world opinion slightly in a way that helps restore/create trust in the culture of humanitarianism? And might it go another inch in the slow building of bridges between radically opposed states/populations? Hence the conundrum: either do nothing, confirming the cynics but keeping international human rights instruments from being *ineffectually* deployed, or deploy such instruments with at best partial success (probably less), yet in a way that generates powerful symbolic appeal, thereby further weakening the instruments. An easy alternative is to award peace prizes to American presidents.

A full-scale congressional inquiry into human rights abuses at Guantánamo and Bagram would be equally daunting. I think the eyes of the world would be keen to see such a thing, and in some cases impressed by it. Beyond the tentative kinds of investigations to date—important as they are for acknowledgment and self-correction—this also seems unlikely. A full-scale investigation would totally polarize the U.S. citizenry. And we have seen from the quality of "debate" (an optimistic word) around health care in the United States that its citizenry seems to prefer Talk Show Democracy of the Jerry Springer/Larry King Live varieties to rational discourse. Aggression seems to have become, along with late-night comedy and personal blogging, the preferred form of public discourse.

There are many human rights instruments and it is worthwhile to consider which might best fit an inquiry internal to the United States. First note this: for the United States to even *consider* adopting an international model for its own use would already be an improvement of sorts, for the United States is a country that steadfastly refuses to acknowledge that any other society or state has very much to teach it (about health care, taxation, whatever). We in the United States immediately assume that our own received systems are the only ones that should be taken seriously.

I have been charged in this essay to ask whether an inquiry of the Truth and Reconciliation type might be an appropriate instrument for investigating putative violations by the Bush Administration. I shall do that in what follows, but then take the question of what South Africa has to teach the United States in a different direction. I shall consider the ideology of "exceptionalism" in international relations shared by South Africa and America—settler societies both—thus holding South Africa up as a distant mirror to the United States. At the end of the essay I shall argue that the lesson learned from this South Africa-U.S. comparison provides a strong reason mandating an *internationally* driven inquiry into recent U.S. abuses, even if it fails. My remarks are tentative, meant to provoke discussion rather than advocate any particular policy.

II

To the TRC then.[2] The South African Truth and Reconciliation Commission was the result of negotiation between warring parties, its goal being to serve the function of political change in a way that would prove tolerable to both. By 1989 it was clear that neither the African National Congress nor the National Party and the South African Defense Forces could win an outright civil war. This, along with the collapse of communism worldwide, brought both sides to the negotiating table. The CODESA talks of 1991–92 ("Coalition for a Democratic South Africa") carried initial negotiations forward in a formal way and resulted in the interim government of Mandela and De Klerk, the timetable for elections (1994), and the Interim Constitution, also of 1994.

The Interim Constitution mandated the Truth and Reconciliation Committees, including the Committee on Amnesty—which was so controversial that its mandate appeared only as a postscript to the Constitution.

The kind of amnesty offered (as is well known) was qualified. Amnesty would be granted in exchange for: first, full disclosure of the truth, and second, demonstration that the crimes committed were, I quote, "in proportion" to the hypothetical goals which motivated the larger scheme of action of which the crime was a part. Full disclosure would be measured by the Amnesty Committee on the basis of the proceedings of the Committee on Truth and Reconciliation hearings. Proportionality would be decided on the basis of whether a gross violation of human rights could be explained in terms of the larger political motive which compelled the perpetrator to act: a motive such as keeping the state intact or "winning the war against the communists." While the concept of proportionality is in one respect absurd— given that the object of investigation was gross violations of human rights which by their nature were *out of proportion* to human decency—the idea was to distinguish between acts directed at "the enemy" from random killings of children, rape of women bystanders, torture of old people, and the like, which could in no way be defended as actions performed "for the cause," as the assassination of presumed "political targets" could be. Proportionality was a way of excluding perpetrators of certain acts from the domain of amnesty and many cases rested on who had raped the bystander as opposed to killing the presumed "terrorist," as the former could not apply for amnesty while the latter in theory could. Note that a small number of applicants out of a large pool received amnesty; it was not at all automatic.

Qualified amnesty emerged from the CODESA talks as a compromise: the African National Congress wanted outright punishment for crimes, while the National Party wanted blanket amnesty. The alternative to qualified amnesty might well have produced a stalemate to the transitional process, even civil war. Moreover, qualified amnesty allowed the TRC to formulate itself as a proceeding motivated by forgiveness, reconciliation, and nation building, rather than the sterner stuff of retribution. There could have been no Desmond Tutu, Alex Boraine, or Bongani Finca in a truth commission of the Nuremberg type, no assimilation of the TRC to the New Testament. In short, and this is my point, the *aura* generated by the players in the TRC and occasioned for so many riveted by the proceedings depended on qualified amnesty. This aura of the biblical—of forgiveness, reparation, and moral nation building—was central to the entire working of the South African Truth and Reconciliation Commission, to this procedure chaired by three men of the cloth, three Anglicans who returned South African concepts of reconciliation from the Hegelian to their original religious context of redemption through suffering and acknowledgment.

This aura was conceptualized in the Commission's *Report* of 1998 as the truth that leads to "restorative justice." "There is also 'healing' truth, the kind of truth that places facts and what they mean within the context of [actual] human relationships—both among citizens and between the state and its citizens."[3] This healing involves in the first instance:

> Acknowledgement . . . acknowledgement refers to placing information that is (or becomes) known on public, national record. It is not mere factual information about past human rights violations that counts; often the basic facts about what happened are already known, at least by those who were affected. What is critical is that these facts be fully and publicly acknowledged. Acknowledgement is an affirmation that a person's pain is real and worthy of attention. It is thus central to the restoration of dignity of victims.[4]

Restorative truth is the *placing* of truth in the human context where it effects, or may point in the direction of, reconciliation. This involves placing "the facts" in the public archive, but goes beyond that to the dynamic power of truth *set to work*, as Heidegger might have put it, in human relations. It is the appropriate recognition of truth which restores. And by truth is meant evidence gathered by the commission's researchers, victim-centered testimony spoken in the drama of the TRC event, truth offered by perpetrators in the hope of qualified amnesty, and truth given by judgment about such perpetrators, all driven by a process which, at the moment of political transition, will set the terms for a new moral regime and change the way South African citizens come to see the past, the future, and each other. A heady road this, indicated by the banner unfurled at each of the Commission's "hearings," namely, "Truth: The Road to Reconciliation."

Restoration carries the idealized thrust of full reconciliation, but it also carries the acknowledgment of losses to which persons may never fully be reconciled. Central to the tensions within the workings of the Commission were tensions between utopian recognition and a sense of irreparable loss. These tensions rendered the concept of reconciliation problematical as a unified concept. But they drove the drama of the event in a way that was central, truthful, to the moment of transition itself, which is a moment defined by multiple and contradictory— or at least opposing—objectives.

The editors of this book have provided an excellent introduction to the topic of transitional justice, which topic is critical to understanding the TRC. A nation in transition from authoritarianism to liberal democracy has a unique set of needs: first, the need to punish perpetrators from the past regime and to thereby strengthen the rule of law against forces of terror remaining in the society; second, the need for the kind of social healing that comes not from punishment but instead from public exercises in reconciliation; third, the need for specific spectacles of transition, often in an international forum or over the media, which will build the moral capital of the new regime and garner support; fourth, the need to delicately appease those from the old regime, so that transition will not be derailed by a coup or other regressive means; fifth, the need to strengthen the new state, while also freeing it of the remnants of the past; sixth, the need to archive the past for the future; and seventh, the need to free persons from the haunting of the past, to lessen its grip by acknowledging the irreparability of loss. These needs are not exactly congruent—hence the *dilemma* of transition. What the theory of transitional justice has right is that the criterion of qualified amnesty cannot be measured against a timeless, universal, and unyielding concept of justice against which it would fail. Rather, the concept of justice itself has to be understood in a more contextual way, with incongruent and conflicting demands (at least sometimes) relevant to specific historical moments.

The conflicting needs and goals of transitional justice are built into the very language Tutu uses when he speaks to victims during the workings of the Commission. On the one hand, it is the language of the religious healer, the utopian Anglican pastor bringing sacrament and miracle, the language of *religious homily,* of the preacher's platitude. The sweet singsong character of Tutu's voice augments these ways of talking. Tutu's language is of such startling obviousness that only Tutu, and only on this kind of occasion, in 1996–98, when most of the drama of the TRC took place throughout South Africa, speaking to an orchestrated visual spectacle, on a stage where the commissioners sit, facing victims and perpetrators, above the crowd, before the television audience, as in a service of the heart or a public confessional, only Tutu, dressed is the glorious robes of the archbishop, can make these remarks, can *mean* these remarks, can *bring them home.* For they are one inch from being preposterous or kitsch. Tutu is a man of the cloth, and not only is he, the chairperson, a man of the cloth, but so also are the vice chairman, Reverend Alex Boraine, and the commissioner, Reverend Bongani Finca.

Then Tutu listens to the testimony of Mrs. Beth Savage, severely hurt during a bomb blast by the Pan African Congress in 1992, who six months later suffered a "nervous breakdown." Mrs. Savage states to the Commission, "[T]here but for the grace of God go I," when asked how she feels about the perpetrators. In response, Tutu says,

> Thank you, I just want to say, we are, I think, a fantastic country. We have some quite extraordinary people. Yesterday, I had spoken about how proud I was to be black in seeing the kind of spirit that people showed in adversity, and now we're seeing another example, and I think it just augers so wonderfully well for our country. We thank you for the spirit that you are showing and pray that those who hear you, who see you will say, "Hey, we do have an incredible country with quite extraordinary people of all races."[5]

This language, abstracted from context, would be an inch from ludicrous. But at the operatic moment of the Commission, it has a different effect. Beth Savage is moved. A choral union is effected after the hearing of things so intense that some faint and must leave, others cannot control their bodily functions. Tutu's voice brings the religious background of strife reconciled through the holy host, of the Christian ritual, to this moment. It is a language whose timing, pulse, tonality, and drama are stunning, but more than that, it is a language whose aesthetic force is internalized by this so very Christian nation. Truth and Reconciliation can happen in South Africa in the language of the ministry because South Africa is already Christian to the core. This should not be underestimated. And it is not only white South Africans who believe—it is African mission churches, apostolic churches, followers of the Shembe cult who in their thousands take to the hills of Natal dressed in flowing white garments to celebrate their prophet, and Anglicanism itself, which is tied to the liberal opposition through Tutu himself and before him, to Bishop Trevor Huddleston, who so opposed the forced removal of black Africans in the 1950s that he was sent home to England.

The anthropologist David Bunn illustrates the point through an example:

> Apartheid's worst torturers relied absolutely on the fact that it was possible to kill, maim and massacre without any record of their actions passing into the public domain. . . . When policemen like Gideon Niewoudt burnt the bodies of Siphiwe Mtimkulu and Topsy Madaka, wrapped the ash and bone fragments in rubbish bags and dumped them into the Fish River, they expected the waters to obliterate all traces of their victims. . . . Some months ago, the widows and children of the men murdered by Gideon Niewoudt finally learned, in confessions before the Truth and Reconcili-

ation Commission, what became of those who were thought erased from the historical record. Some time after the hearing, a simple ceremony was held at the approximate site where the bone ash was thrown into the river. Those who had gathered to remember, tossed wreaths into the water and watched them carried away towards the sea.[6]

To appreciate this story of the widows of Mtimkulu and Madaka, one must understand that many Southern African religions teach that the souls of the dead live in or near the bodies of the dead for a time, after which, gradually, they disperse. Many Africans expressed a desire simply to find the bodies of their loved ones when they gave testimony before the TRC. What they wanted was to be present to the souls of their dead loved ones, which they believed lingered around their bodies. The ritual of casting wreaths into the river is that of making contact with the souls of the dead which hover there, but it is also a means of cleansing sorrow by enacting the gesture of relinquishment, which is, taken literally, exactly what will happen to those souls when they float away toward oblivion. Hegel secularized the project of reconciliation, South Africa showed that in its context, which is a particular religious formation, it is possible to revert to the original religious idea of reconciliation, the Christian ideal, in order to pursue a secular effect: democratic transition. This was what was unique about the occasion, what may or may not be transportable to other contexts of transitional justice.

This story illustrates perfectly the way restorative truth functions: it is about reconciliation, but also about facing irreparable loss and moving on in a way foreign to the language of host, sacrament, and idealized historical finality.

III

Unfortunately a South African-style Truth and Reconciliation Commission is not appropriate to the (former) Bush Administration for reasons related to the soul of that enterprise. Remember: first, the TRC arose from a compromise between warring factions; second, the TRC evolved around victim testimony, which conferred dignity on victim families who were given voice; third, central to the TRC was "qualified amnesty," which occasioned "full confession" by perpetrators seeking it while also allowing the TRC to construct itself as a religious enterprise aspiring to bring about a culture of reconciliation; and fourth, the TRC served the specific demands of transitional justice.

These conditions are largely absent from the circumstances around Guantánamo. First, the prisoners there, and the nations behind them, are globally distributed, not closely linked. They do not believe they are in immediate need of reconciliation so that they can learn to live together. Not enough, anyway. So there is no overriding motivation for a Truth Commission around Guantánamo. Second, it is not clear to whom and for what purpose victims would give testimony, nor even which place or state would host them. Many families refused to participate in the proceedings of the South African TRC, most notably the family of Black Consciousness leader Steven Biko, beaten to death by the apartheid authorities. These families refused the project of amnesty. One could imagine many victims of Guantánamo and/or their families following suit. Third, the TRC was about individual perpetrators and individual victims. But in the case of Guantánamo, the number of individual torturers was small whereas the power of the big U.S. brass was overriding. It is Cheney, Rumsfeld, and Bush who would be the focus of victim, family, and world anger. And in fact the TRC was at its worst when it tried to deal with the big brass: the Church, big business, and higher-ups in the apartheid state. Fourth, regarding religious truth: It is religious difference which is central to the problem of global strife, war, conquest, and terror. There is no overriding Christian/African community deeply invested in forgiveness that would give substance to a project of reconciliation around Guantánamo: just the opposite.

Finally, the question of which party would *grant* qualified amnesty cannot begin to be answered, nor in exchange for what. Different kinds of human rights and/or legal ideologies tenaciously held by differing parties would mandate totally different forms of reprieve/punishment for perpetrators and their regime(s).

IV

Let me therefore turn from the TRC to what I have called the distant mirror of the South African apartheid past and what it shows the United States. Distant mirror indeed, since one might have thought no place could be further from the United States of today than the apartheid South Africa of former times. Apartheid South Africa was the place liberals like me demonstrated against: it was the pariah among pariahs. And yet U.S. foreign policy consistently favored South Africa in its geopolitical interests, seeking to protect South African mineral resources, defend South Africa as a bulwark of anticommunist stability, develop and invest in its free markets. U.S. foreign policy was rooted in the unspoken belief that South Africa was the one civilized corner of the continent, which is what the Nationalist Party believed about itself. U.S. postwar foreign policy applauded South Africa's vision of its *exceptional* status within the African region and vowed to keep it safe from Marxist insurgency. Many of us were engaged in antiapartheid struggle and we recall the sit-ins and demonstrations over divestment, the marches, the speeches by former prisoners from Robben Island, and our endlessly fierce and self-applauding denunciations of persons like Under-Secretary of State for African Affairs, Chester Crocker. But moral outrage against that uniquely racist regime also disguised the uncomfortable fact that South Africa has always been a mirror to the United States. The antiapartheid struggle arose nonviolently against the first construct of the social architecture of apartheid: the Dompass, which all persons of color were required to carry on pain of immediate arrest and which severely restricted their freedom of movement. The early days of struggle within South Africa were also directed against the Group Areas Act, which forced the removal of entire populations to designated areas far enough from European (white) enclaves and urban centers to prevent the intermingling of populations and access to urban culture, and made travel to work a tremendous hardship (when there was work to be had at all). The Defiance Campaign was orchestrated by Nelson Mandela, Walter Sissulu, and others from the para-city of Sophiatown, at the edge of Johannesburg, a city which was like Harlem at the edge of Manhattan in the 1920s and 1930s, and which joyfully proclaimed its connection with that African American culture. That campaign was coterminous with Martin Luther King's marches into the segregated American South (during the 1950s). Here we have two forms of similar response to two forms of racism. To this shared moment of resistance we may attach deeper shared histories of slavery and settling.

Imagine two countries, each scathed by the settler's rapacious knife, each importing slaves by ships which returned to the European center with sugar, tea, and tobacco extracted from the earth by skins burned by salt and welts, two colonies, then two places (the American South of 1900 and the South African colony arising from the conclusion of the Boer war in 1901), each segregationist by law. Then imagine South African segregation morphing into the apartheid state in 1948 and now one is in a position to understand that for both places racial separateness was justified by reference to ideologies of "exceptionalism." Only those who were true inhabitants of each of these places could know what was right for that place, because knowledge supposedly arose only through the long act of settling and habitation. The Bible, soil, people, locality, and identity were one in this myth of special settler knowledge of their respective subject populations. Outsiders were excluded from the understanding of people and place because they were not part of the form of life. This exclusion of all those on the outside, all who might therefore raise a critical voice about settler epistemology, justified the knowledge claim on communalist grounds. Only the community could know who blacks were, only they could know what made them happy, only the community could truly grasp that what looked to the outside as racism was in fact the acknowledgment of what made the native happy. This endless scuttlebutt about the native and his or her ways was the settler's assertion of inner truth, the truth accrued by generations of deep and special experiences. Thus was the status quo justified on *communalist* grounds: only the settler community who grew up with black and/or native could know what was right for black and/or native; and their consensus *proved* that their current form of life was correct. The Bible belt meant Bible *and* belt: the Bible proved racist truth, while the belt lashed out at all who disagreed. The apartheid state particularly had it in for Afrikaners of prominence who broke ranks. Bram Fischer, for example, who led the legal team defending Mandela and his cohort at the Rivonia trial in 1963, helping to secure them life sentences rather than execution, was, when finally arrested as a communist organizer, put in prison for life and humiliated on a daily basis there. My predecessor as Chair in Philosophy at the University of Natal in the early 1990s, Koos Stofberg, taught at that "English" university because he had been barred from Afrikaans universities for life on account of having written a letter to the Head of the Dutch Reformed Church disputing its claim of racist lineage in the Bible. The one who broke ranks was the one who gave the lie to the myth of special knowledge understood only by those who were part of the community, and he had to be humiliated and expunged.

The belief in special knowledge rooted in *exceptional circumstances* is a mark of settler cultures wherever they may be found. Those cultures tend to vacillate between Eurocentrism and exceptionalism. Eurocentrism is the ideology that the settler is superior to the native by virtue of his European origins, and in accord with this the settler represents and performs himself as more European than the European in his drinking of tea, his love of the hunt, his architecture, university culture, monument, park, tone of voice, preference for English literature, Oxbridge education, and so on. Exceptionalism, by contrast, is the ideology of difference: the settler is different from the European and must stake his experiences as special forms of knowledge worthy of his encounter with the new land. Exceptionalist knowledge grows gradually; it is the achievement of generations. At its most creative, exceptionalism is the demand for innovation worthy of the genuinely new conditions of life outside Europe. There are as yet no American scholars, Ralph

Waldo Emerson told the graduating class of Harvard College in the early 1830s, because the new kinds of experiences this new land invokes require new epistemologies, new certainties and uncertainties, and these have not yet, Emerson urged, been imagined or discovered. The alternative to invention is, for Emerson, rank imitation, a failure to become oneself, a failure of occupancy of the land, mere imitation of the European past, a parody of personhood. And so the settler veers between aping the European and setting forth in his or her own ship of knowledge creation.

Eurocentrism is one form of destiny ("from Cape to Cairo, a single British Empire," as Rhodes put it); exceptionalism is another. From the political point of view, exceptionalism defines land as the place of absolute settler sovereignty because the material for settler philosophical self-invention and thus an improvement in the world is mandated by force of destiny, that is, the deity. This is James Madison's doctrine: Manifest Destiny writ large for the new America which, since it is not Europe, is entitled to special dispensations of control. Here the rubber meets the road: settling becomes mandated as something god-given, indelible, and unassailable, for God and Country, a necessity prescribed by the very conditions of origin, by the ship of the future. In South Africa it was the ox wagon, which the Afrikaner Nationalist rewrote as the point of entry into South African history at the moment when, in the 1830s a small group of Afrikaners dissatisfied with English rule in the Cape Colony commandeered their ox wagons into the interior and beat the Zulu. In America it was the horse, with John Wayne riding it into the Hollywood camera. This settling of the South African interior was during the apartheid period—rewritten as the originating moment of the South African nation, the moment when the nation formulated its principle of self and took on its destiny. There was no place for the English, the Portuguese, the colored, nor (above all) for black people in this myth, which empowered the Afrikaner Nationalist as the one and only spiritual force of the nation, the one and only actor capable of grasping its biblical script. It is not for nothing that the place where the first monument to the Great Trek was constructed for the apartheid state (1948–49) was called Valhalla, around the corner from Pretoria and even closer to the home of the gods in the Wagner Ring cycle of operas. America needed no such monument, it had Washington and it had the written decree mandating its political destiny. And it had John Wayne and Custer to make sure the reservation was the place reserved for the Native.

Where there is an exalted destiny inscribed in a mythic past uniquely relevant to a particular group, where that destiny is uniquely blessed by god, where knowledge of right and wrong depends entirely upon being that settler or his progeny with exclusive access to local knowledge (of land, people, past, and future), omnipotence can turn paranoid if not already rooted in paranoia. The National Party arose in response to the decimation of the Afrikaans populations under Lord Kitchener's "salt and burn" policy which wrecked Afrikaans farms as punishment for their refusal to surrender and their excellence at fighting the English. Nothing would ever grow again on those farms. The first use of the concentration camp occurred during the Boer war, and it was introduced by the English: tens of thousands of Afrikaans women and children died of disease in places of group incarceration. And the Afrikaner knew that the Boer war had been launched purely on pretext, as a way for Cecil Rhodes to lay claim to the gold and diamonds in the Transvaal. Because the English "stole" the Transvaal from the Afrikaner, the Afrikaner took it back from the English through a corrupt electoral process in 1948 and held onto it until 1991. During those forty-three years the brutal architecture of apartheid was instituted, Afrikaans was forced on black people as the language of instruction (precipitating the Soweto riots), home, community, and education were destroyed for people of color, and a bloated state bureaucracy allowed Afrikaners to become a sizable middle class. And they had their myths of Great Trek, the beleaguered past, the biblical endorsement.

Sovereignty is God-given, but also that which the settler fights for, and fights hard for. In bombing Saddam, Bush was settling West Texas all over again, doing so through the lens of the John Ford movies in which indomitability is assured because everything is replayed in retrospect. Hollywood invented the Western as a genre when the west was already "won," the Native American was on his reservation, and the "wild West" became the western states. This replay allowed settling to happen a second time, this time as myth, with its resolution already in place. Manifest destiny was confirmed on the silver screen, where it played this second role of history happening after its outcomes had already taken place, with the assurance of a river of yes, destiny. Settler destiny is always also exceptionalism writ large, since what legitimates the settling is the settler's exceptional relation to the land, usually God-given, sometimes earned through this heroic feat or that, more often confirmed as superiority over those already there. Apply this to the Middle East and you get the thought that with 9/11 a similar moment appeared, where the Middle East was the wild West in need of settling, which was the claim that sovereignty could be established through war.

We are the only ones who really know what the world needs at this critical moment, we and the "coalition of the willing." We will demonstrate that we can still play the Cold War game of making dominoes fall by finding the toughest hombre in the Middle East, Saddam Hussein, and kicking the hell out of him. This will subdue Syria and Iran by scaring the hell out of them, thus asserting postwar U.S. hegemony in the Middle East.

Under the Bush Administration, a United States genuinely traumatized by attack asserted this settler response through the claim of our own special communal understanding of what democracy is and how it should be instituted in the world. In that rapid response the United States instituted the paranoid architecture of the *laager* (Guantánamo), the *rendition* (of whoever, for whatever purposes, based on racial profiling), and the subversion of whatever political and civil rights Dick Cheney and John Ashcroft could get away with. The United States proclaimed and reveled in contempt for those outside the country who did not agree with its policies, just as the National Party had done.

One continually asked oneself during the eight years of the George Bush Jr. presidency: Why the level of contempt for every major international organization, be it the United Nations or the European Union? Why the need to constantly put every international humanitarian effort down, to prove that it is weak, stupid, inept, and unworthy? I think the reason was this: by reactivating deeply held myths around settler destiny the Bush Administration was activating raw U.S. nationalism among its citizenry. This will for paranoid grandiosity and the downgrading of international political systems into articles of contempt allowed the Bush Administration to assert a claim of *international sovereignty* in the political sphere. Cheney was, I believe, ready to engineer a new world order with the resoluteness of the Third Reich. Not the same world, of course, but the same *claim of international sovereignty*.

Cheney's was also an assertion of sovereignty on the basis of post–Cold War *realpolitik*. The United States had been accustomed to an international chess match with its opponent, the international world being a set of satellite positions, pawns in this world order. Now, for the moment, there is only one player. Hence the Cheney view that the United States is de facto in a position of sovereignty. Why play ball with weaklings and fools when you have superior knowledge, better morals and family values, inner truth, and the only real understanding of how dangerous the world is. Assert the control you have earned, make the world order your own. It is the only sustainable world order, given terror. This is the Cheney idea. And so Cold War chess became *unilateralism* in the post–Cold War environment.

This combined position of settler ferocity (the world must be settled on one's own terms which are superior and God-given), and post–Cold War unilateralism (play chess with the world because it is the only way to sustain order in the world) had a third aspect: the reactivation of a vision of Manifest Destiny for the United States, a belief as old as settling itself, made dizzy through 9/11 paranoia. Settler communalism is always also xenophobic, since the settler position is based on a perception of outsider threat. Bush drew upon this deep vein of American paranoia which became his fundamentalist quest. The greater the fear Bush could activate, the stronger the fundamentalist position became—hence the Bush-Cheney policy of keeping terror central in every newspaper, at every moment, for everyone. Fox TV made a racket out of this. Keep the temperature of the country febrile and you keep the image of Manifest Destiny active, somewhere between James Madison and John Wayne.

Terrible goings-on which go some way toward explaining why the world turned from sympathy toward the United States to active hatred so soon after the Towers were hit.

V

All the more reason for an *internationally generated response* to the abuses that followed upon the Unites States's bald assertion of sovereignty in international politics. But which response? There have been resolutions by international, nongovernmental organizations such as the Inter-American Commission on Human Rights, whose Resolution No 2/06 of July 28, 2006 resolved to:

"1. INDICATE that the failure of the United States to give effect to the Commission's precautionary measures has resulted in irreparable prejudice to the fundamental rights of the detainees at Guantánamo Bay including their rights to liberty and to humane treatment.
2. URGE the United States to close the Guantánamo Bay facility without delay.
3. URGE the United States to remove the detainees from Guantánamo Bay through a process undertaken in full accordance with applicable forms of international human rights and humanitarian law.
4. URGE the United States to take the measures necessary to ensure that any detainees who may face a risk of torture or other cruel, inhuman or degrading treatment or punishment if transferred, removed or expelled from Guantánamo Bay are provided an adequate, individualized examination of their circumstances through a fair and transparent process before a competent, independent and impartial decision-maker. Further, where

there are substantial grounds for believing that he or she would be in danger of being subjected to torture or other cruel, inhuman or degrading treatment or punishment, the State should ensure that the detainee is not transferred or removed and that diplomatic assurances are not used to circumvent the State's non-refoulement obligation [the obligation in international law that persons not be returned to their place of origin if there is reason to believe their freedoms or lives will be endangered there].

5. URGE the United States to comply with its obligation to investigate, prosecute and punish any instances of torture or other cruel, inhuman or degrading treatment or punishment that may have occurred at the facility, even in the event that Guantánamo Bay facility is closed."7

The Obama Administration has heard some of this and announced closure of Guantánamo (again, not so easy to do). But no international commission of inquiry, much less a case in the International Court of Justice, has transpired. At the beginning of this essay I pointed to a conundrum around the international response to this situation. It might do nothing more than confirm the powerlessness of international human rights instruments to touch the big bully, with a Cheney, a Rumsfeld, or an Ashcroft spitting in the face of the World Court, say. Or it might generate considerable symbolic capital even if it fails. The problems in choice of instrument are daunting. It is not even known which sovereign state would host a commission of inquiry. Guantánamo is unlikely to find itself dwelling in the province of The Hague anytime soon. However, I for one, romantic believer in the power of the media, have a hunch that launching a commission of inquiry or legal case in the International Court of Justice would have real symbolic force, a force worth the probable outcome of procedural failure. Whether through a commission or an actual case in court, facts would emerge (as they did during the Truth and Reconciliation Commission's proceedings), an archive could be (further) constructed, voices would be gifted the symbolic power of speech, such as the voices of detainees, for example. But the real force would come from the media.

Here is one final reason for an international human rights gesture. Until now the vast apparatus of humanitarianism has done precious little in addressing either the United States or China, the current big players. Like the TRC which collapsed when the big players came before it—big business, the church, and the top leaders of the state, including P. W. Botha, "the Crocodile," himself—international instruments have been most productively focused on the smaller players on the world stage. This is a profound inequity in the human rights system. There is symbolic capital to be gained purely from deploying the system in the direction of the all-powerful, the all-exceptional, the force majeure. Such a deployment, even if it leads to probable failure as an instrument, might have the further effect of alienating even the Obama Administration. But it might not. Sometimes a risk is worth taking in spite of it all. I want people to think very seriously, even now, about taking it.

NOTES

1. See David Reiff; *A Bed for the Night: Humanitarianism in Crisis* (New York: Simon & Schuster, 2002).

2. In this section I am relying on work I have published in an earlier book of essays on South Africa. See Daniel Herwitz, *Race and Reconciliation: Essays from the New South Africa* (Minneapolis: University of Minnesota Press, 2003), chapter 2.

3. *Truth and Reconciliation Commission of South Africa Report, Volume 1* (Cape Town: CTP Book Printers and Juta, 1998), 114.

4. Ibid.

5. Ibid., vol. 5, 374.

6. David Bunn, "Whited Sepulchres: On the Reluctance of Monuments," in Hilton Judin and Ivan Vladislavic, eds., *Blank: Architecture, Apartheid and After* (Rotterdam: Architectural Institute, 1998).

7. From the *Inter-American Resolution 2/06,* of July 28, 2006.

3

Universal Jurisdiction as Praxis

An Option to Pursue Legal Accountability
for Superpower Torturers

LISA HAJJAR

> After years of disclosures by government investigations, media
> accounts, and reports from human rights organizations, there
> is no longer any doubt as to whether the [Bush] administration
> has committed war crimes. The only question that remains to
> be answered is whether those who ordered the use of torture
> will be held to account.
>
> —Maj. Gen. (Ret.) Antonio Taguba[1]

In June 2009, Wolfgang Kaleck, a German lawyer and one of the
world's leading proponents of universal jurisdiction (UJ), published an article titled "From Pinochet to Rumsfeld."[2] The focus is on Europe between 1998
(the year former Chilean dictator Augusto Pinochet was arrested in London
on a Spanish warrant) and 2008. During this decade, significant strides in
the development and use—the praxis—of UJ have made it possible to indict
former U.S. Defense Secretary Donald Rumsfeld in a European court for
authorizing and abetting the crime of torture in the context of the post–9/11
"war on terror."

If UJ were merely a fanciful debating point for cocktail party conversations
about impunity for gross crimes, the U.S. State Department (and ministries
of other countries) would not be devoting resources and political capital to
counter efforts to bring officials to justice abroad. Likewise, Rumsfeld would
not have beaten a hasty retreat from France in October 2007 (on a personal
visit after he was out of office) when a criminal complaint was filed against
him in Paris.[3] And John Yoo, a Berkeley law professor who served as deputy
attorney general in the Justice Department's Office of Legal Counsel from
2001 to 2003 and authored some of the most notorious "torture memos"[4]

and participated in the so-called "war council"[5] where U.S. interrogation and detention policy was devised, would not have foregone a planned semester in Italy had he not perceived that this might put his freedom at risk.

In this chapter, I put these events and prospects in context, beginning with the nineteenth-century origins of the doctrine of UJ and its relationship to emergent norms of universal humanity and humane treatment. Those innovations foreshadowed and informed twentieth-century transformations in international law, including the prohibition and criminalization of a growing array of violent and harmful practices. The prosecution of German and Japanese officials in post–World War II tribunals was a groundbreaking event in terms of accountability for crimes of state, albeit a seemingly singular one because impunity for violations of international law was the de facto rule during the Cold War decades. Since the late 1980s, however, new opportunities for accountability have burgeoned, including national prosecutions of perpetrators of previous regimes,[6] and the establishment of international tribunals and courts.

Universal jurisdiction is a distinct method and model of accountability: it permits individuals accused of gross human rights violations and grave breaches of the Geneva Conventions to be prosecuted in foreign national legal systems with no connection to the crime. The "Pinochet precedent" was a landmark in the contemporary praxis of UJ, inspiring governments (mostly in Europe) to incorporate the doctrine into their national systems. However, quests to indict foreign officials, especially from powerful, allied, or important trading-partner states (i.e., the United States, Israel, and China) resulted in political backlash and diplomatic pressure to amend (i.e., narrow) or discard those national UJ laws in some countries. But recent de-universalizing law reforms are rife with logical contradictions and jurisdictional ambiguities, and to the extent that they contravene states' treaty obligations, they will be challenged in the coming months and years by lawyers committed to the enforcement of international law.[7] Consequently, UJ is an evolving legal paradigm and its prospects are a work-in-progress.[8]

As a point of clarification, my interest in UJ is sociolegal rather than (restrictively) doctrinal; I emphasize the concept's analytic and political utility, which derives from its combination of individual criminal accountability, the prosecutability of practices that have come to be defined as core crimes under international law, and the role of national legal systems in international law enforcement. For reasons that I explain, and as demonstrated by the empirical record, of all the crimes subject to UJ, torture stands out for its prosecutability. In this vein, I conclude with an argument about why UJ might be the *best* option among all the alternatives for holding "superpower torturers" legally accountable.

Origins and Foundations

The nineteenth-century "universe" was a racially and politically hier-archical maritime world dominated by European imperial states, and modern international law and order was a nascent project. The origins of the doctrine of universal jurisdiction (UJ) trace back to efforts to deter piracy and the slave trade.[9] These practices were cast as inimi-cal to peace and security for the international community and classi-fied as heinous crimes; perpetrators were condemned as "enemies of all mankind" (*hostis humani generis*) who deserved no sanctuary; and states were vested with additional legal powers and responsibilities to prosecute them or to extradite them to another state for prosecution if petitioned to do so.

Because the high seas were legally *terra nulla* (i.e., a legal black hole, to borrow a contemporary metaphor), in order to enable the prosecution of pirates and slave traders in foreign national court systems, a legal innovation was needed to compensate for gaps in existing jurisdictional doctrines (ter-ritorial, personal, and protective). In contrast, banditry, the dry land analog of piracy, didn't impel any innovation because states already had territorial jurisdictional over (their) land-based crimes.

Despite a flourishing transatlantic antislavery campaign, UJ targeted the trade in slaves rather than the institution of slavery itself. The vaunted Westphalian principle of state sovereignty impeded any possibility of assert-ing foreign criminal jurisdiction over the territorialized ownership and use of slaves. Rather, Britain deployed its dominion over the seas to choke the source by enforcing the newly articulated prohibition of the seaborne trans-port of enslaved Africans to other continents. Notwithstanding the ardent abolitionist sentiment of William Wilberforce and other British human-itarians, the government's primary motivation was to counter labor cost advantages of slave-based economies, not the well-being and freedom of Africans.

Universal jurisdiction epitomizes the logic of a criminal justice approach to law and order. In order to quash the disdained practices of slave trad-ing and piracy, perpetrators had to be made vulnerable to lawful punish-ment. As for victims—actual and would-be—of piracy and the slave trade, any effect that prosecutions may have had on them was indirect, but not insignificant: in criminal law generally, the realistic threat of prosecution aims to deter the practices that "create" victims. In the case of UJ specifi-cally, the practices targeted under this doctrine are those deemed so egregious and internationally significant as to make their perpetrators enemies of all mankind, who may elude justice but for the "universalization" of their prosecutability.

There was no further development of UJ during the nineteenth century, and indeed the concept crusted around these two seafaring crimes. However, two other international legal developments transpired over the subsequent decades that would be critical to the evolution and contemporary praxis of UJ: the creation of a universal category of humanity, and the cultivation of humanitarian norms.

Antislavery campaigns of the nineteenth century hold pride of place in pressing forward the sociolegal construction of people as humans. The ideological motivations and political agendas of those opposing enslavement in the Americas and in King Leopold's Belgian Congo were early and exemplary instances of international humanitarianism—caring about "strangers" because of a sense of shared humanity, and acting purposefully and strategically to alter conditions that cause (normatively) unacceptable human suffering, exploitation, and repression. (As Keck and Sikkink[10] and Hochschild[11] among others have persuasively demonstrated, these campaigns were precursors to the contemporary human rights movement that operates on a global scale.)

International humanitarianism also emanated from responses to modern warfare. The transformation of the laws and customs of war into international humanitarian law (IHL) was prompted by concerns that certain forms of militarized violence were excessively and unnecessarily inhumane.[12] The Lieber Code, a set of rules developed during the American Civil War for the Union army,[13] inspired a line of modern IHL governing belligerents engaged in armed conflict that came to be known as "Hague law." A second line, which came to be known as "Geneva law," grew out of concern for the victims of war and nonbelligerents (the latter including captured, injured, or surrendered enemy combatants). Swiss businessman Henry Dunant, appalled to witness wounded soldiers abandoned on battlefields in a war between Austria and France,[14] founded the Red Cross and called for an international congress that resulted in the first Geneva Convention of 1864 for the amelioration of the wounded in the field. The human toll from asphyxiating, poisonous, and bacteriological weapons during World War I inspired the Geneva Protocol of 1925 prohibiting their use, and the 1929 Geneva Convention expanded rules for the treatment of wounded, sick, and captured soldiers.

A Revolution in International Law

History prior to World War II is replete with exterminations and massacres, forced concentrations, and "cleansings" of populations from territories, torture, slavery, death marches, and systematic rape. But the scale of these acts as well-planned policies by modern states, as well as the toll of military attacks on civilians, constituted the negative inspiration for a revolution in international law to forge greater protections and freedoms for human beings. The postwar initiatives included the establishment of the United Nations (UN) and the creation of a heretofore nonexistent category of international legal entitlements called "human rights" through which people around the globe, for the first time in history, acquired a common international status as *legally human*.

The first human rights law, the Genocide Convention (1948), prohibits acts "committed with intent to destroy, in whole or in part, a national, ethnical, racial or religious group, as such." Consequently, states' sovereign discretion to exterminate populations was circumscribed by dint of the prohibition to engage in or order the practices that constitute the crime, and humans thus gained the right not to be genocidally massacred and destroyed.[15] ("Having" and "enjoying" rights are not the same,[16] as evinced by the many genocides perpetrated since 1948.) However, the crime of genocide as defined and prohibited by the Convention did not attach UJ because it did not authorize the prosecution of perpetrators in *any* legal system, only in "a competent tribunal of the State in the territory of which the act was committed, or by such international penal tribunal as may have jurisdiction with respect to those Contracting Parties which shall have accepted its jurisdiction." In addition to genocide, the postwar catalog of legally proscribed outrageous behavior was expanded to include the newly conceived "crimes against humanity," composed of "murder, extermination, enslavement, deportation and other inhuman acts done against any civilian population, or persecutions on political, racial or religious grounds," whether occurring in times of war or peace.

The prosecution of Axis leaders in the Nuremberg and Tokyo tribunals was a revolutionary contravention of the sacrosanctity of states' sovereign prerogatives to harm humans with impunity. The motto "never again" expressed the aspiration that retributive justice for these twentieth-century enemies of all mankind would have a deterrent effect in the future. As Robert Jackson, chief prosecutor of the Nuremberg tribunal, explained the mission, "[W]hile this law is first applied against German aggressors, . . . if it is to serve a useful purpose it must condemn aggression by any other nations, including those which sit here now in judgment. We are able to do away with domestic tyranny and violence and aggression by those in power against the rights of their own people only when we make all men answerable to the law."[17] In principle, the accused were tried for crimes against "humanity" and "peace," not against the particular victims of their regimes. In principle, the authority of the tribunals derived from the "international community," not the victorious nations. Most importantly, the Nuremberg principles established the prosecutability of state agents, including top officials, who commit, order, or abet gross crimes under international law, and the indefensibility of superior orders or *raisons d'etat*.

Another postwar development was the promulgation of the 1949 Geneva Conventions (GCs), which expanded and refined the rules of armed conflict.[18] Grave breaches of the four GCs—which constitute war crimes—include forced relocations and deportations, torture, collective punishment, hostage taking, extrajudicial killings, the deliberate targeting of civilians in military operations, and the use of excessive force or indiscriminate weaponry. The GCs incorporate a deterrence-through-retributive justice approach to war crimes by imposing an obligation to prosecute violators or to extradite them for prosecution to another jurisdiction (*aut dedere aut judicare*).[19] Ideally, accused war criminals are to be prosecuted in their own country or the country where the crime(s) occurred, but in the likely (and common) event that war crimes were not a deviation but an execution of orders by those up the chain-of-command, *aut dedere aut judicare* aims to foreclose any impunity gap by allowing prosecutions to be undertaken in the legal system of any state party to the GCs (which, by the dawn of the twenty-first century, includes every state in the world).[20] While this obligation to prosecute grave breaches does not specify the kind of jurisdiction to be employed, in practice it overlaps with UJ.

The GCs apply to "international armed conflicts" between and among states.[21] However, one article common to each of the four 1949 GCs explicitly addresses conflicts "not of an international nature" (i.e., not interstatal): Common Article 3 (CA3), often termed a "miniconvention" unto itself, is regarded internationally as the "humanitarian baseline" of all armed conflict, applicable when and where the other articles are not. The provisions of CA3 include rules governing the treatment of prisoners who do not merit prisoner of war status as regulated by GC III, including prohibitions against torture, cruel treatment, and "outrages upon personal dignity, including humiliating and degrading treatment." Serious violations of CA3, like other grave breaches of the GCs, are punishable as war crimes.

The Frozen Decades: Principles without Praxis

The retributive muscularity of the Nuremburg and Tokyo tribunals had the paradoxical effect of establishing principles of international criminal law while chilling its development and use through the decades of the Cold War. Realpolitik exigencies (i.e., states' defense of their sovereign power and prerogatives), and the lack or weakness of international law enforcement mechanisms relegated the principle of accountability to the realm of theory. An obvious example was the refusal to establish an international criminal court to succeed the postwar tribunals. (The International Court of Justice, established through the UN Charter, hears cases brought by states against other states, not individuals.) However, while international law *enforcement* was stymied, law*making* accelerated in the 1960s as most countries across the Global South achieved independence and became member states of the UN. The principles enshrined in the Universal Declaration of Human Rights (1948) were translated into positive law, starting with the Convention on the Elimination of Racial Discrimination (1965).

Most human rights laws incorporate UN-based reporting mechanisms rather than a criminal justice approach to redress violations, and efficacy depends on either the self-enforcement by signatory states or the naming-blaming-shaming approach of monitoring and reporting on violations and advocating for consequences among influential constituencies. However, some practices deemed by international lawmakers to constitute the most grievous violations have been criminalized. In 1966, the General Assembly passed a resolution branding apartheid a crime against humanity. The Apartheid Convention, which was passed in 1973 and entered into force in 1976, attaches international criminal responsibility to "individuals, members of organizations and representatives of the State who commit, incite or conspire to commit the crime of apartheid." This convention incorporates a "permissive" version of UJ by granting any signatory state the right to prosecute a perpetrator of apartheid who comes within its jurisdiction.[22] South Africa, the original but not exclusive subject of the Convention, protested that the prohibition of apartheid assaulted its sovereign autonomy, which of course it did because apartheid is inimical to contemporary standards of international legality.

Torture also attaches criminal liability. Unlike the prohibitions of genocide, crimes against humanity, and apartheid, which were cut from whole cloth in the post–World War II era, the torture prohibition expresses a centuries-old and widely accepted[23]—if pervasively violated and disregarded—legal proscriptions against purposefully harming people who are in custody but have not been found guilty of a crime (i.e., the definition of torture excludes the harms attendant in lawful punishments). Legally, torture occurs (only) in the context of a custodial relationship, and thus the prohibition applies to custodians. This includes state agents as well as anyone acting "under the color of law" (e.g., government-hired private contractors), but it does not exclude nonstate groups; the prohibition of torture is not contingent on legitimacy, jurisdiction, or international recognition. Rather, it is contingent on an organized rather than individualized capacity to take people into custody and then harm them for a purpose that is public rather than personal. The clarity of the custodial relationship (i.e., limited to a situation of imprisonment or detention) distinguishes torture (along with extrajudicial execution of prisoners) from other types of gross human rights violations and war crimes. For example, while the use of indiscriminate weaponry, excessive force, or the deliberate targeting of civilians in a military campaign is no less illegal and prohibited than torturing a person in custody, legally determining if those who caused such death and injury perpetrated a grave breach is often impeded by the "fog of war" and confounded by subjective, rationalizing estimations of proportionality and military necessity.

The grievousness of torture relates to the fact that the power to harm manifests itself in an extreme and distinctive form: the captive condition deprives individuals of any capacity to protect or defend themselves if their custodians purposefully subject them to physical or psychological pain and suffering.[24] Thus, the regulation of that relationship by means of the prohibition of practices that constitute torture (pain- and suffering-causing commissions and omissions) exemplifies the broader human rights project to minimize people's vulnerability to avoidable harms and to guarantee standards of humane treatment.[25]

In the pantheon of international human rights, the right not to be tortured—and the prohibition that constitutes the right—is uniquely strong and universal: first, in comparison to most other rights, which can be derogated from or suspended temporarily in the exigency of an emergency, the torture prohibition is absolutely nonderogable because the law recognizes no exceptions, including in times of war or national emergency. In the words of the UN Convention against Torture and Other Cruel, Inhuman or Degrading Treatment or Punishment (CAT 1984), "No exceptional circumstances whatsoever, whether a state of war or a threat of war, internal political instability or any other public emergency, may be invoked as a justification for torture." Second, the prohibition has ripened into a peremptory norm (*jus cogens*) of customary international law, which means that it is binding regardless of whether or not states have signed relevant conventions. Third, the crime of torture attaches universal jurisdiction; the prosecute or extradite obligation is explicit in both CAT and the GCs. Fourth, the right not to be tortured extends to all people everywhere at all times regardless of their social status, political identity, or affiliations.

The right not to be tortured has one more distinction in contemporary international law and order: rampant violations of that right hold pride of place in catalyzing the activism that evolved into a globalized human rights movement. The 1961 founding of Amnesty International, whose original mission was to ensure the rights of prisoners—foremost the right not to be tortured—was the shot across the bow. Since the late 1970s, there has been a massive proliferation of nongovernmental organizations and activist networks dedicated to international law enforcement. Defense of the right not to be tortured has been the most galvanizing, sustained, and globalized concern.

The Thaw: A New Era of Accountability

In the late 1980s and early 1990s, political transformations in Latin America, Eastern Europe, and South Africa from military, authoritarian, or racist rule to more democratic governance ushered in new prospects for accountability. In many countries, regime changes were accompanied by demands to redress past crimes, which came to be termed "transitional justice."[26] The various avenues of accountability following these national transitions included truth commissions, lustration, and civil damages. *Criminal* retribution was a particularly contentious option for reasons that were exemplified by a public disagreement between two well-known human rights advocates, namely, Jose Zalaquett and Aryeh Neier.[27] In articulating his perspective on transitions to justice, Zalaquett emphasized the need to balance the pursuit of legal retribution for past crimes against other interests, including truth, societal reconciliation, and political stability of a democratic sort.[28] To the extent that victims of the previous regime would want or insist on prosecutions, he argued that they should not be allowed to "hold a veto power or decide on the general rules of society."[29] Neier rebutted this argument by saying that "justice is not democratic,"[30] meaning that prosecution of serious international law violations should not be contingent on domestic opinion or public support in the society of the perpetrating state. While Neier acknowledged the impossibility of predicting with any empirical certainty whether prosecutions would deter future violations, the imperative to hold individuals criminally liable, he reasoned, is essential to (re)affirm the state's commitment to the rule of law and to validate the normative unacceptability and legal liability for such practices.[31]

Whereas accountability for past crimes on a *national* level was enabled by—and contingent on—regime changes, the impetus for *international* criminal prosecution was propelled by gross violations of an exceptionally egregious nature following the collapse of the Soviet Union and, with it, the bipolar realpolitik that had had such an inhibiting effect on international law enforcement during the Cold War. The United Nations, resurrecting an accountability model that had been abandoned since the closure of the Nuremberg and Tokyo tribunals, established ad hoc tribunals for the former Yugoslavia (in 1993) and Rwanda (in 1994) to prosecute suspected perpetrators of genocide, war crimes, and crimes against humanity. These institution-building initiatives breathed new life into the moribund principles of international criminal law. These principles and rules obtained greater clarity and comprehensiveness through the process of drafting the 1998 Rome Statute for the International Criminal Court (ICC), and enforceability was boosted by its establishment in 2002.

International tribunals and courts are important to the evolving praxis of international criminal law enforcement. But because such institutions are established through collective initiatives by governments (usually under the auspices of the UN), they inevitably conform to and reinforce the state-centrism of the international order and prevailing imbalances of global power. For example, in order to finalize the treaty for the ICC, compromises on criminal liability, jurisdiction, and prosecutorial discretion had to be made to accommodate the demands of powerful governments, including granting substantial discretion to the UN Security Council. U.S. representatives involved in the negotiations insisted on treaty language that would minimize if not altogether prevent any prospect that an American might someday find him- or herself in the ICC dock.[32] When George W. Bush came to power, he went so far as to remove the United States's signature from the treaty (which Bill Clinton had signed in his very last hours in office). The Bush Administration pressured dozens of ICC signatories to sign bilateral agreements granting blanket immunity to Americans from the jurisdiction of the ICC.[33]

The Pinochet Precedent

In contrast to the treaty-based jurisdiction and operation of *international* tribunals and courts, UJ prosecutions are pursued through *national* courts, and thus are not contingent—at least not in the same ways—on international consensus or the prior endorsement of powerful states.[34] The case against Pinochet was a landmark because a former head of state was made to face criminal charges in a foreign national legal system. Although often analyzed and discussed in connection with contemporaneous prosecutions in international venues, and lauded as a precursor to the ICC, the "Pinochet precedent" has had distinctive ramifications for the trajectory of international law enforcement in general, and the praxis of UJ in particular.[35]

In Chile, Pinochet enjoyed an immunity (impunity) of his own making, but when he traveled out of the country, he became vulnerable to legal retribution for his regime's crimes. His vulnerability was *produced* through the actions of "legal entrepreneurs," including Spanish lawyer Juan Garces, who represented thousands of victims (some of whom became plaintiffs in the case),[36] Spanish investigating judge Baltazar Garzón, who issued the warrant for Pinochet's arrest and pursued the case against him,[37] and the British officials who honored the warrant and allowed the case to proceed—or in Geoffrey Robertson's words, "who let the law run its course."[38] As a result of these actions, Pinochet was transformed from traveling dignitary to criminal suspect and in the ensuing legal process was stripped of his claim—critics of the indictment would say his right—to sovereign immunity as a former head of state.

The charges against Pinochet that held up in the British legal system were restricted, ultimately, to the crime of torture and contingent on (i.e., limited by) the time frame of British domestic legislation vesting national courts with jurisdiction to prosecute this international crime. The international significance of the Law Lords' decision that Pinochet was indeed indictable (and extraditable) because there is no sovereign immunity for this crime was a stunning validation that torture is a punishable offense regardless of the status of the perpetrator or the geographic location of the crime. This ruling had a larger (precedential) effect of clarifying and fortifying the applicability of UJ to prosecute perpetrators of gross violations. The Pinochet case can be read retrospectively as an example of customary rule-creating processes which "give rules a specificity that enables them to shape future behavior through a sense of obligation, thus constraining and modifying state power."[39]

As the Pinochet case was unfolding, there were those who criticized the Spanish and British governments for acting "imperially" by trouncing Chilean sovereignty (i.e., overriding Pinochet's domestic sovereign immunity). Not only right-wing Pinochet supporters, but some sectors of the Chilean human rights community and even some victims of Pinochet's regime were put off by the idea that European states could intervene in Chilean "national affairs" in this manner.[40] Among some sectors of the left, the targeting of the former leader of Chile resonated with a larger critique of human rights as an instrument of Western power, used selectively against weaker and poorer nations.[41] This criticism, which conflates the fate of Pinochet with that of Chile, aligns in effect if not in spirit with right-wing rationales that would justify the necessity and legitimacy of the actions for which Pinochet was indicted. What gets lost in this reasoning, however, is why "Chile" (or any state government) should be anthropomorphized and conflated with perpetrators of gross crimes.[42] Indeed, the indictment served both metaphorically and literally to separate Pinochet-the-man from Chile, the sovereign state he once governed by military junta.

Another line of critique about the Pinochet case centered on the merits and advisability of retributive justice, especially for countries—like Chile—that had recently undergone political transitions. There was a fear that Chilean democratization might be reversed if the military were to respond to the threat of foreign prosecution against one of its own by mounting a new coup. In retrospect, the case against Pinochet in Britain arguably led to *more* democratization and *stronger* commitment to the rule of law in Chile, not less.[43] When Pinochet was permitted to return home, released from custody in Britain because of a political determination that he was too frail to withstand extradition and trial, he was stripped of his immunity on the grounds that its provisions violated the Chilean constitution. He was then subjected to the prospect of trial in his own country, and was spared that fate by dying.

The Pinochet precedent invigorated and altered debates about how and where justice for gross crimes should be pursued, and who decides if justice has been done.[44] One effort to advance the use of UJ was undertaken by a group of international law scholars and practitioners who met at Princeton University in 2000 and 2001. *The Princeton Principles on Universal Jurisdiction*, according to the introduction,

> are intended to be useful to legislators seeking to ensure that national laws conform to international law, to judges called upon to interpret and apply international law and to consider whether national law conforms to

their state's international legal obligations, to government officials of all kinds exercising their powers under both national and international law, to non-governmental organizations and members of civil society active in the promotion of international criminal justice and human rights, and to citizens who wish to better understand what international law is and what international legal order might become.[45]

Those who prioritize the preservation of domestic autonomy and sovereign immunity were critical of (and in some cases personally anxious about) the expansion and efficacy of UJ.[46] For example, Lord Browne-Wilkinson, a member of the British House of Lords who participated in the Princeton Principles project, dissented from the final text because it "[does] not recognize any form of sovereign immunity. . . . If the law were to be so established, states antipathetic to Western powers would be likely to seize both active and retired officials and military personnel of such Western powers and stage a show trial for alleged international crimes."[47]

From Precedent to Praxis

In 1999, the government of Belgium was inspired by the Pinochet precedent to reform a 1993 law (which itself had been inspired by the creation of the UN ad hoc tribunals for the former Yugoslavia and Rwanda) enabling national courts to prosecute gross violations of international law without any connection to Belgium. A special investigative unit was created to gather evidence and pursue UJ cases and investigations could be initiated at the request of victims from any country—*universal* jurisdiction in its truest sense. In effect, Belgium committed its courts and resources for the prosecution of a comprehensive range of gross violations under international human rights and humanitarian law. In short order, more than a dozen foreign officials became targets of lawsuits in Belgium.

In February 2002, the International Court of Justice issued a decision in *Democratic Republic of Congo v. Belgium* that a person *currently in office* (in that case Yerodia Ndombasi, Congolese foreign minister, alleged to have incited and abetted crimes against humanity during a rebellion against the Congolese president, Laurent Kabila) could not be indicted by a foreign national court (Belgium) because this would interfere with his capacity to discharge his official duties.[48] Human rights advocates criticized this ICJ decision as a step backward in the era of the Pinochet precedent. According to Reed Brody of Human Rights Watch, "This decision goes against the international trend towards accountability for the worst abuses, but it should not stop Belgium from pursuing cases against perpetrators no longer covered by immunity [i.e., once they leave power]."[49]

In June 2002, the Belgian Court of Appeals issued a ruling that a case against Israeli Prime Minister Ariel Sharon for war crimes in Lebanon in 1982 (i.e., abetment of the massacre of between 900 and 2,500 Palestinian civilians in the Sabra and Shatila refugee camps) could not proceed. This decision was based not on the fact that Sharon was then in office but rather that he was not present in Belgium. The ruling galvanized a broad-based coalition of Belgian and international human rights organizations, members of the Belgian Parliament and government, and victims from a variety of countries.[50] In July, there was a political agreement among Belgian parties to put forward an interpretive law to clarify and strengthen Belgium's UJ law (also referred to as the "antiatrocity law"). Despite vigorous foreign diplomatic pressure, the interpretative law was passed by the Belgian parliament. And in February 2003, the Belgian Supreme Court reversed the appeals court decision in the Sharon case, holding that presence in the country was not a requirement to pursue a UJ case.

Shortly after this landmark ruling, several serving and former U.S. officials became subjects of lawsuits in Belgium. As a result, so much pressure was brought to bear—including Rumsfeld's threat to relocate NATO headquarters from Brussels to Warsaw—that the law was amended to restrict jurisdiction to cases involving Belgian citizens or residents (i.e., active and passive personality jurisdiction),[51] to eliminate foreign victims' rights to initiate criminal complaints, and to guarantee immunity to visiting officials, regardless of allegations against them.[52] However, UJ remains authorized for criminal offenses that Belgium is obligated by treaty to prosecute, which includes torture.[53]

The sharp narrowing of Belgium's domestic law as a result of political pressure generated the widespread perception that UJ was "in its death throes."[54] But, as it turns out, news of its death was greatly exaggerated. Later that year, the Council of the European Union declared that gross crimes "must not go unpunished and that their effective prosecution must be ensured by taking measures at the national level and by enhancing international cooperation."[55] Since 2003, courts in Spain, France, Belgium, the United Kingdom, and the Netherlands have successfully prosecuted dozens of foreign nationals for international crimes, and cases are currently underway in a number of European countries.[56]

Superpower Torture

For the United States, the prohibition of torture was black letter law at the end of the twentieth century. The 1949 GCs were incorporated into the Uniform Code of Military Justice (UCMJ), which governs all branches of the uniformed military. Congress passed a federal antitorture statute in 1994 following the ratification of CAT (albeit the ratification contains restrictive understandings regarding the interpretation of "cruel, inhumane and degrading treatment"), and the War Crimes Act in 1996 that gives U.S. courts jurisdiction to prosecute grave breaches of the GCs; together, these laws established criminal liability for torture in times of war or peace. In the 1983 landmark decision in *Filartiga v. Peña*, a U.S. court validated the customary international law status of the torture prohibition by ruling on behalf of foreign (Paraguayan) plaintiffs who sued a foreign (Paraguayan) torturer using the centuries-old Alien Torts Claim Act. In 1992, Congress took further steps to acknowledge the customary international law status of the right not to be tortured by passing the Torture Victims Protection Act (TVPA).

Following the terrorist attacks of September 11, 2001, the Bush Administration understandably and legitimately emphasized the importance of interrogation as one means of acquiring intelligence about al-Qaida. But the formulation of policies and the authorization of practices that disregard the nation's treaty obligations, domestic laws, and jurisprudence was not a necessity but a choice. The administration's posture for waging the "war on terror" was exemplified by the oft-quoted phrases of Vice President Dick Cheney, who said in a *Meet the Press* interview on September 16 that we would have to work "the dark side," and counterterrorism expert Cofer Black, who testified before Congress on September 26 that there "was a before 9/11 and an after 9/11, and after 9/11 the gloves came off." These statements signaled rather succinctly that officials regarded legal rules unsuitable for waging the "war on terror" and inimical to national security.

The Bush Administration, under the direction of Cheney and his legal counsel David Addington, divined the need for a "new paradigm" to rationalize the executive branch's autonomy from the constraints of law and the separation of powers. [57] To these ends, Yoo and other OLC lawyers authored memos opining that the president, as commander-in-chief, should have unfettered powers to wage war; that any efforts to constrain executive discretion in accordance with federal, military, or international law would violate Article 2 of the Constitution; that U.S. agents serving at the behest of the commander-in-chief could capture, detain, and interrogate people from anywhere in the world; and that the president could classify prisoners as "unlawful combatants" (by fiat rather than on the basis of a status review) and hold them incommunicado indefinitely. Other OLC memos asserted that federal laws guaranteeing the right of habeas corpus and prohibiting cruel, inhumane, and degrating treatment were unenforceable outside the United States. In order to evade future consequences for grave breaches, government lawyers including then-White House counsel Alberto Gonzales advised President Bush to "declare" that the GCs are inapplicable to the "war on terror," which he did in a secret directive to his national security team on February 7, 2002.

Two OLC memos dated August 1, 2002—written for the CIA to ameliorate anxieties about the risk of future prosecution because agents and contractors were already torturing several captured (presumptively) "high value" terror suspects—interpreted the applicable definition of "physical torture" to exclude anything less than "the pain accompanying serious physical injury, such as organ failure, impairment of bodily function, or even death." They also opined that cruel, inhuman, or degrading treatment would not constitute "mental torture" unless it caused effects that lasted "months or even years." This torture-permissive reasoning was passed on and adapted by the Pentagon for the military's interrogation and detention operations in Guantánamo Bay, Cuba (GITMO), Afghanistan, and Iraq. The torture policy thus involved an elaborate set of legal interpretations and security rationales to authorize violent and painful interrogation tactics, and to negate the risk of criminal liability for doing so. However, the copious work by government lawyers was a backhanded homage to the torture prohibition, evidenced by the fact that the imagined subject in key memos is repeatedly referred to as "the defendant."

Details about the administration's interrogation and detention policies and practices were exposed in mid-2004 following the publication of shocking photos from the Abu Ghraib prison in Iraq. The scandal that ensued from those photos created political pressure which led to the declassification or leaking of the first batch of secret legal memos and policy documents revealing the extent to which and the rationalizations upon which the pervasive and systematic use of torture had been authorized from the top. Over the following months the public learned that in 2002 and 2003 the State Department and top-ranking military lawyers had registered strong opposition to the authorization of torture and disregard for the GCs and that dissenters were subsequently excluded from policymaking circles.

The exposure of facts about the torture policy exacerbated the rancorous partisanship of public discourse. Defenders of the administration accused critics of being "terrorist sympathizers" and made other spurious allegations. However, the "torture debate"[58] did not comport with the usual party-line dichotomy because the ranks of opponents included many members of the military officer corps, the legal profession, and some people who had served in previous administrations of both political parties. Despite strong and sustained criticism, the Bush Administration refused to end the torture policy. Rather, officials and spokespeople engaged in "we don't torture" denial-through-euphemism by characterizing government-authorized tactics as "enhanced interrogation" methods, and propounding their efficacy and necessity in defeating terrorism.

Although many states defy the international prohibition to engage in torture, the American case is exceptional in two regards. First, by "legalizing" practices that constitute torture (e.g., waterboarding; protracted sleep deprivation, stress positions, isolation, sensory and temperature manipulations; and non-maiming violence such as throwing prisoners against walls) as well as cruel and degrading treatment (e.g., forced nudity and other sexual and religious humiliations), Bush Administration officials deviated from the "normal" pattern of torturing regimes, including pre–9/11 patterns of American torture,[59] to perpetrate these practices without the cover of law. Second, the superpower status and influence of the United States makes American torture more deleterious than torture by less powerful regimes because of its capacity to influence international legal norms and standards of treatment for prisoners.[60] To comprehend the gap between the Bush Administration's practices and the *jus cogens* principle of the absolute and universal right not to be tortured, one need only consider the official U.S. position—sustained through the end of the Bush years—that prisoners in U.S. custody would be treated "humanely" as a matter of *policy*, but that they have no *legal right* to humane treatment.

(Not) Coming to Terms with Torture

During the 2008 presidential primaries, neither the torture policy nor the issue of accountability for its authors featured in the debates and statements of candidates from the two major parties. In the presidential campaign, however, to their credit both contenders publicly vaunted their antitorture credentials: Republican candidate John McCain, a torture survivor from the Vietnam War, had distinguished himself during the Bush years as one of the "Republican dissenters" in the Senate (along with Lindsey Graham and John Warner) to criticize and contest the torture policy, although he had buckled under partisan pressure (spearheaded by Cheney) by conceding to a "CIA exception" to the 2005 McCain Amendment that resurrected the applicability of the UCMJ to military interrogators. Democratic candidate Barack Obama campaigned on the promise to end torture and restore the rule of law. But he sought to demonstrate his aspirational "postpartisanship" and national security bona fides by dodging the issue of legal accountability for the authors of the torture policy with the rhetoric of wanting to "look forward, not backward."

Victorious Obama has been true to his word in both senses: he took important steps to end the torture policy, including imposing on the CIA the requirement that it adhere to the 2006-revised *Army Field Manual for Human Intelligence Collector Operations*, and ordering the closure of their "black sites." But (to date) he has declined calls to initiate any investigation or accountability measures against anyone other than CIA interrogators who may have "deviated" from the policy by engaging in practices that were not explicitly authorized by Bush Administration officials or sanctioned in memos (e.g., mock executions).[61] This commitment to official *unaccountability* has been rationalized by arguing, variously, that criminal procedures or even a noncriminal "truth commission" would be too politically divisive and disruptive of the Obama Administration's agenda (e.g., economic recovery, health care reform) and, that the policymakers of the previous administration and those who followed them had acted in "good faith." Political disagreements in Congress and within the administration undermined the fulfillment of Obama's promise to close GITMO within one year. The Justice Department's decision to try five 9/11 suspects, including "mastermind" Khalid Sheikh Mohammed, in federal court in New York City spurred waves of criticism that appear likely to derail the plan and push the trials back into the widely discredited military commissions, which Obama had promised to cancel when he came to office.[62]

The actions and inactions of the executive and legislative branches have heightened the importance of the courts. During the Bush years, the Supreme Court overturned lower court decisions to rule against the administration in several cases involving the legal rights and treatment of "unlawful combatants" (i.e., *Rasul v. Bush* [2004] and *Boumediene v. Bush* [2008] on the habeas rights of GITMO prisoners, and *Hamdan v. Rumsfeld* [2006] on the unconstitutionality of the military commissions and the applicability of CA3). But in civil suits involving plaintiffs who were tortured by U.S. agents or government-hired contractors, or extraordinarily rendered by the

United States to other countries for torture, none of the court decisions (to date) have provided meaningful redress for victims or accountability for individual perpetrators.[63] In several cases, the Obama Administration simply assumed the position of the Bush Administration. In a civil suit by five victims of extraordinary rendition against Jeppesen Dataplan, the company whose planes were used to transport them to torture, government lawyers invoked the state secrets privilege to derail adjudication rather than taking the opportunity to restore the meaning of the "privilege" as the government's right to limit specific sensitive pieces of information or evidence. In regard to the rights of prisoners held overseas, Obama replicated the most disdained and dubious position of the Bush Administration by denying habeas corpus rights to prisoners in U.S. custody at the Bagram facility in Afghanistan. Bagram has been nicknamed "Obama's GITMO." The protracted delay in releasing the Office of Professional Responsibility (OPR) report on the role that Justice Department lawyers played in formulating the torture policy—revealed evidence of a criminal conspiracy but recommended no action—is a collusion with the unlawful behavior of the previous administration and a manifestation of enduring unaccountability.[64]

The most committed and substantial opposition to U.S. torture has come from legal professionals (civilian and military) who have involved themselves in a variety of cases and other kinds of strategies to contest the use of torture and pursue justice and the rule of law.[65] Among people involved in this loose but dedicated antitorture legal campaign, there is no consensus on the issue of accountability: some concur with Obama's preference to "look forward" and are content with the changes in policy. Others advocate some form of domestic accountability, although they disagree about whether it should take the form of criminal prosecutions or a noncriminal alternative. A smaller group, spearheaded by the Center for Constitutional Rights (CCR) and attorney Scott Horton, has been working with European lawyers (including Kaleck) to pursue UJ prosecutions of U.S. officials abroad. For them, although the ideal is domestic accountability, Europe-based litigation is perceived as a means of building pressure for this outcome.

International Crime, Universal Justice

While prosecution of the intellectual authors of the U.S. torture policy in Europe is not an inevitability, it is a possibility. American torture is *not* a "foreign" matter in which Europeans have no vested stake: some torture and torture-abetting practices occurred on the continent.[66] In November 2005, the *Washington Post* reported that the CIA engaged in kidnappings and ran black sites in Europe (subsequently revealed to be in Poland, Rumania, and Lithuania). The Council of Europe report on its investigation into illegal U.S. activities on the continent, released in June 2006, concluded that a hundred people had been kidnapped in Europe, and recommended a review of all U.S.-EU bilateral military basing agreements. The European Parliament report, released in February 2007 and endorsed by a large majority, exposed extensive collusion with the CIA's extraordinary rendition program by European security services and other government agencies.

In 2005, an Italian court issued indictments for twenty-three CIA agents (along with four Italians) who had kidnapped Hassan Mustafa Osama Nasr (aka Abu Omar) in Milan in February 2003 and transported him to Egypt for torture. This is not a UJ case because the crime actually occurred *in Italy*. But as an accountability measure, it overlaps with UJ in holding officials legally accountable in a foreign national court system. Despite U.S. diplomatic pressure and refusal to cooperate, and political opposition by the Berlusconi government, the trial-in-absentia proceeded because Italian prosecutors are autonomous law enforcement agents. One of the defendants, Sabrina de Souza, brought a suit in May 2009 in a U.S. court petitioning the U.S. government to invoke diplomatic immunity on her behalf to shield her from the Italian charges. In September, the Justice Department filed a motion to dismiss the suit, presumably because any immunity request would constitute an admission of criminal culpability.

On November 4, 2009, the Italian court handed down guilty verdicts for most of the indicted CIA agents. The heaviest sentence, eight years, went to the former head of the CIA's Milan station, Robert Seldon Lady, while twenty-one others got five years each. Judge Oscar Magi did not convict (but also did not acquit) the three highest-ranking U.S. agents because their defense was stymied by the unavailability (i.e., secrecy) of relevant evidence pertaining to their roles in the crime. The Berlusconi government has refused to enforce the court's ruling by issuing Interpol warrants or requesting extradition, but Italian prosecutors have the authority to issue a European Arrest Warrant if any of the convicted sets foot in any EU nation.[67] The timing of this verdict was particularly propitious because the previous week the European Union and the United States had approved a new extradition agreement.

In 2007, a German court issued arrest warrants for thirteen CIA agents involved in the December 2003 kidnapping of Khaled El-Masri, a German citizen, from Macedonia. El-Masri was transported to Afghanistan where he was tortured and held incommunicado for months. When the CIA realized that El-Masri was not who they thought he was and decided to release him, they dumped him in a remote area of Albania, from which he eventually made it back to Germany. Because El-Masri is a German citizen, the case involves passive personality jurisdiction (i.e., the victim is a national), but like the Italian case, the foreign identities of the accused resonate with the praxis of UJ.

The British government is implicated in the torture of Binyam Mohamed, a resident of the United Kingdom who was arrested in Pakistan in 2002 and extraordinarily rendered by the CIA to Afghanistan, then to Morocco where he was subject to torture-by-proxy for eighteen months, then back to Afghanistan where he was held in the so-called "dark prison" (a black site near Kabul), and then transferred to GITMO in 2004. After he was finally released and returned to Britain in March 2009, public disclosures about his brutal torture and British intelligence agencies' involvement sparked intense political controversy and led to the first criminal investigation against British agents for their collusion in CIA torture. In Mohamed's suit against the British government, the High Court initially determined that it had to be dismissed "in the public interest" because the Obama Administration threatened to interrupt bilateral counterterrorism cooperation if documents detailing his torture by the CIA were revealed. In October 2009, this dismissal was reversed, although seven paragraphs in key documents remained blacked out for "security reasons" and the British government appealed the court's order to declassify them. On February 10, 2010, the Appeals Court rejected the government's arguments and forced the publication of the summary, thus "marking a turn in judicial doctrine that had up to this point been extremely accommodating of government views about secrecy."[68]

French criminal procedures require that a suspect be present in the country in order to issue an indictment, but allow a case to proceed even if s/he leaves France. In a pre–9/11 incident, on May 31, 2001 former U.S. National Security Advisor and Secretary of State Henry Kissinger was in Paris when he was summoned for questioning by a French magistrate for his role in Operation Condor (a U.S.-supported Latin American transnational campaign of torture and extrajudicial execution during the 1970s). He refused the summons and left the country (and reportedly no longer travels without checking whether there are pending indictments against him).

As noted above, on October 26, 2007 efforts were made to indict Rumsfeld while he was in Paris on a personal visit to speak at a *Foreign Policy*-sponsored conference. His movement was being tracked by nongovernmental organizations who knew he was coming and had readied a complaint.[69]

When he heard of the complaint, Rumsfeld left the building through a door adjoining the U.S. embassy to avoid the human rights lawyers and journalists waiting for him outside. The complaint was dismissed and an appeal of the dismissal to the General Prosecutor of Paris was dismissed in 2008 on erroneous legal reasoning that officials have blanket immunity for activities connected to their work.[70] This "imagined immunity"[71] contravenes France's obligations under CAT and contradicts France's own record in which both a former head of state (Mauritanian General Ely Ould Dah) and a former Tunisian police official were successfully convicted for torture through the exercise of UJ.

In 2004 an explicitly UJ-based case was brought in Germany by Kaleck and other German lawyers, working in close collaboration with CCR, against Rumsfeld and a number of U.S. officials on behalf of Iraqi torture victims. Under intense diplomatic pressure from the United States, the prosecutor dismissed the case on the principle of subsidiarity (i.e., that a foreign state cannot assert jurisdiction for a case that is being pursued in a more appropriate venue), despite the fact that there was no case against Rumsfeld or the others in the United States at the time. A second UJ case was brought in 2006 against Rumsfeld along with several government lawyers who were accused of being the architects of the torture policy; the 2006 complaint contained substantial new information about Rumsfeld's role in the torture of GITMO prisoners, including the treatment of Muhammad al-Qahtani.[72] The criminal complaint pointed out that there was no domestic U.S. investigation, let alone criminal procedures underway against the accused. The German prosecutor dismissed this case in 2007 on the grounds that, because none of those named in the indictment were present in the country, there was no reasonable likelihood of conviction. In May 2009, a motion was submitted to reconsider the dismissal in light of new evidence of torture and the persistent refusal of the United States to undertake domestic investigations and prosecutions.

Currently, Spain is the most active and feasible site for UJ prosecutions of U.S. officials. Two Spanish investigating judges are developing cases against six U.S. lawyers who helped author the torture policy and provide its legal cover.[73] One case, in the hands of Judge Eloy Velasco, arises from a complaint by Spanish human rights organizations on behalf of Spanish nationals who were tortured at GITMO; like the El-Masri case in Germany, the jurisdiction is passive personality rather than universal. The other case, in which Garzón is the investigating judge, derives from the overturning of convictions of those former GITMO prisoners by the Spanish Supreme Court because the evidence used by the prosecution was elicited through torture and ruled inadmissible. Following that decision, the Supreme Court directed a more detailed investigation to be conducted into their claims of torture.

In September 2009, Garzón and Velasco submitted questions to U.S. Attorney General Eric Holder, and asked for responses by the end of October 2009 (a deadline that passed without results). According to Scott Horton, "The questions focus on the treatment of the Spanish subjects held at Guantánamo and the specific authority and approval for that treatment. They also probe in more detail into the role played by [former Attorney General Alberto] Gonzales, [former head of the OLC Jay] Bybee and Yoo in the process, reflecting a view that the U.S. Justice Department was itself the locus of much of the criminal conduct connected to introduction of a system of torture and cruel treatment of Spanish subjects, in violation of the Spanish criminal code using its universal jurisdiction arm."[74]

As occurred in Belgium in 2003 in response to diplomatic and political pressure, in October 2009 Spanish legislators changed their domestic UJ law,[75] restricting criminal cases to those involving Spanish nationals and/or requiring the alleged perpetrators to be present in Spain and/or the crime to have some direct connection to Spain.[76] However, this change is not retroactive for cases already underway, and moreover it does not affect the so-called "Gonzales Six" case against U.S. lawyers because the victims are Spanish nationals and the case has the sanction of the Spanish Supreme Court.

If the United States were to initiate a criminal investigation into these "torture lawyers," in all likelihood the Spanish case would be dropped because of subsidiarity. But the failure to pursue domestic accountability in the United States sustains and legitimizes the case in Spain.[77] At this juncture, the only two *legal* options for the Obama Administration are either to answer the Spanish judges' questions or to open a domestic criminal investigation that would have international credibility. (The OPR report provided at least some of the answers the Spanish judges are seeking.)

Why Universal Jurisdiction Might Be the Best Option

Putting an end to the torture policy has been an important but inadequate response to the law-violating legacy of the Bush Administration. But "looking forward, not backward" resistance to accountability for the serious crime of torture is inconsistent with President Obama's proclaimed goal of restoring the rule of law. As Neier argued, holding individuals, including government officials, accountable for their crimes is essential to (re)affirm the state's commitment to the rule of law and to validate the normative unacceptability and legal liability for such practices. Moreover, there is a "looking forward" reason to prosecute violators: deterrence of future crimes. The choices that Bush Administration officials made to authorize torture suggests that they were not deterred by the fact that their actions were illegal and punishable. Indeed, why would they be deterred? With few exceptions, U.S. officials have not been prosecuted for gross violations of international law perpetrated abroad. Punishing this generation's torturers may not guarantee that tomorrow's would-be torturers will be deterred, but impunity for past crimes of state probably contributed to the will to torture that drove the Bush Administration's unlawful treatment of prisoners.

In order to conclude with an argument about why UJ might be the best of all possible options, it is necessary to begin with a frank appraisal of the factors that contribute to domestic unaccountability for this crime. The U.S. record on international law is mixed: it includes, on the one hand, a leading role in the post–World War II tribunals and support for the UN ad hoc tribunals (whose jurisdiction would not affect Americans). On the other hand, the U.S. is an outlier among its allies for not signing a number of human rights conventions and for working actively to undermine the ICC. Starting with the Eisenhower Administration, for decades official disengagement was driven initially by the political influence of constituencies intent on preserving domestic autonomy for de jure segregation (which by definition is inimical to international law principles of equality before the law and equal rights for all). Throughout the Cold War, realpolitikers from both major parties and their neoliberal and neoconservative successors would brook no legal constraints on the global pursuit of national military, political, and economic interests. This "American exceptionalist" stance drew succor from the Federalist Society, a right-wing legal organization dedicated to countering the "liberal bias" in law schools and judicial decision making, which has nurtured an ethos to "defend" society against the ostensible infringements that international law would pose to democratic institutions and U.S. sovereignty.[78] Since the 1980s, many judicial appointments and government lawyer positions have gone to international law-averse Federalist Society people. Bush Administration lawyers, whose handiwork is enshrined in the "torture memos,"[79] made mistakes about international law, such as the erroneous assumption that the applicability of IHL is contingent on reciprocity, or the claim that the executive is somehow not bound by customary international law.

The record of U.S. courts as interpreters and enforcers of international law is a mixed bag. The United States pioneered the availability of civil damages against *foreign* defendants who can be sued for torture and other customary international law violations, albeit the jurisprudence is inconsistent. But in cases involving U.S. officials and those acting under the color of law, as well as U.S.-based corporations, the jurisprudence reveals pervasive antipathy toward international law and inexperience interpreting treaty obligations, including those that require legal accountability for violators. While there have been several important Supreme Court decisions on matters related to the Bush Administration's "war on terror" policies (each passed by a slim majority), there has been no ruling to date that recognizes liability let alone exacts a penalty from top-ranking perpetrators. To rationalize or applaud this as judicial restraint misses the point that law enforcement by courts is an obligation, not a choice.

Congress's record on the issue of international law violations over the last decade displays a pattern of sanctioning official impunity. In August 2002, one month after the establishment of the ICC, Congress passed the "American Service-Members' Protection Act" which authorizes the president to "use all means necessary and appropriate to bring about the release of U.S. or allied personnel being detained or imprisoned by, on behalf of, or at the request of" the ICC. In 2003, the House of Representatives passed the "Universal Jurisdiction Rejection Act" which includes the claim that "the very concept of universal jurisdiction is a threat to the sovereignty of the United States." [80] In response to the *Hamdan* decision, in October 2006 Congress passed the Military Commissions Act which took the extraordinary step of granting ex post facto immunity (back to 1997) for violations of CA3 and other grave breaches of the GCs. There has been no congressional action in response to the findings of the bipartisan Senate Armed Services Committee (SASC) report (2008) which concluded that "senior officials in the United States government solicited information on how to use aggressive techniques, redefined the law to create the appearance of their legality, and authorized their use against detainees." [81]

At the popular level, the public's uninformed attitudes about international law provide no counterweight to the record of Congress. Indifference or ignorance about the criminality of torture is exemplified by the ease with which criticisms of the Bush Administration's torture policies could be construed as "un-American" and critics (mis)characterized as representing (only) "the far left of the Democratic Party" and condemned for wanting to "coddle terrorists." This public posture has inflected official responses to calls for domestic accountability for the authors of the torture policy. Even a nonretributive commission of inquiry is deemed a threat to Obama's striving postpartisanship, and combines with other political realities and public attitudes to block prospects for domestic accountability.

Another factor is the empirically dubious but popular perception that "torture works"—that it is an effective means of producing true and useful actionable intelligence, and that its use in the "war on terror" has "kept America safe."[82] In fact, available evidence indicates that not only did torture *not* produce valuable and actionable intelligence,[83] but that the torture policy has had serious adverse consequences *for Americans* and for national interests abroad; according to the 2008 SASC report, the Bush Administration's interrogation and detention practices "damaged our ability to collect accurate intelligence that could save lives, strengthened the hand of our enemies, and compromised our moral authority." A related factor militating against accountability is the public's understandable and legitimate animus toward terrorists, but that label has been conflated with all those who have been held in U.S. custody, despite evidence (known by the Bush Administration since the summer of 2002) that the vast majority of prisoners were either entirely innocent or of no threat or intelligence value. Indifference toward the suffering of those who have been subjected to U.S. torture as the just deserts for terror translates into broad opposition to holding officials responsible for their torture.

Accountability in an international venue is not an option because the United States is not a signatory to the ICC—and even if it were, the Security Council veto would work, as it was planned to do, to prevent Americans from being indicted. Thus, UJ prosecutions are not just *an* option but the only conceivable option at this juncture due to the factors outlined above. I would go further to argue that it is the best option for two reasons. First, because of the relatively advanced understanding and extensive use of international criminal law in Europe, the prosecution of any U.S. officials in foreign courts would provide a learning experience for American jurists and politicians about the applicability and enforceability of international criminal laws that prohibit torture. Of course, the political pressure to drop indictments would be fierce, but as the Italian case against the CIA agents demonstrated, some countries might be willing to let the law run its course. Second, to the extent that the American exceptionalist legacy has included the perpetration or collusion in some gross human rights violations and grave breaches of the GCs, the prosecution of torturers from the world's lone superpower would be an important demonstration that no one is above the law, and this might deter such behavior by other regimes in the future, to the benefit of international peace and security and the global rule of law.

Although the Obama Administration's reluctance to prosecute the intellectual authors of the U.S. torture policy grants them (de facto) impunity within the United States, the praxis of UJ makes them potentially vulnerable to prosecution abroad. Indeed, if this were to materialize, there would be domestic *benefits*—as happened in Chile after Pinochet's indictment—in strengthening public understanding of the importance and value of the prohibition against torture, and the criminal consequences for its violation. Contrary to the claims of those who warn that the pursuit of legal accountability of Americans abroad would be a politicized use of the law, *not* holding Americans accountable for torture is a politicized affront to the rule of law. For universal norms to be *universal*, every perpetrator of gross crimes must be vulnerable to prosecution, those from powerful nations as well as weaker ones.

NOTES

1. Antonio Taguba, "Preface," *Broken Laws, Broken Lives: Medical Evidence of Torture by the US* (Cambridge, Mass.: Physicians for Human Rights, 2008); available at: http://brokenlives.info/?page_id=23

2. Wolfgang Kaleck, "From Pinochet to Rumsfeld: Universal Jurisdiction in Europe 1998–2008," *Michigan Journal of International Law* 30 (June 2009).

3. See Katherine Gallagher, "Universal Jurisdiction in Practice: Efforts to Hold Donald Rumsfeld and Other High Level United States Officials Accountable for Torture," *Journal of International Criminal Law* (2009); Michael Ratner and the Center for Constitutional Rights, *The Trial of Donald Rumsfeld: A Prosecution by the Book* (New York: New Press, 2008).

4. See Jameel Jaffer and Amrit Singh, eds., *The Administration of Torture: A Documentary Record from Washington to Abu Ghraib and Beyond* (New York: Columbia University Press, 2007).

5. John Yoo, *War by Other Means: An Insider's Account of the War on Terror* (New York: Atlantic Monthly Press, 2006).

6. Since 1990, sixty-seven heads of state have been prosecuted for serious human rights violations or financial crimes, most by courts in their own countries. See Ellen L. Lutz and Caitlin Reiger, eds., *Prosecuting Heads of State* (New York: Cambridge University Press, 2009).

7. The ranks of lawyers committed to (and expert in) international criminal law enforcement have grown dramatically over the last decade because hundreds have spent parts of their careers working in one or more of the international tribunals and courts.

8. For example, a conference on "Universal Jurisdiction Trial Strategies: Focus on Victims and Witnesses," held in Brussels on November 9–11, 2009, and sponsored by two European nongovernmental organizations (Redress and the International Federation for Human Rights), brought together dozens of lawyers, prosecutors, and human rights activists to discuss the current state of affairs and to strategize the advancement of this mode of accountability. (The author was in attendance.)

9. The broad principle of UJ traces back to canon law in the sixteenth century and international law in the seventeenth. See Luc Reydams, *Universal Jurisdiction: International and Municipal Perspectives* (New York: Oxford University Press, 2004), 29, 35.

10. Margaret Keck and Kathryn Sikkink, *Activists beyond Borders: Advocacy Networks in International Politics* (Ithaca: Cornell University Press, 1998).

11. Adam Hochschild, *King Leopold's Ghost: A Story of Greed, Terror and Heroism in Colonial Africa* (Boston: Mariner Books, 1999); see also Adam Hochschild, *Bury the Chains: Prophets and Rebels in the Fight to Free an Empire's Slaves* (Boston: Mariner Books, 2006).

12. As *lex specialis*, IHL comes into effect when the peace has been broken. It is agnostic on the causes of conflict (*jus ad bellum*) but governs the conduct of war (*jus in bellum*).

13. Francis Lieber, *Instructions for the Government of Armies of the United States in the Field* (Originally issued as General Orders No. 100, Adjutant General's Office, April 24, 1863).

14. Henry Dunant, *A Memory of Solferino* (published first in 1862; Geneva: International Committee of the Red Cross, 1986).

15. The Convention's authors did not include—indeed, purposefully excluded—political groups in the definition of the crime, nor did they extend the legal prohibition to "nongenocidal" violence as delimited by the intent requirement and the insertion of the phrase "as such."

16. See Lisa Hajjar, "Rights at Risk: Why the Right Not to Be Tortured Is Important to You," *Studies in Law, Politics and Society* 48 (2009).

17. *Office of the US Chief Prosecution of Axis Criminality, Nazi Conspiracy and Aggression*, vol. 1 (1946), 172.

18. These include *civilian immunity* (i.e., the prohibition against deliberately targeting civilians in military operations or otherwise treating them as combatants); *distinction* (i.e., the imperative to distinguish between civilians and combatants, and for combatants to distinguish themselves by wearing visible insignia and carrying arms openly); *proportionality* (i.e., the injunction to limit the use of force in a manner that is proportional to the value of the military target); *necessity* (i.e., the imperative to restrict targets or tactics to those necessary to achieve legitimate military objectives); and *humane treatment* (i.e., the prohibition against torture and cruel, inhumane, and degrading treatment of prisoners and civilians in militarily occupied territories).

19. Culpability for violations includes the direct perpetrators and their commanding officers (military and civilian) in the chain of command.

20. Jakob Kellenberger, "International Humanitarian Law at the Beginning of the 21st Century," May 9, 2002; available at: http://www.icrc.org/web/eng/siteengo.nsf/htmlall/5e2c8v

21. Since World War II, the majority of wars have not been fought between or among states but rather between states and nonstate groups (including wars of liberation against colonial and racist regimes and foreign occupations) or within states (e.g., civil and secessionist wars and uprisings). In order to extend the humanitarian principles of warfare to "asymmetrical" or "unconventional" armed conflicts, the GCs were further expanded through the promulgation of Additional Protocols I and II (1977). These protocols incorporated many elements deemed customary in IHL, but because they grant combatant status and a right to fight to nonstate groups that commit to IHL compliance, they are less widely signed or acceded to, thereby remaining conventional international law and applicable only to signatories.

22. There is a class action case underway in a New York federal court in which victims of apartheid in South Africa are suing multinational corporations, including IBM, Fujitsu, Ford, General Motors, and banking giants UBS and Barclays. The corporations are accused of "knowing participation in and/or aiding and abetting the crimes of apartheid; extrajudicial killing; torture; prolonged unlawful detention; and cruel, inhuman and degrading treatment." See "Holding Corporations Accountable for Apartheid Crimes," *Democracy Now!* January 13, 2010.

23. See Edward Peters, *Torture,* expanded edition (Philadelphia: University of Pennsylvania Press, 1996).

24. See Elaine Scarry, *The Body in Pain: The Making and Unmaking of the World* (New York: Oxford University Press, 1985); Henry Shue, "Torture," in *Torture: A Collection,* ed. Sanford Levinson (New York: Oxford University Press, 2004).

25. See Hajjar, "Rights at Risk."

26. See Stanley Cohen, "State Crimes of Previous Regimes: Knowledge, Accountability, and the Policing of the Past," *Law and Social Inquiry* 20 (1995); Priscilla Hayner, *Unspeakable Truths: Confronting State Terror and Atrocity* (New York: Routledge, 2001); Neil Kritz, ed., *Transitional Justice: How Emerging Democracies Reckon with Former Regimes: General Considerations,* vol. 1 (Washington, D.C.: United States Institute of Peace, 1995); Neil Kritz, ed., *Transitional Justice: How Emerging Democracies Reckon with Former Regimes: Country Studies,* vol. 2 (Washington, D.C.: United States Institute of Peace, 1995); Neil Kritz, ed.., *Transitional Justice: How Emerging Democracies Reckon with Former Regimes: Laws, Rulings, and Reports,* vol. 3 (Washington, D.C.: United States Institute of Peace, 1995); Juan Mendez, "Accountability for Past Abuses," Kellogg Institute for International Studies Working Paper Series no. 233 (1996); Martha Minow, *Between Vengeance and Forgiveness: Facing History after Genocide and Mass Violence* (Boston: Beacon Press, 1998); Diane Orentlicher, "Settling Accounts: The Duty to Prosecute Human Rights Violations of a Prior Regime," *Yale Law Journal* 100 (1997); Ruti Teitel, *Transitional Justice* (New York: Oxford University Press, 2000); Lawrence Weschler, *A Miracle, a Universe: Settling Accounts with Torturers,* 2d. ed. (Chicago: University of Chicago Press, 1998).

27. Zalaquett is a Chilean lawyer who defended political prisoners during Pinochet's military regime until he was expelled from the country. He returned following the transition and served on the country's National Truth and Reconciliation Commission. Neier, who was born in Nazi Germany, became a refugee at the age of two when his family fled to the United States. At the time of this debate, he was the executive director of HRW.

28. Jose Zalaquett, "Balancing Ethical Imperatives and Political Constraints: The Dilemma of New Democracies Confronting Past Human Rights Violations," *Hastings Law Journal* 43 (1992).

29. Alex Boraine, Janet Levy, and Ronel Scheffer, eds., *Dealing with the Past: Truth and Reconciliation in South Africa* (Pretoria: Institute for Democracy in South Africa, 1994), 103.

30. Ibid., 99.

31. See Aryeh Neier, "What Should Be Done about the Guilty?" *New York Review of Books,* February 1, 1990; see also Aryeh Neier, *War Crimes: Brutality, Genocide, Terror, and the Struggle for Justice* (New York: Random House, 1998).

32. See Michael P. Scharf, "The United States and the International Criminal Court: The ICC's Jurisdiction over the Nationals of Non-Party States: A Critique of the US Position," *Law and Contemporary Problems* 64 (2001).

33. Diane Orentlicher, "Unilateral Multilateralism: United States Policy toward the International Criminal Court," *Cornell International Law Journal* 36 (2004).

34. See Kaleck, "From Pinochet to Rumsfeld," 930–31.

35. See William J. Aceves, "Liberalism and International Legal Scholarship: The Pinochet Case and the Move toward a Universal System of Transnational Law Litigation," *Harvard International Law Journal* 41 (2000); Lisa Hajjar, "Chaos as Utopia: International Criminal Prosecutions as a Challenge to State Power," *Studies in Law, Politics and Society* 31 (2004); Christopher Hitchens, *The Trial of Henry Kissinger* (London: Verso, 2001); Naomi Roht-Arriaza, "The Pinochet Precedent and Universal Jurisdiction," *New England Law Review* 35 (2001); David Sugarman, "The Pinochet Precedent and the 'Garzon Effect': On Catalysts, Contestations and Loose Ends," *Amicus Curiae* 42 (2002); Ruth Wedgwood, "International Criminal Law and Augusto Pinochet," *Virginia Journal of International Law* 40 (2000); Richard Wilson, "Prosecuting Pinochet: International Crimes in Spanish Domestic Law," *Human Rights Quarterly* 21 (1999).

36. See "Pinochet—Interview with Plaintiffs' Attorney Juan Garces," *Democracy Now!* October 21, 1998.

37. See Daniel Rothenberg, "'Let Justice Judge': An Interview with Judge Baltazar Garzón and Analysis of His Ideas," *Human Rights Quarterly* 24 (2002).

38. Geoffrey Robertson, *Crimes against Humanity: The Struggle for Global Justice* (New York: New Press, 1999), 361.

39. Ann-Marie Slaughter, Andrew Tulumello, and Stepan Wood, "International Law and International Relations Theory: A New Generation of Interdisciplinary Scholarship," *American Journal of International Law* 92 (1998): 380. See also Naomi Roht-Arriaza, "The Pinochet Effect and the Spanish Contribution to Universal Jurisdiction," in *International Prosecution of Human Rights Crimes*, eds. Wolfgang Kaleck, Michael Ratner, Tobias Singelnstein, and Peter Weiss (Berlin: Springer Verlag, 2007).

40. See Ariel Dorfman, *Exorcising Terror: The Incredible Unending Trial of General Augusto Pinochet* (London: Pluto Press, 2003).

41. See Lama Abu Odeh, "A Radical Rejection of Universal Jurisdiction," *Yale Law Journal* 116 (2007).

42. See Adamntia Pollis, "Cultural Relativism Revisited: Through a State Prism," *Human Rights Quarterly* 18 (1996).

43. See Naomi Roht-Arriaza, *The Pinochet Effect: Transnational Justice in the Age of Human Rights* (Philadelphia: University of Pennsylvania Press, 2005). See also Sebastian Brett, *The Pinochet Effect: Ten Years on from London 1998* (report of proceedings of a conference held at the Universidad Diego Portales, Santiago, Chile, October 8–10, 2008); available at http://www.icso.cl/archivos/the-pinochet-effect-english.pdf.

44. See John Bolton, "Is There Really 'Law' in International Affairs?" *Transnational Law and Contemporary Problems* 10 (2000); Reed Brody, "Prosecution of Hissène Habré: An 'African Pinochet,'" *New England Law Review* 35 (2001); Bruce Broomhall, "Towards the Development of an Effective System of Universal Jurisdiction for Crimes under International Law," *New England Law Review* 35 (2001); Benjamin Ferencz, "A Nuremberg Prosecutor's Response to Henry Kissinger," *Brown Journal of World Affairs* 8 (2001); Henry Kissinger, "The Pitfalls of Universal Jurisdiction," *Foreign Affairs* 80 (2001); Harold Hongju Koh, "How International Human Rights Law Is Enforced," *Indiana Law Journal* 74 (1999).

45. Stephen Macedo, ed., *The Princeton Principles on Universal Jurisdiction* (Princeton University Program in Law and Public Affairs, 2001), 26; see also Stephen Macedo, *Universal Jurisdiction: National Courts and the Prosecution of Serious Crimes under International Law* (Philadelphia: University of Pennsylvania Press, 2003).

46. See John Bolton, "The Global Prosecutors: Hunting War Criminals in the Name of Utopia," *Foreign Affairs* 78 (1999); Curtis A. Bradley and Jack L. Goldsmith, "Pinochet and International Human Rights Litigation," *Michigan Law Review* 97 (1999); Kissinger, "The Pitfalls of Universal Jurisdiction."

47. Macedo, *The Princeton Principles on Universal Jurisdiction*, 49n.

48. Even though the ICJ decision did not reach the question of UJ, ten (out of sixteen) justices discussed the issue in separate opinions, with five in favor of UJ, four opposed, and one "abstention" on the grounds that the law is currently insufficiently developed to opine authoritatively on the matter.

49. Human Rights Watch, "Disappointment on Belgian War-Crimes Law Ruling" (press release), February 14, 2002.

50. Laurie King-Irani, "Universal Jurisdiction: Still Trying to Try Sharon," *MERIP Press Information Note* no. 102 (July 30, 2002).

51. The active personality principle refers to a state's competence to judge crimes committed *by* its own nationals, and the passive personality principle refers to the power of the state to judge crimes committed *against* its own nationals.

52. In September 2003, the Belgian Supreme Court ruled to close the case against Sharon. See Deena Hurwitz, "Universal Jurisdiction and the Dilemmas of International Criminal Justice: The Sabra and Shatila Case in Belgium," in *Human Rights Advocacy Stories,* eds. Deena Hurwitz, Margaret Satterwaite, and Doug Ford (New York: Foundation Press, 2009); available at SSRN: http://ssrn.com/abstract=1314940

53. Belgium remains actively involved in efforts to prosecute former Chadian dictator Hissène Habré. See Human Rights Watch, "Chronology of the Habré Case," February 2009; available at: http://www.hrw.org/fr/news/2009/02/12/chronology-habr-case

54. Antonio Cassese, "Is the Bell Tolling for Universality? A Plea for a Sensible Notion of Universal Jurisdiction," *Journal of International Criminal Justice* 1 (2003): 589. See also Michael Verhaeghe, "The Political Funeral Procession for the Belgian UJ Statute," in *International Prosecution of Human Rights Crimes*, eds. Kaleck et al., op. cit.

55. Human Rights Watch, *Universal Jurisdiction in Europe: The State of the Art* (June 27, 2006), 10; available at: http://www.hrw.org/en/reports/2006/06/27/universal-jurisdiction-europe

56. The Netherlands was the first state to successfully prosecute and convict a person (Congolese national Sebastian Nzapali) for torture on the basis of UJ.

57. See Jane Mayer, *The Dark Side: The Inside Story of How the War on Terror Turned into a War on American Ideals* (New York: Doubleday, 2008).

58. See Karen Greenberg, ed., *The Torture Debate in America* (New York: Cambridge University Press, 2005).

59. See John Parry, "Torture Nation, Torture Law," *Georgetown Law Journal* 97 (2009).

60. See Kenneth Anderson, "Who Owns the Rules of War?" *New York Times Magazine,* April 13, 2003; Knut Dormann, "The Legal Situation of 'Unlawful/Unprivileged' Combatants," *International Review of the Red Cross* 85 (2003); Lisa Hajjar, "International Humanitarian Law and 'Wars on Terror': A Comparative Analysis of Israeli and American

Doctrines and Policies," *Journal of Palestine Studies* 36 (2006); Philippe Sands, *Lawless World: America and the Making and Breaking of Global Rules—From FDR's Atlantic Charter to George W. Bush's Illegal War* (New York: Viking, 2005).

61. In August 2009, Attorney General Eric Holder appointed a special prosecutor to investigate such "excesses."

62. See Jodi Kantor and Charlie Savage, "After 9/11 Trial Plan, Holder Hones Political Ear," *New York Times*, February 14, 2010; Jane Mayer, "The Trial: Eric Holder and the Battle over Khalid Sheikh Mohammed," *New Yorker*, February 15, 2010.

63. The most illustrative example of the failure to provide justice for victims of U.S. torture is the case of Maher Arar, a Canadian citizen, who was taken into incommunicado custody while transiting through a New York airport in September 2002, then extraordinarily rendered to Syria where he was tortured for ten months until this innocent man was released and returned home. In *Arar v. Ashcroft,* the defendants are former Attorney General John Ashcroft, FBI Director Robert Mueller, and Secretary of Homeland Security Tom Ridge, as well as other immigration officials involved in Arar's illegal extradition and rendition to torture. The case alleges that his treatment violated U.S. obligations under CAT, and proffered his right to sue under TVPA. In 2005, the Bush Administration sought to dismiss the case on the grounds that any response to his allegations would violate "state secrets," and would be harmful to national security and foreign policy. The District Court that heard the suit accepted the government's claims and dismissed the case as nonjusticiable. The case was appealed to the Second Circuit in 2006 around the same time that the Canadian government, which had colluded in the rendition, released a report of their exhaustive investigation which acknowledged that there was no evidence that Arar had been involved in terror, and officially apologized and paid him compensation of $10 million. Despite his uncontested innocence, Arar was not permitted to enter the United States to testify before Congress (he testified by video link) because he remains on the "no fly" list. On June 30, 2008, the Second Circuit's majority opinion found that adjudication of this suit would interfere with national security and foreign policy, and that because he was a foreigner who had not technically "entered" the United States (he was detained in the border control area of the airport), he had no constitutional due process rights—and thus no violation had occurred; and on the issue of his torture, the majority decided that U.S. officials could not be held accountable for torture in Syria. In August 2008, the Second Circuit decided to rehear the case en banc, and the 7-4 decision, issued on November 2, 2009, affirmed the dismissal. Guido Calabresi, one of the dissenting judges (who had dissented on the first appeal too), said, "When the history of this distinguished court is written, today's majority decision will be viewed with dismay." Arar's attorneys filed an appeal to the Supreme Court in February 2010.

In *Saleh v. Titan/CACI,* Iraqi torture victims sued the security contractors from two firms which were most directly responsible for their abuse at Abu Ghraib. A District Court had provided a summary judgment against one of the two firms, but on September 11, 2009, the Federal Court of Appeals in Washington, D.C., ruled that both contractors are immunized from any liability, including for torture. For a critique of this decision, see Scott Horton, "Security Contractors Immune from Torture Charges, Judge Rules," No Comment blog, www.harpers.com, September 14, 2009.

64. The OPR report was released on February 19, 2010.

65. This includes hundreds of lawyers who have worked as habeas counsels for GITMO detainees (the so-called "GITMO bar"); military and civilian defense counsels for people charged or slated for prosecution; legal counsels in civil suits brought by victims of torture against officials, contractors, and corporations; and lawyers litigating under the Freedom of Information Act for the release of documents and photos. See Mark P. Denbeaux and Jonathan Hafetz, eds., *The Guantánamo Lawyers: Inside a Prison, Outside the Law* (New York: NYU Press, 2009); Lisa Hajjar, "An Army of Lawyers," *Nation*, December 7, 2005.

66. See *CIA-Extraordinary Rendition Flights, Torture and Accountability* (Berlin: ECCHR, 2008); available at http://www.ecchr.de/index.php/cia_flights.html

67. See "Italian Prosecutor in Case against CIA Operatives Hails Convictions for '03 Kidnapping of Egyptian Cleric," *Democracy Now!* November 5, 2009. See also Scott Horton, "Judgment in Milan," No Comment blog, www.harpers.org, November 4, 2009, and Scott Horton, "More on the Verdict in Milan," No Comment blog, www.harpers.org, November 6, 2009.

68. Scott Horton, "British Appeals Court Forces Release of Torture Details," No Comment Blog, www.harpers.org, February 11, 201.

69. The NGOs involved in the French complaint against Rumsfeld are the U.S.-based Center for Constitutional Rights, the International Federation for Human Rights (FIDH), the European Center for Constitutional and Human Rights (ECCHR), and the French League for Human Rights. Documents relating to this complaint are available at http://ccrjustice.org/ourcases/current-cases/french-war-crimes-complaint-against-donald-rumsfeld

70. The holding that a former Secretary of Defense would have immunity was based on a misreading of the ICJ's 2002 decision in the *Congo v. Belgium* case, which deals only with sitting officials.

71. The phrase and examples of France's "imagined immunity" were provided by Patrick Baudouin, honorary president of FIDH, at a conference on universal jurisdiction in Brussels in November 2009.

72. See Philippe Sands, *Torture Team: Rumsfeld's Memo and the Betrayal of American Values* (New York: Palgrave Macmillan, 2008).

73. The six lawyers are Alberto Gonzales, former White House counsel and then Attorney General; Jay Bybee, formerly head of the OLC (now a judge on the Ninth Circuit); Douglas Feith, former Undersecretary of Defense for Planning; William J. Haynes II, former general counsel for the Defense Department; and Addington and Yoo.

74. Scott Horton, "Spanish Investigators Push Justice Department on Torture Role: How Will Holder Answer?" Huffingtonpost.com, September 11, 2009.

75. In this instance, the Spanish government was responding to political and diplomatic pressure from Israel. On January 29, 2009 the Spanish *Audencia National* announced an investigation into the 2002 Israeli bombing of a multistory apartment building in Gaza where a Hamas leader resided; the bombing destroyed the building and killed fourteen people, including eleven women and children. Following this announcement, the Spanish foreign minister apologized to Israel and promised that the law would be changed. On June 30, the Spanish Appeals Court voted to close the investigation into the 2002 bombing and in October the Spanish Parliament voted to change the law. However this change does not preclude other cases against Israeli officials for war crimes perpetrated during

the 2009 war in Gaza because at least one thousand Gazans hold Spanish nationality. For information about UJ cases pertaining to Israel/Palestine, see the Palestine Human Rights Center, "Universal Jurisdiction: The Case against Impunity," available at www.pchrgaza. org/files/campaigns/english/almog/main.html.

76. According to several Spanish lawyers, the new law is rife with "technical mistakes" and logical inconsistencies because it was rushed through parliament and not subject to extensive discussion and debate. For example, the new "presence" requirement will make it impossible for Spain to continue its policy of prosecuting drug traffickers interdicted on the high seas.

77. In May 2010, Spanish prosecutors requested a judicial arrest order for the same 13 CIA agents under investigation in Germany for the kidnapping and torture of El-Masri because they transited through Spain using forged documents. See Scott Horton, "Arrest of 13 CIA Agents Sought in Spain," No Comment Blog, www.harpers.org, May 12, 2010.

78, See Ann Southworth, *Lawyers of the Right: Professionalizing the Conservative Coalition* (Chicago: University of Chicago Press, 2008).

79. See David Cole, *The Torture Memos: Rationalizing the Unthinkable* (New York: New Press: 2009).

80. In a similar measure, in November 2009 an overwhelming majority in the House of Representatives passed Resolution 867 "Condemning Goldstone Report" (which pertains to the UN commission headed by South African justice Richard Goldstone that investigated international law violations by Israelis and Palestinians during the Gaza war in January 2009). This resolution includes the claim that "the concept of 'universal jurisdiction' has frequently been used in attempts to detain, charge, and prosecute Israeli and United States officials and former officials in connection with unfounded allegations of war crimes and has often unfairly impeded travel of those individuals."

81. US Senate Armed Services Committee, "Inquiry into the Treatment of Detainees in U.S. Custody," November 22, 2008, xii.

82. See Lisa Hajjar, "American Torture: The Price Paid, the Lessons Learned," *Middle East Report* 251 (2009); Lisa Hajjar,, "Does Torture Work? A Sociolegal Assessment of the Practice in Historical and Global Perspective," *Annual Review of Law and Social Science* 5 (2009).

83. See David Rose, "Tortured Reasoning," *Vanity Fair web exclusive*, December 16, 2008.

4

The Spider's Web

How Government Lawbreakers
Routinely Elude the Law

STEPHEN HOLMES

Laws are like cobwebs, which may catch small flies,
but let wasps and hornets break through.[1]

A debate is raging, and not only within this volume, about the wisdom of prosecuting Bush Administration officials for serious violations of the law, domestic and international. Both opponents and advocates of prosecution make dire predictions about what will happen if their conflicting imperatives are not heeded. Conservatives allege that any prosecution of illegal behavior by counterterrorism officials will disarm the country in the face of its deadliest enemies; liberals retort that a failure to prosecute will fatally weaken hitherto robust principles of the American legal and political system.[2] This debate is theoretically fascinating and politically resonant, but it remains somewhat disconnected from historical realities.

High-ranking American officials have never been held legally accountable for lawbreaking in the pursuit of public safety, as they have understood it. Seen in historical perspective, letting cabinet-level and White House officials off the hook or slapping their wrists, despite ample evidence of illegal behavior, is no aberration, but exactly what we should (and do) expect. Thus, the fears and the hopes that swirl around the current debate are equally misplaced. If the past is prologue, no high-level Bush Administration officials will be successfully prosecuted for serious violations of indelible rights. Perjury convictions remain a hypothetical possibility but even they seem improbable. Nor is any high-level Bush Administration official likely to be successfully sued for money damages. Incredibly, progressives are now reduced to pleading for some kind of commission of inquiry, simply to establish a clear historical record of what laws were broken by whom and for what reasons.

And even such an anodyne form of accountability seems unlikely to materialize, at least not anytime soon.

American officials may have committed war crimes; but the Nuremburg precedent is obviously irrelevant to their misdeeds, since the great power they recently governed has not been militarily conquered and occupied by a foreign power. So what about domestic law? Seldom do countries try and convict their own top leaders for war crimes. Not having been installed by the Nazis against the will of the vast majority of his country's citizens, Dick Cheney will not be punished by his countrymen in the manner of Quisling. Not facing victor's justice administered by the Soviet Union's local proxies, he will escape the fate of the leaders of Hungary and Slovakia after World War II. And not having ordered the killings of citizens and inhabitants of his own country, Cheney will not end up like Alberto Fujimori or Augusto Pinochet. Thus, after asserting forcefully that "Investigators need to be allowed to follow the evidence all the way to the top—into the White House, if that is where the trail leads," an influential liberal columnist immediately concedes that his imaginary campaign for accountability is bootless: "I'm under no illusion that George W. Bush or Dick Cheney is actually going to be prosecuted by the Justice Department."[3] Ideal justice is one thing, political reality is another.

I

Before examining the various legal strategies which Bush Administration lawbreakers can and do use to slip the noose and avoid legal jeopardy, we need to examine briefly the meaning of "the rule of law." Indeed, the first step toward understanding the disheartening but historically customary impunity of high-ranking executive officials is to replace an idealized picture of the rule of law with a more realistic understanding. Greater realism about law's habitual leniency toward the powerful, as I will argue in conclusion, may also help us control the public narrative about why high-ranking Bush Administration officials are not being held accountable for their crimes.

The rule of law is classically said to rely on general rules (not ad hoc instructions) that are spelled out publicly and in advance, and that are understandable, mutually consistent, stable over time (though changeable), not retroactive, and enforced reliably by the various professional agencies that make up the system of justice, including an independent judiciary. Such idealizations, along with venerable maxims such as "no one is above the law,"[4] play an important role in the self-presentation of liberal societies and legal professionals. But they leave out some unsavory details. They say nothing, for example, about the specific content of laws or about who makes them, interprets them, and applies them for what purposes. The easiest way to approach these touchy issues is to ask about the relation between the rule of law and special-interest legislation.

Deluded or deluding theorists are free to depict the rule of law as intrinsically incompatible with special-interest legislation. But they will then have imagined a system that has never been observed. We can view this as a defect of their conceptualization or a deficiency of the world. I prefer the former approach, which has many classical proponents. One of them is that saint of legal liberalism, John Locke: "a great part of the municipal laws of countries" are truly "the fancies and intricate contrivances of men, following contrary and hidden interests put into words."[5]

An even more cutting account of the peculiar sensitivity of the rule of law to the interests of a few was advanced by Jean-Jacques Rousseau: "The universal spirit of the Laws of all countries is always to favor the strong against the weak, and the one who has against the one who has nothing. This inconvenience is inevitable, and it is without exception."[6] Far from being neutral and impartial, law is soaked through with partiality and favoritism. In every known society, therefore, "iniquitous decrees whose only goal is the private interest are falsely passed under the false name of laws."[7] Partiality and favoritism seep into law not only via the lawmaking process, it should be emphasized, but also through the institutions and procedures created and designed to interpret and apply the law.

Judicial impartiality and professionalism are not completely illusory, of course. But even if judges demonstrated no class bias, their ability to provide equal justice for all would be limited because they necessarily operate in an environment characterized by massive and enduring asymmetries of power. What the law declares permissible and impermissible depends first of all on the interests and prejudices of the lawmakers. Before the Civil War, to choose an egregious example, the refusal to return a runaway slave was a criminal offense. During the war, the Thirteenth Amendment outlawed slavery, it is true. But soon afterward, throughout much of the South, procedurally immaculate legal instruments were put in place to stabilize a system of peonage for many former slaves. The laws in question were reliably enforced by impartial judges in independent courts. It may be scandalous, therefore, but it is not particularly surprising when, even today, mainly white legislators attach harsh penalties to the consumption of drugs by blacks and lenient penalties to the consumption of drugs by whites. Those who make, interpret, and apply America's laws would not be so easily reconciled to America's high per capita incarceration rate, in fact, were their own children being as frequently locked up as the children of those with little or no political clout.

These examples lend support to Rousseau's claim that "laws are always useful to those who have possessions and harmful to those who have nothing."[8] His point is overstated to some extent and even verges on the cartoonish. Nevertheless, it is a welcome corrective to overidealistic views. President Obama himself has lent credence to the rather cynical thesis that corporations do not have to break the law because, as it turns out, they find it relatively easy to make and remake the law. When an interviewer asked him if someone at AIG should not go to jail for the financial shenanigans that seriously damaged the national and world economies, Obama answered frankly: "Here's the dirty little secret, though: most of the stuff that got us into trouble was perfectly legal."[9] Highly risky banking practices (such as the trading of mortgage-backed securities) were perfectly legal because myopic profit seekers in the investment banking sector had successfully lobbied Congress to repeal, in 1999, certain sections of the Glass-Steagall Act (1933) and other restrictions that had been designed to reduce the risk of a financial meltdown.

As a group's influence over the creation, interpretation, and application of the law increases, its members have less and less need to break the law to pursue their interests and achieve their aspirations. From this analysis it follows that cognizable lawbreaking will be observed more frequently among the socially disenfranchised than among those who wield substantial social influence. The fact that this is exactly what we observe does not prove the analysis correct, needless to say. But it is highly suggestive.

So what about equality before the law? Rousseau denies the possibility of equality before the law because he does not believe that society is composed of dissociated individuals who can, one at a time, be treated fairly by the legal system. Society is composed not of dissociated individuals, but of individuals woven into networks of greater and lesser power. Depending on your social network and the leverage it supplies, you will be treated better or worse by political authorities and that includes political authorities acting under color of law. A present-day example is the unequal treatment meted out to the original eight hundred or so Guantánamo detainees. More than five hundred were released in dribs and drabs over the past seven years. But the difference between those released early and those released late had nothing whatsoever to do with guilt or innocence, but only with their social and political affiliations. Those who were citizens of important U.S. allies, such as the United

Kingdom or Australia, were the first to be released. Political pressure was decisive, while due process had no role in restoring their freedom.

In general, individuals who are plugged into especially powerful networks receive considerable advantages through the legal system administered by members of privileged networks, who went to the same universities, belong to the same congregations and clubs, vacation in the same locales, and so forth. The same cannot be said for their socially marginalized or dispossessed cocitizens. Well-connected insiders usually receive more indulgent treatment than poorly connected outsiders, even in the case of undeniable lawbreaking. The effect of this skewed distribution of leniency and severity on legal liability of government malefactors goes without saying.

An important exception to impunity for the rich and powerful occurs when a member of a socially influential network seriously injures a member of the same or another socially powerful network. (Bernie Madoff is a recent example.) Unable to inject much fairness into relations between the strong and the weak, impartial justice nevertheless has a serious role to play in governing relations among groups of roughly equal power. This cynical-sounding but not unrealistic pattern was described, more than two millennia ago, by the Athenian envoys to Melos, who agreed that parties of equal strength may settle their disputes according to justice, but that relations between unequal parties are determined by force.[10]

This is an overly dramatic way to make the point. But asymmetries of power cannot be ignored by any realistic understanding of the rule of law. Crucial for the purposes of this volume are two common observations. First, while the well-to-do can often rely upon law to defend their interests, socially disadvantaged groups frequently encounter "the law" only in the form of erratic police violence. And second, crimes committed up the social ladder are usually punished more severely than crimes committed down the social ladder. We will return to both points below, especially to the observable impunity of powerfully networked people when those they injure are palpably weak.

The importance of informal networks for the distribution of legal rights and remedies is crucial for our topic because the government itself is one of the most powerful social networks. Indeed, there is perhaps no more influential network in American society than that into which the U.S. president, his cabinet, and his main advisors are plugged in. As John Stuart Mill, another authority on the asymmetries of power that characterize every known society, said, the greatest source of social power is the capacity to organize, "and the advantage in organization is necessarily with those who are in possession of the government."[11] The network occupied by political elites may even be considered the network of networks. Their membership may be relatively small, but, if well-disciplined, they can prevail over a large majority that is poorly organized and incapable of coordinated action. They can do this by taking and maintaining control of the machinery of state, especially the machinery for producing, revising, interpreting, and applying the law.

Before turning to the legal strategies by which Bush Administration officials will predictably manage to avoid accountability, I need to make a final theoretical point about "the rule of law." It concerns the way many criminal statutes contain broad grants of discretionary authority, implicitly allowing the executive to make many unaccountable ad hoc decisions. No one expects the police to stop every driver who exceeds the speed limit by a small amount. But the police can apply a vague public safety standard to decide that a driver who has barely exceeded the speed limit is driving recklessly and to stop him for that reason, using his easily clockable rule violation as an excuse. In effect, the rule against speeding is a loaded-gun statute which policemen can apply or not, as they choose. This makes good practical sense, given the variability of human affairs. But a problem arises when the rules in place are enforced or disregarded not to promote public safety, impartially understood, but in the furtherance of class interests or racial prejudice.

What is true for the police is also true for public prosecutors. The discretion to prosecute or not to prosecute is easy to justify. But it is nevertheless disturbing, from the vantage point of ideal justice, especially if the distribution of liability and impunity hinges unjustifiably on the relative weakness or strength of the networks to which perpetrator and victim belong. If the crimes committed by Important Persons—that is, by politically well-connected individuals—produce injury and suffering only among politically marginalized and weakly networked groups, then such are very unlikely to be prosecuted and, if prosecuted, they are very unlikely to be convicted. Needless to say, low-level operatives may well be (indeed, already have been) thrown to the lions. Lynndie England, who grew up in a trailer park, is a case in point. On the other hand, anti-Castro terrorists who bring down civilian Cuban aircraft, but who have influential friends in the U.S. intelligence community, will not be prosecuted in American courts. This is how network favoritism shapes or misshapes the legal system. The same bias explains why there will probably be no successful prosecutions of high-level Bush officials for lawbreaking. But of course this is far from being the last word on the subject.

II

That serious lawbreaking occurred during the Bush presidency cannot be doubted. Statutes, constitutional rights, and binding treaty obligations were all violated in undeniable ways. One example is the destruction of CIA videotapes showing the waterboarding of terrorist suspects—done with the acknowledged purpose of protecting CIA personnel from criminal liability.[12] But this perfectly clear case of obstruction of justice in a criminal investigation is only the beginning: "by one count, the administration has broken 269 laws, both domestic and international."[13]

Among the most salient statutory violations, where the involvement of high-level officials cannot be doubted, were warrantless eavesdropping in knowing disregard of the express and unequivocal language of the FISA statute,[14] and the physical abuse of detainees with the aim of extracting actionable intelligence[15] in contravention of the War Crimes Statute, 18 U.S.C. § 2441, the Torture Statute, 18 U.S.C. § 2340, and (when military personnel were involved) the UCMJ. These statutes were violated in both letter and spirit by government policymakers and operatives, many of whom were fully aware that the actions being authorized and performed were illegal under settled law. Detainees in U.S. custody were stripped naked, exposed to hypothermia, hung by their arms till their shoulders became dislocated, threatened with ferocious dogs, and placed in the cramped confinement of boxes for hours. Their heads were smashed against walls, and they were threatened with guns to the neck and with the revving of an electrical drill. Some were told that their children would be killed and their mothers raped. Taken together, the Abu Ghraib debacle and the evidence that more than a hundred detainees have died in U.S. custody in Iraq and Afghanistan suggest why such abusive behavior had never before been made into official policy from on high.

For our purposes, perhaps, the most instructive detail is former Vice President Cheney's more-or-less direct public admission that he personally authorized waterboarding. This only slightly garbled confession is important because the current Attorney General, Eric Holder, has said unequivocally that waterboarding is torture and therefore a crime under U.S. law.[16] So Cheney's legal culpability, in principle, as opposed to his real legal jeopardy, is not seriously in doubt. Along the same lines, Secretary of Defense Donald Rumsfeld, his General Counsel, Jim Haynes, Cheney's General Counsel, David Addington, not to mention President Bush himself, consciously designed and implemented an interrogation policy that involved abuses equivalent to torture. A high-ranking official in Ashcroft's Justice Department signed off on the decision to "render" Maher Arar, detained at JFK airport, to Syria (a country known for torture) where he was held for almost a year and tortured.[17] The Deputy Attorney General who signed this order for the "extraordinary rendition" of Arar is presumably guilty of a serious crime,[18] especially because he did so after a determination was made by a hearing board that Arar would more likely than not be tortured if returned to Syria. The designers of the policy of harsh interrogation likewise broke the law. On paper, their actions seem to expose Cheney and his entourage to serious criminal penalties. The Torture Statute, for example, reads:

> Whoever outside the United States commits or attempts to commit torture shall be fined under this title or imprisoned not more than 20 years, or both, and if death results to any person from conduct prohibited by this subsection, shall be punished by death or imprisoned for any term of years or for life.[19]

But we can safely predict that neither Jim Haynes nor Richard Addington nor any other high-level Bush official will be charged with a capital offense, or even with conspiracy to commit torture, for which the death penalty is not contemplated. Why not?

III

"Law is a spider's web that ensnares small flies but lets more forceful hornets escape." Swift's quip, cited in the epigraph, is amusing and accurate so far as it goes. But it does not go far enough. Law is not simply too weak to punish the lawbreaking of powerfully networked malefactors. Rather, law provides such individuals with numerous well-marked pathways to immunity.

An analogy may help clarify the point. Regular democratic elections were originally designed to inject a degree of insecurity into the lives of rulers and to make them, thereby, more attentive to the needs and concerns of ordinary citizens. In response to this attempt to hold elites *politically* accountable, elites throughout the world have developed a variety of counterstrategies, aimed at insulating themselves from insecurities inflicted from the bottom up. These counterstrategies include rigged elections, safe districts, lucrative lobbying careers available to unseated officeholders, and so forth.

Attempts to hold political elites *legally* accountable have met with the same kind of resistance and equally inventive counterstrategies. When trying to explain why high-ranking Bush officials are unlikely to face legal jeopardy, in fact, we need to give credit where credit is due. One reason why Dick Cheney and his circle are unlikely to be held accountable for their lawbreaking is that they worked long and hard (with malice aforethought) to avoid it. Cheney himself lived through Watergate and Iran-Contra and plotted carefully about how to prevent the recurrence of embarrassments of the sort that befell the entourages of Nixon and Reagan. To keep the public asleep, and thereby to maximize executive discretion in the deployment of U.S. combat troops abroad, it was essential to maintain an all-volunteer army. Vietnam had taught or retaught the lesson that antiwar sentiments are fueled by antidraft sentiments. Avoiding conscription therefore lessened the effervescence of any emerging antiwar movement, which in turn meant reduced public attention to the government's military adventures abroad. The antidemocratic impulse to reduce the government's obligation to explain its actions to the public also helps explain the Bush Administration's decision to borrow money from the Chinese Central Bank (loans to be repaid by taxpayers yet unborn) instead of raising taxes on current taxpaying voters. These policies were deliberately adopted to decrease government accountability by reducing public sensitivity to policy choices made in their name.

More pertinent to our theme are the ways in which Bush Administration lawbreakers have been making, and will continue to make, use of resources furnished by the law itself to reduce their criminal and civil liability. Modern American law, like the law of most modern states, makes available various forms of immunity, starting with sovereign immunity, which means that the government itself cannot be criminally prosecuted or civilly sued unless it explicitly waives its immunity. Modern American law also provides for absolute and qualified immunity for public officials acting in their official capacity, and even for the possibility that the government will "substitute" itself for a civilly sued government official and then shut down the case by declaring sovereign immunity. Admittedly, international war crimes tribunals (as well as the ICC) assume that official immunity is inoperative, at least when it comes to war crimes and crimes against humanity, including torture. But domestic American courts make no such assumption. Immunity is not a travesty of law, therefore, but a *part of law*, an unsurprising fact given the ample opportunities that government officials have long enjoyed of shaping law to favor the interests of government officials.

Immunity from prosecution may also derive from decisions that the president makes pursuant to his authority as commander-in-chief and chief executive of the United States. One such was Bush's February 7, 2002 decision that "common Article 3 [minimum humanitarian standards] does not apply to either al-Qaeda or Taliban detainees"[20] To understand the purpose of this presidential decision that effectively removed all legal limits on detainee interrogation, we need to reexamine a memo that Alberto Gonzales had sent to Bush on January 25, 2002 giving reasons why the president could plausibly reject Secretary of State Powell's request that the Geneva Convention on Prisoners of War (GPW) apply to al-Qaida and the Taliban. Gonzales's principal point is that ruling the GPW inapplicable would "substantially reduce the threat of domestic criminal prosecutions under the War Crimes Act."[21] Indeed, "A determination that the GPW does not apply . . . would provide a solid defense to any future prosecution."[22] Formulated differently, government officials do not have to worry about breaking the law if the president exempts them from it by executive fiat first.

Another way in which the law provides selective immunity from prosecution for instigating or engaging in torture has to do with evidentiary problems, unreliable and missing witnesses, sloppy or belated forensic work, the impossibility of maintaining a chain of custody in the chaotic environments of Iraq and Afghanistan, and the notorious difficulty of proving criminal intent. Soldiers accused of war crimes in Iraq are routinely acquitted or given negligible sentences on the grounds that establishing guilt beyond a reasonable doubt is almost impossible in a war zone, where witnesses are prone to disappear and the chain of custody cannot be maintained.[23]

The application of such procedural rules to Americans but not to similarly situated non-Americans corroborates the suggestion that, in the war on terror, the just-unjust distinction has been replaced by the us-them distinction. When those whose voices are inaudible within American networks of power are being accused of grave crimes, no procedural safeguards are necessary and no judicial second-guessing of the executive decision to incarcerate is allowed. By contrast, when American personnel, especially high-level policymakers, are accused of grave crimes, *their* procedural safeguards suddenly become all-important. In the latter case, the judiciary is not ousted, but, on the contrary, judicial oversight of procedural niceties suddenly becomes a sacred right. That is to say, the government lawbreakers are shielded from legal liability not by going around the law but through a selective application of core institutions of the rule of law. One such institution is the jury system and its unanimity rule. Could a prosecutor find a unanimous jury, even in Washington, D.C., willing to convict Dick Cheney of authorizing torture? If not, then the rule of law itself becomes an instrument not for meting out but for tiptoeing around serious punishment for serious war crimes.

Another perfectly legal strategy for conferring immunity on otherwise felonious or torturous acts involves territoriality and citizenship. Based on both the Justice Department's ruling that Guantánamo Bay Naval Base was outside U.S. legal jurisdiction and the long-standing constitutional doctrine that noncitizens held outside the United States have no constitutional rights, the decision to locate foreign terrorist suspects at Guantánamo was dictated in large part by a desire to avoid legal accountability for the executive branch's handling of the detainees. Even if the Supreme Court has now cast doubt on both assumptions, good-faith reliance upon them will almost certainly be sufficient to immunize any government official who acted on the assumption that they were valid.[24]

From the standpoint of the Bush Administration officials most involved in the war on terror, in other words, procedural protections administered by independent judges are systematically ambivalent. They are welcomed when they protect government lawbreakers from legal liability, but they are scorned when they make government lawbreaking itself more difficult. In the second case, they conspire to oust the judiciary from any role. That was the gist of the president's Military Order of November 13, 2001,[25] legalizing the transfer of all foreign terrorist suspects to the Department of Defense, thereby marginalizing the DOJ, with its professional investment in legality, in the struggle against the terrorist threat. Notice that this determination to oust or subdue the judiciary was justified by appeal to military necessity. But its more immediate effect was to shield members of the executive branch from any criminal liability for actions undertaken in response to 9/11.

This brings us to the famous torture memos written by John Yoo, among others. Early in 2002, the CIA informed the White House that its interrogators would continue to engage in what the War Crimes Statute and the Torture Statute defined as criminal conduct only if they were granted full-scale immunity ahead of time by the Department of Justice. If these secret Office of Legal Counsel memoranda, written to assuage the anxieties of the CIA, were really crafted to provide ex ante advice, they would probably constitute malpractice, since they do not explain to the DOJ's client any of the plausible legal arguments against detainee abuse. Instead, the memos rehearse the defenses available to any executive official who had violated the War Crimes Statute or the Torture Statute. Yoo seems to have been helping the executive branch stockpile defenses in case of prosecution, just as a black market pharmacist might help his rich clients stockpile CIPRO or other scarce drugs in case of an epidemic. Yoo's secret memoranda seem awkwardly contrived to immunize executive officials who had been acting outside the law. This curious effort at preemptive exculpation becomes comprehensible only when we realize that detainee abuse began in the spring of 2002, before the OLC had been able to provide a patina of legality to patently felonious conduct. Thus, Yoo's memos were scripted as after-the-fact get-out-of-jail-free cards for CIA interrogators who were already engaged in behavior that clearly violated 18 U.S.C. § 2340, which applies to any U.S. national who "outside the United States commits or attempts to commit torture."

As mentioned, an interrogator who participates in such techniques, according to this law, "shall be fined under this title or imprisoned not more than 20 years, or both, and if death results to any person from conduct prohibited by this subsection, shall be punished by death or imprisoned for any term of years or for life." The acknowledged fact that over a hundred detainees have died in U.S. custody, many from abusive interrogations, makes this a threatening statute indeed.

This "preemptive" strategy was politically shrewd. Soliciting OLC memoranda to shelter the CIA from legal liability would provide immunity all around, because the Justice Department has strong institutional reasons not to prosecute the lawyers who wrote the memos authorizing otherwise illegal interrogation methods. The Justice Department is well constructed for prosecuting malefactors in other branches of the executive, but poorly constructed for prosecuting its own personnel, especially when they are working directly for the White House. As Scott Horton says, "[S]o many high-level figures at Justice were involved in creating the legal mechanism for torture that the Justice Department has effectively disqualified itself as an investigative vehicle, even under a new administration."[26] The reason the problem is so acute, it should be said, is that the Office of Independent Counsel, a prosecutor distinct from, and independent of, the Attorney General was terminated in 1999.

The memos themselves arguably violate the United States's treaty obligations, which outlaw the legalization of torture. Nevertheless, Eric Holder has instructed the Special Prosecutor charged with investigating possible criminal behavior by CIA interrogators to treat the subsequently disavowed memos as binding law that provides full-scale immunity to any CIA agent operating in good faith under their guidance. This deference toward the shoddy legal reasoning of John Yoo is revealing, not least of all because the Bush Administration kept the memos hidden from legal professionals within the executive branch (some were locked in Addington's safe), engaging thereby in the forbidden practice of secret lawmaking, and showing their fear that the legal reasoning the memos contained would not survive scrutiny even by conservative lawyers inside the executive (such as William Taft and Alberto Mora), so long as they were not operating under David Addington's thumb.

IV

Law-and-order conservatives frequently complain about the way obvious criminals exploit legal technicalities, such as the fruit-of-the-poisoned-tree doctrine, to escape the punishment they patently deserve. The misuse of law by inveterate lawbreakers is a domestic version of "lawfare," or the instrumentalization of law by enemies of the United States. The most interesting discussion of lawfare, in the area of counterterrorism that concerns us here, can be found in Jack Goldsmith's *The Terror Presidency*.[27] The book is a fierce polemic against what Goldsmith disparagingly refers to as the "end impunity" philosophy promulgated by American liberals, among others.[28] Indeed, it is an all-out attack on anyone who wants to hold government officials criminally and civilly liable for their felonious or torturous actions while in office. In some passages describing the atmosphere in Washington after 9/11, Goldsmith seems to portray the Bush officials responsible for fighting terrorism as more afraid of prosecution by a future Democratic administration than of a follow-up al-Qaida attack.[29]

In chapter 2, revealingly entitled "The Commander in Chief Ensnared by Law," Goldsmith reproduces an interesting passage from a memo that he wrote to Rumsfeld during his stint at the Pentagon. He presumably did not have Jonathan Swift in mind, but (as if to illustrate Swift's point) he casts himself as a professional lawyer whose job it is to run interference for honorable terrorism fighters, helping them escape the cobweb of laws spun by politically correct international lawyers and human rights activists and providing get-out-of-jail-free cards in the form of reliably crafted legal opinions that will block future legal culpability:

> In the past quarter century, various nations, NGOs, academics, international organizations, and others in the "international community" have been busy weaving a web of international laws and institutions that today threatens USG interests. . . . The USG has seriously underestimated this threat, and has mistakenly assumed that confronting the threat will worsen it. . . . Unless we tackle the problem head-on, it will continue to grow. The issue is especially urgent because of the unusual challenges we face in the war on terrorism.[30]

The problem which needs to be tackled head-on is the problem of accountability for government lawbreaking. Tackling it head-on means ripping through the legal restraints that the Lilliputians have been using to tie Gulliver down. The essence of Goldsmith's approach to the question comes through in the following passage:

> Enemies like al Qaeda who cannot match the United States militarily instead criticize it for purported legal violations, especially violations of human rights or the laws of war. They hide in mosques so that they can decry U.S. destruction of religious objects when attacked. They describe civilian deaths as "war crimes" even when the deaths are legally permissible "collateral damage." Or they complain falsely that they were tortured, as we now know al Qaeda training manuals advise them to do. Lawfare works because it manipulates something Americans value: respect for law.[31]

But al-Qaida is not the only anti-American group to resort to "lawfare" in an effort to weaken the United States and impede effective executive action. The terrorists are joined in this pernicious effort, Goldsmith claims, by "the human rights industry."[32]

Several paradoxes implicit in this excoriation of lawfare are worth pointing out. First, Goldsmith complains bitterly about the unconscionable vagueness of the laws of war, especially about crimes such as outrages upon human dignity, which may be interpreted in any number of ways. This is a fair criticism, but it did not stop Bush's Justice Department from using unconscionably vague material-support statutes (in the Lackawanna case, for example) to prosecute mixed-up youngsters for what are basically thought crimes.[33] If conservative critics of vague international laws also object to vague material-support statutes, granting unaccountable discretion to federal prosecutors in search of limelight and career advancement, they have largely kept their scruples to themselves.

Second, conservative fury about the minuscule number of lower-class criminals who escape punishment because of legal technicalities does not prevent conservatives from selectively clinging to the legal technicalities that help government lawbreakers, such as Oliver North and John Poindexter, avoid accountability for their proven crimes.[34] Just as one man's terrorist is another man's freedom fighter, so one man's lawfare is another man's constitutional right.

To explain the double standard at work here, it might be helpful to distinguish between *anticipatory* and *reactive lawfare*. Ordinary criminals, and presumably suspected terrorists being tried in civilian courts or military tribunals, will use whatever legal defenses they find available. Their version of lawfare, in other words, is primarily reactive. That is natural because, before they have benefit of counsel, they are unlikely to understand the variety of intricate legal defenses provided by American law. Bush Administration officials, by contrast, were perfectly familiar with the technical ins-and-outs of the U.S. legal system even before they took office. That is what allowed them to conspire in advance to manipulate America's vaunted rule-of-law system to minimize the chances that they would be successfully prosecuted or sued.

Finally, Goldsmith makes it easy for himself by his uncritical association of flexibility with effectiveness. To be effective in the fight against terrorism, he argues, the executive branch must break free of legal rules that impede nimble adaptation to an agile and lethal enemy. He then identifies the flexibility, and therefore the effectiveness, of the executive branch with grants of legal immunity to counterterrorism policymakers and agents from all criminal and civil liability. This analysis seems like self-dealing by immunity-seeking officialdom, however, because of what it carefully omits to mention. Enforceable legal rules may limit flexibility, but the lack of enforceable legal rules may encourage recklessness.

Goldsmith is perfectly right to point out that legal restrictions on the executive can occasionally prevent effective action, in other words. But his analysis is one-sided and too narrowly focused. He neglects to mention that the absence of legal restrictions on the executive, in turn, can encourage irresponsible, wasteful, and self-defeating choices. This is a significant omission, given that the Bush Administration's refusal to submit its decision making processes to the normal sanity checks led to one national security disaster after another. The challenge is to balance the symmetrical risks of sticking blindly to the Constitution and recklessly subverting it, not to pretend that following rules is risky while circumventing rules is not.

V

The complicity of the DOJ, or of a few key actors within the DOJ, in the war crime of torture brings me to the general question of organizing complicity or "risk spreading," and the role that it too plays in obstructing criminal prosecution of former Bush officials. In a multibranch and multiparty political system, one way to buy insurance against the threat of future prosecution is for the executive branch and the incumbent party to implicate Congress and the opposition party in its legally dubious behavior. The Military Commissions Act of 2006 is the perfectly legal fruit of this perfectly legal strategy for avoiding accountability. In that Act, Congress denied the Guantánamo detainees the right to question the reasons for their detention. In 2008, the Supreme Court, in *Boumediene*, ruled that this denial was unconstitutional. The D.C. Circuit has now begun to hear the habeas petitions of these detainees and, so far, in 29 out of 36 cases the court has found that the government was unable to produce any serious evidence that supported continued detention.[35] This raises the disturbing possibility that the administration fought judicial review in the past not in order to preserve sensitive intelligence but to disguise the arbitrariness of its initial decisions (made without any procedural checks) about whom to incarcerate. Such a suspicion is unlikely to be tested in court, however, since Congress gave its strong imprimatur to the administration's claim that it could legally detain Guantánamo detainees (many of whom were not captured on a battlefield, thereby giving rise to a high risk of mistaken identity) for life with no judicial oversight.

From the very beginning of the war on terror, the Bush Administration devoted considerable effort to immunizing itself, via constitutionally favored congressional approval, from any form of judicial oversight that might find executive officials guilty for violations of law. This strategy was first visible in the AUMF passed as a Joint Resolution of House and Senate on September 14, 2001. This "Authorization for Use of Military Force" declared

> [t]hat the president is authorized to use all necessary and appropriate force against those nations, organizations, or persons *he determines* [my emphasis] planned, authorized, committed, or aided the terrorist attacks that occurred on Sept. 11, 2001, or harbored such organizations or persons, in order to prevent any future acts of international terrorism against the United States by such nations, organizations or persons.

The key phrase in this passage is "he determines." That is to say, Congress gave the president, or executive branch officials acting in his name, the right to use force against anyone he wants without having to provide the factual basis for the application of force before an independent tribunal of any sort. Some such broad grant of war-making discretion might make sense in a normal war, waged on fields of battle against an enemy state. Aimed against difficult-to-identify stateless terrorists who deliberately blend into civilian populations, such unmonitored and unaccountable discretion was almost certain to be misdirected and abused.

The importance of congressional complicity for shielding executive branch lawbreakers from criminal liability is also revealed in the 2002 AUMF, authorizing the invasion of Iraq. In the run-up to the November 2002 midterm elections, the administration spread false rumors about the involvement of Saddam Hussein in the 9/11 attacks, making it very difficult for representatives to oppose the authorization to go to war. In his book on the former vice president, Barton Gellman details a private briefing in late September 2002 that Cheney provided to Republican Congressman Dick Armey, then majority leader of the House. Armey opposed an invasion of Iraq on the reasonable grounds that the United States should not attack a country that had not attacked it. Usually hawkish, Armey presented an embarrassing hurdle to the war party in the administration. As Gellman says, "If Armey could oppose the war, he gave cover to every doubter in waiting," making him "the center of gravity of the political opposition."[36] Something had to be done, and Cheney did it. According to Gellman, Cheney, brandishing top-secret satellite photos, made statements about Saddam Hussein's nuclear arsenal and ties to al-Qaida that he knew to be erroneous: "In the privacy of his office, for this one crucial vote, Cheney leveled claims he had not made before and did not make again." Some of these claims "crossed so far beyond the known universe of fact that they were simply without foundation."[37] Gellman concludes that Cheney deliberately told Armey "things he knew to be untrue,"[38] bamboozling a congressional leader of his own party just long enough to extract a go-ahead vote. Having been preapproved on false pretenses by a gullible or complicit Congress, the misbegotten invasion was launched six months later. Naturally enough, congressmen who had voted in favor of the 2002 AUMF were later reluctant to criticize the war, just as they were reluctant to discredit themselves by publicly announcing that they had been duped and played for fools by the administration.

Cheney's lies to Armey may resemble treason in a moral sense, although they do not fall under the narrow constitutional definition of treason. He apparently lied, but not under oath, so there is no question of perjury. The vice president's actions could also be described as an attempt to subvert the democratic order. This once again might be an impeachable offense, although the administration successfully ran out the clock on impeachment. It is not, however, the kind of criminal violation that is likely to be prosecuted in court. It is an offense without a remedy, exactly as Cheney had anticipated.

The roots of this de facto immunity lie deep in American constitutional history, it should be said, in the rejection of bills of attainder, and other techniques by which the legislature could exercise independent quasi-prosecutorial and quasi-judicial functions. In the U.S. system, as a result, the executive branch controls the prosecutors (except in the case of impeachment). Because it is not in the executive's interest to open its own personnel to criminal or civil liability, it happens only rarely.

VI

Just as congressional Democrats have a very weak incentive to support the prosecution of former high-level Bush Administration officials for war crimes (having been involved just enough in the key decisions to make them enablers, if not coconspirators), so the Obama Administration has a strong incentive to avoid such prosecutions, while perhaps allowing the scapegoating of low-level operatives to go forward. For one thing, impunity for lawbreaking by Bush, Cheney, Rumsfeld, Tenet, Addington, Haynes, and so forth fits in with Obama's heavy domestic agenda (health care and saving the economy) and postpartisan agenda: "I would not want my first term consumed by what was perceived on the part of Republicans as a partisan witch hunt, because I think we've got too many problems we've got to solve."[39] Obama wants, as he has said, to look forward, to avoid recriminations, and to eschew partisan rancor, although his Justice Department, allegedly asserting its independence from the White House, has opened the way for the prosecution of some low-level CIA operatives who disobeyed explicit instructions.[40]

An influential columnist, who sides with the CIA operatives being investigated by Holder's Special Prosecutor, has objected that investigating detainee abuse by such low-level personnel, even those who violated instructions from above, would inevitably look like "political payback."[41] Along the same lines, Minority Leader John Boehner issued a statement warning that such prosecutions would leave ordinary CIA agents worrying that "they will face criminal prosecution as a result of a political election."[42] Such arguments against prosecutions speak implicitly to the worry that singling out more low-level operatives, on the Abu Ghraib or "bad apples" model, would be the worst of both worlds, punishing the weak while immunizing the strong. Hence, norms of fairness themselves may contribute to an eventual decision not to prosecute anyone at all for the grave war crime of torture.

But let us return to Obama and the reasons for his reluctance to support prosecutions. Yes, he wants to avoid the appearance of a partisan witch-hunt. But it is also true that Obama bears the special burden of liberals, that is, the need to prove that he is not weak on national security, not prone to coddling terrorists, and not unappreciative of those who have been risking their lives to protect the country from lethal enemies. Prosecuting anyone for torture, including those who designed the torture policy and authorized the use of torture, is counterindicated politically. It would suggest that Obama sides with those who were tortured—the victims— and not those who did the torturing, the interrogators as well as those who designed the torture policy. That is not a politically comfortable position to occupy. Moreover, Obama cannot govern without conciliating the military especially, but also the CIA to his presidency. This is a good example of the way an elected president can become captive to career officers in one of the government's own subunits. It also helps us understand why we are not seeing transitional justice in the United States today. There will be no transitional justice because there has been no real transition. The continuity, especially of CIA and DOD personnel, even when the partisan affiliation of the president changes, means that prosecution of wrongdoing by the previous administration will always be inhibited by the new administration's reluctance to prosecute itself. Obama sees this, which is why he is eager for this whole issue to fade from memory.

It is also worth mentioning again, in this context, Obama's decision to recycle many of Bush's techniques for avoiding legal accountability, especially the State Secrets doctrine. The current president is apparently determined to legalize the preventive detention of foreign nationals who have committed no crime but who, in the opinion of the executive branch, are dangerous to America and Americans.[43] Earlier he was reported to be considering the possibility of creating a National Security Court to handle terrorism cases, with special rules to insure the safe handling of classified information.[44] Both "reforms" would send a clear message, namely, that the Bush Administration did not have the legal tools necessary to fight the terrorists. In other words, if Bush officials went outside the bounds of the law, as it existed at the time, it was only because they had to do so. If the Obama Administration sends such a message, its DOJ would be additionally debilitated from prosecuting behavior which, in the president's own opinion, was technically illegal but necessary for the sake of national security.

Another strong constituency against prosecution is formed by those who believe, correctly in my view, that a trial of high-level Bush officials would quickly turn into a political trial. Prosecutors living in a bubble of legal professionalism might think that they have a purely legal case, that the law is the law and violations of the law "must" be punished and that prosecutions for legal trespasses automatically vindicate the rule of law. But they would not be able to control the political symbolism of such trials. In a multiparty democracy, legal prosecution of a former head of state and other high-ranking officials of a former administration, especially when initiated by a Justice Department now controlled by a rival political party, will not remain an aseptically legal affair. The trial of such officials will be fiercely politicized, first of all by the accused and their counsel. And, partly as an allergic response to political trials, a jury would likely acquit, an outcome that would paradoxically vindicate high-official immunity, as I have been arguing, via the rule of law.

Many advocates of closing the books on Bush-era lawbreaking have argued against prosecutions, invoking the folly of initiating political trials. The clearest statement was made by Alan Dershowitz. I cite at length:

> No reasonable person can disagree with the important principle under-lying these statements by the democratic nominees [Obama and Biden] that "no one is above the law." But there is a countervailing principle at play here that is equally important— namely that the results of an election should not determine who is to be prosecuted. These principles inevitably clash when the winners of a presidential election investigate and prosecute the losers, even if the winners honestly believe that the losers committed "genuine crimes" rather than having pursued merely "bad policies." Under our particular system of government, it is nearly impossible for a winning administration to prosecute those it defeated without it being perceived, quite understandably, as "a partisan witch hunt." This is because the attor-ney general of the United States, the official who a President Obama would ask to review his predecessors' actions, plays two roles simultaneously— that of political adviser to the president, and that of chief law enforce-ment officer of the United States. . . . We simply cannot trust a politically appointed and partisan attorney general of either party to investigate his political predecessors in a manner that is both fair in fact and in appear-ance. . . . The real question is whether investigating one's political oppo-nents poses too great a risk of criminalizing policy differences—especially when these differences are highly emotional and contentious, as they are with regard to Iraq, terrorism and the like. The fear of being criminally prosecuted by one's political adversaries has a chilling effect on creative policy making and implementation. . . . Most "political" crimes are matters of degree, hinging on "mens rea," the mental state of the alleged perpe-trator. The criminal law is a blunderbuss, not a scalpel, and in the hands of a partisan prosecutor it is too blunt an instrument to distinguish "gen-uine crimes" from "really bad policies" on the part of defeated political enemies.[45]

A political trial, moreover, would split the nation, making a unanimous jury verdict impossible, as well as making it much more difficult to deal with the many other issues facing the country. That, I take it, is Obama's position, a position shared by many political commentators, arguing that it would be a dangerous precedent if a change in power were to lead to criminal investigation of previous incumbents.[46] And such arguments seem to have carried the day, perhaps because some civil liberties groups, fearing acquittals even more than the failure to prosecute, have quietly abandoned the fight.

This is not to deny that there is something disturbing about Dershowitz's argument. What makes it irritating is not the argument itself, which is reasonable enough, but the fact that it is being made on behalf of an administration that, as is now well-known, deliberately politicized the DOJ, using "the rule of law" to selectively prosecute six times as many Democrats as Republicans and in a way designed to influence electoral outcomes.

VII

In November 2009, a federal appeals court ruled that Maher Arar, the Canadian citizen who had been rendered to torture in Syria by U.S. officials, could not sue for damages because no cause of action existed in the absence of an explicit congressional authorization.[47] This is a nice example of legally conferred impunity. Suits seeking money damages for constitutional violations by federal officials can be, and regularly are, blocked by the legal system itself. Interestingly enough, Obama's Justice Department started off supporting a motion to dismiss a lawsuit against John Yoo on the grounds that legal counsel to a president in wartime should not be subject to judicial second-guessing. José Padilla is suing Yoo for nominal damages ($1) for his part in shaping the policies to which he, Padilla, was subject while detained in a military brig.[48] Another and different lawsuit has also been brought against John Ashcroft.[49] In that case, Ashcroft is being sued for doing something he openly bragged of doing, that is, abusing material witness law to jail suspected terrorists without having to show probable cause of criminal conduct. Despite administration requests that both suits be dismissed, the lower court judges in the cases are (so far) letting them proceed. When looking ahead, moreover, we should remember that the Bush Administration had eight years to stack the appeals courts with conservative judges, so that any eventual finding in favor of the plaintiffs would very likely be reversed on appeal. And, yes, the right to appeal is another essential feature of the rule of law.

Conservative appointees to the appellate bench provide another perfectly legal route to effective executive branch impunity. The politicized process of appointing judges is yet another layer in a multilayer system designed to make difficult successful criminal prosecutions or civil suits. Bivens actions,[50] in light of the Supreme Court's increasingly restrictive understanding of the right to sue government officials, are often overturned on appeal. Along these lines, the U.S. Court of Appeals for the District of Columbia Circuit, with Dick Cheney's close friend Lawrence Silberman writing for the court, disallowed a suit against private contractors accused of beating, raping, and electrocuting prisoners, as well as attacking them with dogs, on the grounds that employees of the firm were under military command authority (a claim that is arguably inaccurate).[51]

Lawyers can be sued for malpractice. They cannot be sued for a simple mistake, but they can be sued, say, for negligent misrepresentation. Such suits, however, are almost always brought by the lawyers' clients. John Yoo's client was the U.S. government, and therefore an ordinary malpractice suit is not going to be brought. His memos nevertheless do seem grossly negligent. They do not explain that other lawyers might disagree with his claims. They do not explain what would happen if his advice proved legally mistaken. These professional shortcomings remain a live issue because, today, a third-party suit is legally possible. I can sue the lawyer for giving bad advice to a client who then harmed me in a way the lawyer should have foreseen. So the law, in principle, allows Yoo to be sued for the misconduct of other government officials who relied on his legal reasoning. But the law simultaneously makes it very difficult for such suits to succeed. For example, the plaintiff has to show that no reasonable official would have believed that the conduct approved by the lawyer being sued was lawful. Good faith is always available as a defense. And that is a formidable barrier to overcome in the absence of documentary evidence that Yoo falsified his own considered views to satisfy, say, Addington's demands for a specific piece of advice.[52]

Disbarment remains possible, but the disciplinary boards of state bar associations, used to dealing with lawyers who have stolen from clients and so forth, have no experience with this sort of case, where matters of high policy are involved. Moreover, "the five-year statute of limitations for allegations of attorney misconduct in Pennsylvania, where Yoo is licensed to practice law, has expired. That makes it unlikely the state bar will take up an ethics inquiry into his work at the Justice Department, which he left in 2003."[53] At this point in the argument, there should be no need to add that statutes of limitation are an integral feature of the rule of law.

Censure without disbarment is another possible response to a major ethics violation such as client laundering, that is, providing the client with a bogus legal rationale, a piece of paper that can be waved in the face of regulators to get them off the case. (This was presumably an unethical tactic brought into a CEO government from the private sector.) And censure remains possible, but only because it is a fairly tepid response, given the shocking nature of the conduct in question.

VIII

High-level officials in the Bush Administration regularly used proxies to carry out their illegal and unconstitutional instructions. Gellman's book on Cheney provides plenty of examples. Understanding how legal liability is proved in court, Cheney and his coconspirators were careful to keep their fingerprints off controversial decisions and to leave no incriminating paper trail. When one agency or office came under scrutiny, moreover, it proved easy enough to transfer the questionable task to another agency or office that, for the time being, was able to act under the radar. Privatization of government functions was very helpful in this regard, because private companies have a different set of methods than public agencies for keeping their activities secret. The ever-present possibility of shifting back and forth between public sector and private sector proxies provided a kind of "recombinant immunity" to Bush's war cabinet.

At a certain point, however, leaks are certain to occur and the machinery of accountability will grind laboriously into action. Take the complicity of American telecom companies in the government's violation of the FISA statute. A private company, in principle, has no right to sign a contract with the government to break the law. On the other hand, Congress, following legally correct procedures, can retroactively shield telecommunications companies from lawsuits for past or future cooperation with federal law enforcement authorities engaged in spying on the public.[54] Two years earlier, in 2006, Congress had amended the War Crimes Statute to immunize CIA interrogators from prosecution for abusive treatment of detainees.[55] Such statutes are subject to constitutional challenge, but until they are overturned (which is unlikely, given the political and ideological makeup of the Supreme Court) they remain valid law.

By first acting through proxies and then immunizing them when they come under legal assault, government lawbreakers manage, more often than not, to disentangle themselves from law's gossamer web. The Obama Administration, for instance, is trying to block a civil suit against a Boeing subsidiary for cooperating in an illegal conspiracy to "render" detainees in U.S. custody to countries known for torture.[56] The administration is attempting to grant the Boeing subsidiary a kind of de facto immunity to civil suit by invoking the State Secrets privilege. True, the administration has announced a new, more demanding procedure, involving the Attorney General himself, before the State Secrets privilege can be invoked.[57] But it has not backed away from the privilege itself. And it has not renounced the most controversial aspect of the privilege, namely, the government's right to block the adjudication of an entire case (rather than simply excluding certain classified materials) on the grounds that even discussing the case in court would put national security at risk. In the Boeing case, the government continues to allege that such an airing would severely damage relations of trust with the intelligence services of certain Muslim countries.

The flipside of the State Secrets doctrine, it is worth noting, is "graymail" whereby an indicted official can force the government to dismiss its case by convincing the judge that a credible defense cannot be mounted without access to classified materials that the government is not willing to disclose. The deeper a government official is involved in top-secret affairs, therefore, the more thoroughly his eventual lawbreaking will prove beyond the reach of law. The possibility of complicity between an indicted official and the government that seeks to avoid embarrassing prosecutions cannot be ruled out.

IX

A final source of lawbreakers' impunity is dismayingly democratic. The American electorate elected Bush and Cheney in 2004, after at least some of the information about their lawbreaking, especially the sickening photographs from Abu Ghraib, had become public knowledge.[58] In 2008, the Republicans were ousted from the White House and lost in Congress as well. But there is no evidence that the public turned to the Democrats out of moral revulsion at the Bush Administration's war crimes. The public seems divided about the justifiability of torture,[59] perhaps because of the lessons they imbibed from television shows such as "24." True, the administration waged a deliberate and successful campaign to mislead the public into associating Saddam Hussein and Osama bin Laden in order to create support for the invasion of Iraq. But Bush's public assertions that "we do not torture" were not necessarily believed by those who voted for him in 2004.

To understand the role of public opinion in the effective immunization of high level Bush officials for lawbreaking in the name of national security, we need to look back at the self-presentation of the makers of the war on terror. Although they checked all the rule-of-law boxes, seeking congressional rubber stamps and OLC authorizations, Cheney and the others also sent the message that they were more than willing to break the law (to take off the gloves, as Stalin liked to say) in order to defeat the terrorists. Defending the nation was simply more important than hewing to legal rules, such as the presumption of innocence, created for less dangerous times.

So far I have been arguing that legally culpable officials have been able to invoke basic rule-of-law principles to secure their immunity from prosecution. What I now want to suggest is that they also used the opposite strategy, that is, they obtained effective immunity from prosecution by winning public assent to the theory, or myth, that governmental lawbreaking makes the country safe.

This is a somewhat odd theory, but a rhetorically powerful one nonetheless, at least in the United States. It is mirrored in Guantánamo as well as the CIA's ghost prisons or black sites.[60] Both express the truly bizarre belief that the best terrain on which to meet and defeat the terrorist enemy is the domain of illegality, that is, in places where no law applies, and especially where the executive does not have to give reasons for its actions to an independent and impartial tribunal.

Americans were culturally conditioned to accept this sort of reasoning, prepared by popular culture to believe that governmental lawbreaking can make the country safe. A cultural historian could probably reveal the roots of this idea in the vigilante myths inculcated in American self-understanding by experiences on the Western frontier.[61] The most familiar example is Dirty Harry who can protect innocent civilians against predaceous killers only by acting decisively outside the law and in bold defiance of irresponsible sticklers for civil liberties. The hero of "24," a TV series watched and rewatched by American personnel at Guantánamo, is another example of this same pattern. To follow procedural niceties when faced with homicidal maniacs is to communicate weakness. Who do you want watching your back during a murderous firefight, Dirty Harry and Jack Bauer or a bunch of civil libertarians and judges in robes? There is something hallucinatory about describing America's criminal justice system, as Cheney regularly did, as "our soft side." But that is the implication of the cultural myth that, when push comes to shove, civilization can be reliably protected only by lawbreakers.

The idea that due process is a luxury which we cannot afford in wartime is closely related to the dim notion that individual liberty can make no positive contribution to national security. Such beliefs provide the mythical underpinning of Bush-era lawbreaking. They even make their way into semiacademic works, such as Goldsmith's *The Terror Presidency*. The book's central claim, remember, is that America's "super-legalistic culture"[62] is a major obstacle to defeating al-Qaida. We cannot afford to be "strangled by law,"[63] he says, if we want to win this war. This is the context in which he takes credit, shockingly, for the classification of "law" as another "weapon of the weak," alongside terrorism itself, contained in a notorious Department of Defense document.[64] There is something strange, as mentioned, about viewing legality as a preferred tool of international terrorists. If the terrorists are using our own laws to do us harm, however, we have no choice but to disarm them, that is, to break our own laws. Superlegalistic attempts to punish counterterrorism officials for heroic lawbreaking, from this perspective, is equivalent to traitorous surrender to the enemy.

Such myths shape the cultural atmosphere in which President Obama is now confronting the Bush legacy. They make it very difficult for him to reassert the simplest principles of due process such as the presumption of innocence. For political reasons he cannot appear to take sides with those suspected of attacking America. This would be tantamount to sympathizing with the aggressors and snubbing the victims. His dilemma was captured neatly in that old newspaper cartoon of two liberals who come upon the victim of a mugging, unconscious and bleeding on the sidewalk. One liberal says to the other: "The person who did this needs our help." Many registered voters in the United States subscribe to this mocking image of liberals. As a vote seeker, Obama is not about to invite their ire. At the very least, a public taught to believe in such caricatures will put no pressure on prosecutors to indict officials who have broken the law in the name of national security.

To be sure, the Bush Administration's exploitation of such inculcated public mythologies was to some extent cynical and opportunistic. Evidence of bad faith is plentiful, especially when we look closely at the most common defense of lawbreaking, namely, that government officials are allowed to break the law when it is necessary for national security. That is a superficially plausible claim, but it raises the question, how do we know that the government, behind a veil of secrecy, is not feigning necessity to win approval of a policy that is merely optional and (in someone's untested opinion) desirable? To preserve democratic accountability, the government's claims of necessity have to be tested before some independent body that has no incentive to cover up executive branch dissimulations. This seldom happened during the Bush Administration. Secrecy expanded to unprecedented levels, allowing the government to spread baseless lies, particularly the claim that waterboarding prevented another 9/11, without anyone being able to refute them on the basis of verifiable information. This is what it means to say that Cheney and his entourage are guilty of subverting the democratic order, an offense which, as I mentioned, has no effective legal remedy short of impeachment, which is no longer possible.

Bush's failure or refusal to issue pardons to any high level member of his war cabinet is suggestive about the way Bush officials who had been involved in what can only be construed as illegal behavior may have been thinking at the tail end of Bush's term. An exclusive focus on strained relations between Bush and Cheney, which left Cheney's former deputy Scooter Libby with a felony perjury conviction on his record, despite his having to serve no time in prison, is not sufficient to explain the no-pardons decision. Bush's father had behaved quite differently, one should recall. Although several members of the Reagan Administration involved in the Iran-Contra affair were convicted of obstruction of justice, lying to the Independent Counsel, destruction of documents pertinent to an ongoing criminal investigation, and so forth, none of them served time in prison, either because their convictions were vacated on appeal or because they received a presidential pardon from George H. W. Bush.

If prosecutions and convictions had been deemed likely at the end of George W. Bush's term, many powerful people (not Cheney alone) would presumably have been pushing hard for pardons. But if they assumed that successful criminal prosecutions or civil suits were highly unlikely, former Bush officials may have, on the contrary, lobbied against pardons. One possible reason is that a full-scale pardon would spell the exhaustion of legal remedies within the United States for crimes against international law, a trigger for "universal jurisdiction," or gadfly prosecutions by European prosecutors, who may never bring anyone to court but who can effectively prevent indicted individuals from traveling freely, for business or pleasure, in the world. Even more importantly, pardons would have lifted all legal jeopardy and would consequently have barred high level Bush officials from taking the Fifth when summoned before congressional commissions of inquiry. In other words, the no-pardons decision makes probing investigations of Bush Administration illegalities more difficult. Is that an accident? I am speculating here, obviously. But the curious lack of pressure for pardons and even perhaps some behind-the-scenes pressure not to pardon, may possibly be explained by a strategic commitment to avoid political accountability for illegal behavior, always assuming that no one influential seriously expected successful prosecutions or civil suits.

X

This chapter attempts to address two questions: What legal and extralegal tactics and resources have high level Bush officials mobilized to avoid being prosecuted for what is, after all, demonstrable lawbreaking? And second, What does their predictable evasion of criminal and civil liability tell us about the rule of law? To answer the first question, I have enumerated the principal formal strategies that American law makes available to those with sufficient informal resources, for avoiding legal liability. These preprepared escape routes include doctrines of absolute and qualified immunity from both criminal prosecution and civil suit for government officials acting in their official capacity. If we managed to take government lawbreakers to criminal court, we will have to give them all the legal defenses available to the bank robber, and it would be wrong not to give them these rights. But the executive branch has additional resources unique to itself that it can apply to such cases. It can, for example, use the State Secrets doctrine to provide a kind of ad hoc immunity, preventing unwanted trials of public officials or private contractors working for the government. When a two-term president manages to stack the appeals courts with sympathetic judges, the chances that any successful prosecutions or suits would be overturned on appeal are greatly increased. That additional layer of protection is undeniably judicial, even if it is not especially moral. Legality can also serve to exculpate culpable parties when the underlying wrongdoing, such as torture, cannot be easily proved beyond a reasonable doubt due to gaps in the chain of custody, the disappearance of witnesses, and so forth. Complicity by the Office of Legal Counsel, in the form of memos ostensibly authorizing facially criminal conduct, also makes it hard to prosecute anyone who relied on the findings in good faith. To prosecute the lawyers who wrote the memos is also difficult, since the Justice Department has not been organized to enable it to prosecute itself.[65] Suits for money damages against the memo writers run up against similar obstacles. Moreover, the Bush Administration also shrewdly used the legislative oversight process to decrease executive branch accountability. By deliberately misleading key members of Congress in the few weeks before the November 2002 election, the administration managed to obtain congressional approval for the Iraq war. Lying to congressmen, but not under oath, turns out to have been a "clever" move because the senators and representatives who voted for the war could not easily turn against the war later on without explaining that they had allowed themselves to be duped—not the sort of slip-up to which politicians like to draw attention. And finally, the administration tapped into deep-rooted American myths about the virtues of extralegal vigilantes. Because it was culturally prepared to believe that governmental lawbreaking makes us safe, the public was also willing to vote for Bush in

2004, knowing a lot about his administration's illegal behavior. The public's strong support for governmental lawbreaking, including the use of torture, may be the most important factor in explaining the predictable failure or refusal to prosecute.

What does all this tell us about the rule of law? It illustrates the way law itself provides plenty of instruments which the powerful can use to avoid accountability; and it corroborates the obvious fact (routinely obscured by a failure or refusal to distinguish between the ideal and the real) that the rule of law is biased toward the interests of well-networked individuals, especially when the harms they have caused are mostly felt by poorly-networked individuals. This is not an encouraging lesson, but it is true.

Pestering the former Bush officials most responsible for the torture policy (Cheney, Addington, Rumsfeld, Haynes, and Yoo) with lawsuits and foreign gadfly prosecutions is a perfectly legitimate form of political activism. Those who engage in such legal tactics may successfully express their own and our disgust. But neither we nor they should exaggerate their power or believe that such legal assaults can overcome the unassailable fortress of defenses behind which government lawbreakers will predictably find shelter. That is why, in my opinion, it is better, both politically and morally, to admit the inherent bias of the law, to recognize clearly the multiple pathways that the law provides to government lawbreakers to avoid accountability, that is, the ease with which hornets can break free of the rule of law's unevenly woven web. This approach, at least, will help rebut the narrative favored by the government lawbreakers themselves, namely, that the observable failure to prosecute or sue them successfully amounts to vindication, that it is prima facie evidence that they did nothing wrong. This may not be an optimal outcome, but it is at least something, and it may well be the best that we can do.

NOTES

1. Jonathan Swift, *A Tritical* [*sic*] *Essay Upon the Faculties of the Mind* (1707), in *The Works of Jonathan Swift* (Edinburgh: Archibald Constable, 1824), vol. IX, 134.

2. Paul Kane and Carrie Johnson, "GOP Leader Calls CIA Probe 'Witch Hunt'; Democrats Say It's Too Narrow," *Washington Post* (August 26, 2009).

3. Eugene Robinson, "History That Obama Can't Ignore," *Washington Post* (August 25, 2009).

4. During the campaign, famously, vice presidential candidate Joe Biden said: "If there has been a basis upon which you can pursue someone for a criminal violation, they will be pursued—not out of vengeance, not out of retribution, out of the need to preserve the notion that no one, no attorney general, no president—no one is above the law." Cited

in Elana Schor, "Obama Might Pursue Criminal Charges against Bush Administration," *Guardian* (September 3, 2008).

5. John Locke, *The Second Treatise of Government* (Indianapolis: Bobbs-Merrill, 1952), chapter 2, section 11, 9.

6. Jean-Jacques Rousseau, *Émile*, in *Oeuvres complètes* (Paris: Pléiade, 1969), vol. IV, 524.

7. Jean-Jacques Rousseau, *On the Social Contract* (New York: St. Martin's Press, 1978), book IV, chapter 1, 109.

8. Ibid., Part I, chapter 9, 58n.

9. "Transcript: President Barack Obama on 'The Tonight Show with Jay Leno,'" *New York Times* (March 20, 2009).

10. Thucydides, *The Peloponnesian War* (Harmondsworth: Penguin, 1972), book V, chapter 89, 402.

11. John Stuart Mill, *Considerations on Representative Government*, in *Collected Works* (Toronto: University of Toronto Press, 1977), vol. XVIII, 381.

12. Mark Mazzetti, "C.I.A. Destroyed Tapes of Interrogations," *New York Times* (December 6, 2007).

13. Karen Greenberg, "The People vs. Dick Cheney," *Mother Jones* (January–February 2009), 57.

14. For the story, see Eric Lichtblau, *Bush's Law: The Remaking of American Justice* (New York: Pantheon, 2008).

15. Joby Warrick, Peter Finn, and Julie Tate, "CIA Releases Its Instructions for Breaking a Detainee's Will," *Washington Post* (August 26, 2009).

16. David Stout, "Holder Tells Senators Waterboarding Is Torture," *New York Times* (January 16, 2009).

17. Jane Mayer, "Outsourcing Torture: The Secret History of America's 'Extraordinary Rendition' Program," *New Yorker* (February 14, 2005).

18. Namely, a violation of 18 U.S.C. § 2340A.yulaw.

19. 18 U.S.C. § 2340A.

20. Memorandum from President, to the Vice President, the Secretary of State, the Attorney General, Chief of Staff to the President, Director of Central Intelligence, Assistant to the President for National Security Affairs, Chairman of the Joint Chiefs of Staff (February 7, 2002), reprinted in Karen J. Greenberg and Joshua L. Dratel, eds., *The Torture Papers: The Road to Abu Ghraib* (Cambridge: Cambridge University Press, 2005), 134.

21. Memorandum from Alberto R, Gonzales, Counsel to the President, to George W. Bush (January 25, 2002), reprinted in Greenberg and Dratel, eds., *The Torture Papers*, 119.

22. Memorandum from Alberto R. Gonzales, in ibid., 119–20.

23. Paul von Zielbauer, "The Erosion of a Murder Case against Marines in the Killing of 24 Iraqi Civilians," *New York Times* (October 6, 2007).

24. In *Boumediene v. Bush* (2008), the Supreme Court ruled that the Guantánamo detainees had a constitutionally protected right to have their habeas petitions considered in U.S. courts. But the decision did not substantially increase the probability that high-ranking officials would be held legally accountable for violations of U.S. or international law.

25. Reprinted in Greenberg and Dratel (eds.), *The Torture Papers*, 25–28.

26. Scott Horton, "Justice after Bush: Prosecuting an Outlaw Administration," *Harper's* (December 2008).

27. Jack Goldsmith, *The Terror Presidency: Law and Judgment inside the Bush Administration* (New York: W. W. Norton, 2007).

28. Ibid., 55.

29. Ibid., 69.

30. Ibid., 60.

31. Ibid., 58–59.

32. Ibid., 59.

33. Dina Temple-Raston, *The Jihad Next Door: The Lackawanna Six and Rough Justice in the Age of Terror* (New York: Public Affairs, 2007).

34. The only person to serve jail time in the Iran-Contra affair was a protester who stole a street sign in Odon, Indiana, for a street named after Poindexter, as recounted in Howard Zinn, *A People's History of the United States* (New York: Perennial, 2003), 587–88.

35. Carol Rosenberg, "Guantánamo Captives Winning Lawsuits 29–27," *Miami Herald* (September 7, 2009). As of November 2009, the number seems to be 30 out of 38.

36. Barton Gellman, *Angler: The Cheney Vice Presidency* (New York: Penguin, 2008), 216.

37. Ibid., 217.

38. Ibid., 221.

39. Cited in Charlie Savage, "Bush, Out of Office, Could Oppose Inquiries," *New York Times* (November 13, 2008).

40. Carrie Johnson, "Prosecutor to Probe CIA Interrogations," *Washington Post* (August 25, 2009).

41. David Ignatius, "Kicking the CIA (Again)," *Washington Post* (July 15, 2009).

42. Paul Kane and Carrie Johnson, "GOP Leader Calls CIA Probe 'Witch Hunt'; Democrats Say It's Too Narrow," *Washington Post* (August 26, 2009).

43. Robert Chesney, "A Detention Debate in Black and White," *Washington Post* (September 10, 2009). Chesney served on President Obama's Detainee Policy Task Force during the summer of 2009.

44. Jack L. Goldsmith and Neal Katyal, "The Terrorists' Court," *New York Times* (July 11, 2007). Katyal is now Obama's Deputy Solicitor General.

45. Alan Dershowitz, "Indictments Are Not the Best Revenge," *Wall Street Journal* (September 12, 2008), A17.

46. David S. Broder, "Why Holder Is Wrong," *Washington Post* (September 3, 2009).

47. Benjamin Weiser, "Appeals Court Rejects Suit by Canadian Man over Detention and Torture Claim," *New York Times* (November 2, 2009).

48. Adam Liptak, "Padilla Sues U.S. Lawyer over Detention," *New York Times* (January 5, 2008). The fact that the DOJ was willing, at the outset, to represent both Ashcroft and Yoo, suggests that it has no intention of ever pursuing claims against them.

49. Carrie Johnson, "Court Allows Lawsuit against Ashcroft," *Washington Post* (September 5, 2009).

50. *Bivens v. Six Unknown Named Agents*, 403 U.S. 388 (1971).

51. Mike Musgrove, "Court Rejects Suit against CACI over Abu Ghraib—Torture Contractor Granted Wartime Immunity," *Washington Post* (September 12, 2009).

52. As Daniel Richman, a professor at Columbia Law School told a reporter, "Any punishment against Bush lawyers is unlikely unless e-mail messages or early drafts turn up proving that they blatantly altered their legal conclusions to fit a policy agenda," cited

in Charkie Savage and Scott Shane, "Terror-War Fallout Lingers over Bush Lawyers," *New York Times* (March 9, 2009).

53. Carrie Johnson, "Amid Scrutiny, Yoo Pushes Back," *Washington Post* (July 27, 2009).

54. The FISA Amendments Act of 2008.

55. The Military Commissions Act of 2006.

56. John Schwartz, "Obama Backs Off a Reversal on Secrets," *New York Times* (February 10, 2009).

57. Charlie Savage, "Justice Dept. to Limit Use of State Secrets Privilege," *New York Times* (September 22, 2009).

58. The Yoo/Bybee "torture memo" had also been made public by the summer of 2004.

59. Chris McGreal, "Americans Split on Torture as Polls Approve Obama's First 100 Days," *Guardian* (April 26, 2009).

60. Mark Danner, "U.S. Torture: Voices from the Black Sites," *New York Review of Books*, 56, no. 6 (April 9, 2009).

61. Richard Slotkin, *Gunfighter Nation: The Myth of the Frontier in Twentieth-Century America* (Norman: University of Oklahoma Press, 1998).

62. Goldsmith, *The Terror Presidency*, 79.

63. Goldsmith, *The Terror Presidency*, 69.

64. "Our strength as a nation will continue to be challenged by those who employ a strategy of the weak, focusing on international fora, judicial processes and terrorism," *National Defense Strategy of the United States of America*, March 18th, 2005.

65. "After five years of often bitter internal debate, the Justice Department concluded in a report released Friday that the lawyers who gave legal justification to the Bush administration's brutal interrogation tactics for terrorism suspects used flawed legal reasoning but were not guilty of professional misconduct." Eric Lichtblau and Scott Shane, "Report Faults 2 Authors of Bush Terror Memos," *New York Times* (February 19, 2010).

5

Democracy as the Rule of Law

PAUL HORWITZ[1]

Introduction

In American politics and political culture, eight years is not an eternity, but it can feel like one. In that time, a presidential administration and its politics can become entrenched as the regnant political culture and orient our political landscape around what comes to feel like a fixed point. It is long enough to make the transition to a new administration, especially one of a different party, seem like a significant change, a meaningful reorientation of our political culture.

We are in the midst of such a change in political culture, in two senses. We are in the post-Bush era. The players in the executive branch have changed. The names that drew such controversy have lost some of their power to provoke, like a magnet that has lost its charge. John Yoo has returned to academia; Jay Bybee sits on the federal bench, more powerful but less notorious; Donald Rumsfeld has retired to the world of foundations, think tanks, and the like. Even former Vice President Dick Cheney, who has spoken out quite visibly since his transition from power, now possesses only as much influence as others see fit to grant him.

We are also in the Bush transition era. We are still dealing with the hangover from that era. Voices that were raised in opposition to the actions of the Bush Administration in the context of post–9/11 national security issues are still asking not only what to do next, but also what is to be done in securing accountability for the actions of those who have left office.

These are, of course, related questions, and they raise deep issues. These issues might be thought of in terms of three guiding concepts: democracy, the rule of law, and transitional justice. These concepts, interrelated and yet, from the conventional viewpoint, distinct, share one thing in common: they are unhelpful. They are all essentially contested concepts.[2] Democracy is a concept of storied vagueness and disagreement.[3] The rule of law is more often invoked as a rhetorical flourish than a thickly defined concept, and those who give it serious thought find it almost obligatory to begin their discussions by acknowledging its "will-o'-the-wisp" nature.[4] Transitional justice fares no better, having been described as an "enigma" that "defines the contours of an entire field of intellectual inquiry, yet at the same time. . . . hides more than it illuminates. No one is exactly sure what it means."[5]

In short, to hope for an answer to the question what we should do about alleged abuses of legal authority by the Bush Administration during the war on terror by simply invoking concepts like democracy, the rule of law, or transitional justice is to hope in vain. That is not to say these concepts cannot start us down the road to answering that question. But they do not provide us with a clear map to any useful destination.

In what follows, I ask what the question of "prosecuting Bush," or any of the members of his administration, says about the relationship between these essentially contested concepts, and the relationship between democracy and the rule of law in particular. I will take a fairly unsentimental look at these issues. I will assume that these labels suggest little and answer nothing; that simply invoking them in an impassioned way is akin to invoking motherhood, and just as unhelpful. I will assume that these values are not metaphysical goods or ends in themselves, but rather should be viewed pragmatically in terms of how they cash out in the real world. As such, they must be weighed, balanced, and implemented by considering the costs and benefits of particular approaches in particular contexts. I will assume, in short, that what "the rule of law," "democracy," or "justice" (transitional or otherwise) demand is not absolute or sacred, but depends on the particular costs and benefits of given actions in specific circumstances.

I draw two conclusions from this analysis. First, as many others have concluded, transitional justice itself consists largely if not entirely of a pragmatic and political balance between democracy and the rule of law. It does not privilege "justice," or any other value, but involves an effort to build or preserve a reasonably healthy political environment in societies under transition. It requires a consideration of what I will call the "costs of settlement"—a balancing of past investments in and future costs to the stability and viability of both democracy and the rule of law. As such, both transitional justice and the "rule of law" itself, despite the latter term's usual assumption of universality, may require different approaches and different compromises in different societies. The rule of law, in short, at least viewed from a nonideal perspective, is not a single value with a single solution. The same actions—say, the torture of military and/or political prisoners—may, consistently with the rule of law, be dealt with in different ways at different times.

Second, the conventional view of the relationship between democracy and the rule of law treats these as distinct, if related, concepts, and tends to treat the rule of law itself in largely, if not entirely, legalistic terms. It thinks of the *rule* of law as demanding the *remedy* of law, particularly in a juridical form: a courtroom, a judge, and so on. This is understandable, but it risks missing something important. It fails to recognize that there may be a distinction between the rule of law and its implementation; and it obscures or neglects the possibility of treating *democracy itself* as one method of implementing the rule of law. The rule of law can be and, especially in stable democratic societies, often is implemented not just by and within the judicial process, but in the ordinary operation of the political process itself. Those critics of the Bush Administration who argue that the rule of law demands a legal response to that administration's allegedly lawless actions may neglect the degree to which the very fact of that administration's passage out of power has itself provided a sufficient response, albeit perhaps an incomplete one. Democracy, in short, can be seen not as distinct from the rule of law, but as a *form* of the rule of law.

Let me note at the outset that I am making a set of factual assumptions in this essay. I assume that the Bush Administration, or some of its high officials, contravened domestic and/or international law in its national security conduct involving 9/11 and the wars in Afghanistan and Iraq. Although I will mention figures such as John Yoo, who provided the apparent legal cover for these actions, they are exemplars and need not be the only relevant figures embraced by this assumption. I also assume that the actions of the Obama Administration going forward might subject its officials to the same legal liability. But I do not focus closely on these assumptions or examine at length the arguments over whether Yoo or others in fact violated the law. These are, of course, important and controversial issues, but I simply assume them for purposes of my broader discussion.

The Rule of Law and Its Implementation

Although the rule of law is a protean term, attempts to define it tend to coalesce around a standard, if broad, set of values. Lon Fuller lists its attributes as "generality, publicity, prospectivity, clarity, noncontradictoriness, capability of being followed, stability, and congruence between norms as stated and norms as applied."[6] Richard Fallon offers five elements: the capacity of legal rules to be understood, efficacy, stability, the supremacy of legal authority, and the availability of impartial legal procedures.[7] Judith Shklar writes of the rule of law as demanding that law be "general, promulgated, not retroactive, clear, consistent, not impossible to perform, enduring[,] and officials must abide by its rules."[8] More abstractly, Allan Hutchinson and Patrick Monahan describe the rule of law's "central core" as "compris[ing] the enduring values of regularity and restraint, embodied in the slogan of 'a government of laws, not men.'"[9] At a still greater level of generality, Brian Tamanaha writes that "[t]he broadest understanding of the rule of law . . . is that the sovereign, and the state and its officials, are limited by the law."[10] In general terms, then, the rule of law can be said to comprise some bundle of goods that includes generally applicable, publicly available laws that are enforced against citizens and leaders alike through some form of due judicial process.

None of these goods, one will quickly notice, necessarily depends on the existence of a democratic structure. It is common practice, in the literature on transitional justice and elsewhere, to view democracy and the rule of law as intimately connected goods.[11] Yet most serious students of the rule of law take it as a given that the rule of law is a distinct value from democracy itself. By democracy, I have in mind a fairly thin definition, involving popular rule through some form of representative and electoral government.

Many democratic theorists might argue that it is impossible to have democracy without the rule of law[12]—although that conclusion may turn as much on the substantive commitments that underwrite the spongy term "democracy" as it does on any consensus about what "democracy" itself actually requires. But it is widely agreed that the rule of law does not in turn require democracy. Thus, Brian Tamanaha observes that "[l]egal theorists have often made the point that legal liberty (as the rule of law) may exist without political liberty (democracy)."[13] José María Maravall argues that "[t]he nature of the political regime is indifferent; democracy or dictatorship is irrelevant, as long as the laws are respected and enforced."[14] Similarly, Joseph Raz writes that "if the rule of law is to have any meaning, it cannot overlap with a theory of justice or normative political philosophy."[15]

Taking things one step further, other critics have observed that the rule of law and democracy may not just be distinct concepts; they may actually *conflict*. This conflict stems from the apparent tension between the regularity and general applicability of the rule of law, with its focus on the judicial resolution of disputes, and the more free-flowing, context-dependent, and popular nature of democratic change.[16] Thus, Ian Shapiro writes that "[w]hereas democracy revolves around infusing the law with the will of the majority, the appeal of the rule of law is an appeal to its supremacy over the wills of persons, however measured or aggregated."[17] On this view, even if democracy requires the rule of law, the relationship between the two is not simply complementary, but involves a certain tension.[18]

We are left, then, with a view of democracy and the rule of law as distinct goods with an asymmetric relationship, in which one needs the other but the reverse is not necessarily true, and in which the relationship is as much one of tension as of complementarity. If we leave things at this point, we seem to have run aground, to have taken these concepts and their relationship as far as they are likely to travel together. That is, in fact, where many scholars of both democracy and the rule of law leave things.

But this is a decidedly incomplete picture. Such an approach tends to treat both democracy and the rule of law as fixed and absolute values, goods that are complete in and of themselves and whose good lies, as it were, in their very existence. It tends to treat both democracy and the rule of law as ideal theories. There is another way to think of them, however. We may think of them as nonideal theories,[19] or as theories whose ultimate meaning only crystallizes when they are implemented in some nonideal form. If we make this move, a number of further steps are possible.

In particular, we can think in terms of an important distinction: between the rule of law as an ideal, and the *implementation* of the rule of law. In American constitutional law, the distinction between the Constitution in its ideal form and the Constitution as implemented has fueled a rich and important scholarly literature, sometimes described in terms of constitutional "decision rules."[20] The crucial point of this literature is that there is a gap between the Constitution in its ideal state, or as a series of bare textual provisions, and the Constitution as judges (and others) implement it through doctrine. Similarly, we might say that whatever the rule of law demands as an absolute or abstract principle or set of principles, it still requires implementation in practical forms, and those mechanisms of implementation may vary depending on the context. On this view, whether or not there is a unitary concept known as the "rule of law," there is no one absolute form of *implementation* of the rule of law. Its applications will be as varied as the occasions which give rise to them.

Democracy and the Rule of Law

The same perspective can deepen and complicate our understanding of democracy, and of the relationship between democracy and the rule of law. Understood in nonideal terms, democracy can have a host of meanings and implementing devices. The relationship between the two concepts will also be complicated and contextual. Their relationship will not necessarily be a matter of either complementarity or conflict, but rather will depend on a variety of circumstances. How to evaluate the relationship between the two concepts, or to decide whether one concept or the other should prevail in a particular instance—that is, whether "rule of law" values or "democratic" values, roughly defined, should predominate with respect to a particular circumstance—will itself be a highly contested, contextual, and political matter.[21]

We might go a step beyond this and say that democracy, rather than being treated as utterly distinct from the rule of law, as dependent on the rule of law, or as constrained by the rule of law, can be seen as being one of a number of possible means of *implementing* the rule of law. In other words, rather than viewing the democratic process as a different matter entirely from the values such as regularity and accountability that are usually used in describing rule of law values, we can see the democratic process as one of the means of achieving rule of law values. Perhaps somewhat counterintuitively in light of the legalism that usually surrounds discussions of the rule of law, we might conclude that one of the ways in which the rule of law can be implemented is through *political* rather than legal means.

This might seem like an obvious point. Taking experience as our guide, it seems clear that the democratic process is generally viewed as one of the mechanisms by which we achieve the values—generality, publicity, and so on—that people usually have in mind when they invoke the rule of law. Yet this possibility is often neglected in the rule of law literature.[22] Instead, democracy and the rule of law are seen as being distinct concepts. The two are often linked, but mostly in the sense of both being part of a larger package of social goods that includes both democracy and the rule of law.

This tendency to treat the two as distinct goods may be a consequence of the spirit of legalism that tends to surround discussions of the rule of law, a spirit that emphasizes the need for juridical means of implementing that value and thus understates or opposes other, nonlegal methods of implementing the rule of law. This vision of the two values as distinct goods may also be reinforced by the treatment of both democracy and the rule of law as ideal theories that are more metaphysical than practical. Or it might flow from a tendency to think of the rule of law as a value that is all about *process*, while democracy is viewed as a means (albeit a procedural means) of hashing out *substantive* disputes; that is, the rule of law is seen as being a process that is primarily *about* process, while democracy is seen as a process that is ultimately about substance. Whatever the precise reason for this tendency to view the rule of law as being both juridical in nature and distinct from democracy, it remains true that more needs to be said about democracy as a means of implementing the rule of law.

Something of this idea is present in Jean Hampton's important essay on democracy and the rule of law. Hampton draws a distinction between citizens of democratic and nondemocratic societies that may help us to understand the notion of democracy as a means of implementing the rule of law that I have described here, and that will also resonate below when I bring in the concept of transitional justice. Hampton argues that in nondemocratic societies, the citizen's role in maintaining or altering the metarules that govern that society is "ill-defined, often little understood, often thwarted by the rule to any extent possible, and something she and her fellow citizens 'make up as they go along.'"[23] This may be seen as a problem for which one remedy is the implementation of the rule of law. But because there are no clear means within the existing system of achieving that goal, generally the only way to do so is through revolution.

In contrast, in a democratic society, the system, as set out in a written or unwritten constitution, allows the people "not only [to] define the object of the political game but also [to] determine the system by which the people can revise that game, and under what circumstances they will be warranted to do so."[24] It does so by creating democratic mechanisms through which the people can not only displace current officeholders by nonviolent means, but can also change both the current second-order rules (what we might call ordinary legislation, along with nonconstitutional court decisions, administrative rules, and so forth) and, through constitutional amendment, the first-order rules that constitute the operating system of that society, as it were. Thus, Hampton writes, "Those who fashioned modern democracies came to see that not only such activities as criminal punishment and tort litigation but also the very process of adding to or changing the political game itself could be made part of a larger conception of the 'political game.'"[25] Put starkly, in a democratic society, "[v]oting is . . . a form of controlled revolutionary activity."[26]

We can restate Hampton's insight in a form that underscores and reinforces the idea of democracy *as* the rule of law, or as one form of the rule of law. As we saw above, on the conventional view the rule of law, defined in a relatively narrow and legalistic fashion, can exist without democracy. It can display all the features of regularity, publicity, and so on that comprise the rule of law. What a nondemocratic society lacks, however, is a regularized means of altering the rules and metarules that govern that society. This is the missing feature that is supplied by a democratic society. Without it, the rule of law exists only by sufferance. In the long run, that is not an effective means of guaranteeing its stability and ensuring that it continues to command the respect and obedience of the people who are subject to it. By regularizing and routinizing "revolutionary activity" on this level, by ensuring that the rules of the game are ultimately subject to popular control, democracy thus serves as both an important component of, and an implementing device for, the rule of law.

Again, on the conventional view this may seem paradoxical. Politics seems to defy the qualities of regularity and general applicability that characterize the common understanding of the rule of law. Political resolutions of controversial issues can favor a particular individual or interest group or segment of the community over others. Although politics is importantly about a fair and regular process, that process certainly does not resemble the kind of juridical framework we usually have in mind when we think about the rule of law. As I have been at some pains to argue, however, the juridical framework is only one of the many means by which we realize the rule of law. And it can be an unsatisfactory one. Grant Gilmore famously observed: "The worse the society, the more law there will be. In Hell there will be nothing but law, and due process will be meticulously observed."[27] As we have seen, the rule of law, defined simply as a system of legal regularity, can be observed punctiliously in a nondemocratic society. As Hampton points out, however, in the long run such a system may come to little if it does not present a means of altering the rules and metarules that govern that system. Ultimately, then, democracy is or should be one of the central mechanisms by which the rule of law is established and by which it can evolve and be perpetuated.

Some examples may bear this out, and I will offer two. The first is prosecutorial discretion. Decisions not to prosecute may seem to be in some tension with the rule of law, since they suggest that the sovereign is violating the central rule of law principle that the law should apply equally and with equal rigor to everyone. Yet such decisions are a routine part of any prosecutor's daily work, driven by factors ranging from the practical (the difficulty of proving particular charges in court, or the necessity of husbanding scarce prosecutorial resources) to the qualitative and philosophical (declining to prosecute out of mercy, or because a particular individual acted out of addiction, deprivation, or some other influence) to the seemingly arbitrary. The routine and (largely) uncontroversial nature of such decisions, the fact that they are viewed as "bring[ing] us to law's limit" without necessarily undermining the very existence of the rule of law, suggests that something more than a mere tension is at work here.[28] Prosecutorial discretion is not just a matter of the "gaps, fissures, and failures" of the rule of law—although it may seem to be just that if viewed from a juridically oriented understanding of the rule of law.[29] Rather, it represents a recognition that the rule of law cannot function at all in the long run if its only means of implementation is an unstinting absoluteness of application. It will not command allegiance if its rigor allows no room at all for mercy; and neither it nor society as a whole can long function if its claim on resources is absolute. The rule of law, like everything else in a finite universe of scarce resources, requires some suppleness of application. We thus permit prosecutors, subject to some fundamental limitations, to choose how they will allocate those resources. At the same time, we retain some democratic hold over the prosecutors—either directly, in the case of elected prosecutors, or indirectly through those who appoint them—to ensure that the rules and metarules by which those resource allocation decisions are made are acceptable.

A second example is that of impeachment. In the American constitutional system, impeachment of federal officials is reserved for "high crimes and misdemeanors," and the system of impeachment, with respect to both the charging process and the trial process, is reserved for a political branch, the U.S. Congress (with an assist in the case of presidential impeachments from the Chief Justice of the United States, who presides at the president's Senate trial).[30] In some respects, impeachment follows the rule of law model. It redresses the violation of the law through a juridical process of sorts. In other respects, however, the impeachment mechanism is largely a political one, and the trial that results is a political trial.[31] For one thing, the "charges" that constitute the articles of impeachment often include "political as well as legal claims."[32] For another, the decision whether to impeach or convict is ultimately in the hands of political officials and may be made for political reasons. Finally, the "trial" process for an impeachment is virtually uncabined, so much so that the Supreme Court has held that the nature and scope of that process is itself a political question.[33]

The impeachment of President Bill Clinton, which was followed by an unsuccessful attempt at conviction in the Senate, serves as an illuminating example—not least because it reveals a fairly neat reversal in the lineup of views on the necessity and merits of prosecuting members of the former Bush Administration. In that instance, the champions of impeachment insisted that the rule of law did not just permit, but required, Clinton's impeachment and (on what they believed was ample evidence) his conviction. He had, on this view, clearly committed crimes, both in the broad sense of having committed specific statutory offenses and in the sense of having committed more difficult to define "high crimes and misdemeanors." To censure him, to publicly condemn his behavior, or to simply allow him to slide into historical disgrace as his tenure in office expired, was viewed as an insufficient response to the demands of the rule of law, which requires all to suffer its penalties equally. His defenders, on the other hand, in addition to arguing the facts and arguing over whether the president's actions, even if proved, constituted "high crimes" or "misdemeanors," maintained that the rule of law either did not require the president's impeachment or conviction or would be sufficiently served by his censure or public condemnation, or by his being forced to serve out the remainder of his lame-duck presidency in a state of weakened political power.

From a perspective that treats the rule of law as an absolute and ideal good, those who argued for impeachment might be viewed as having some justification for that position. There was indeed evidence (whether or not it was sufficient to merit conviction at a regular judicial trial) that Clinton had committed federal offenses, and there were sound arguments that those offenses formed a constitutional basis for impeachment and conviction.[34] The charges and evidence *could* have merited conviction following a Senate trial. If the rule of law is an end in itself that requires impeachment and conviction when the facts merit it, as proponents of prosecutions of the Bush Administration have argued, then we might reasonably object to Clinton's eventual acquittal.

But the impeachment process has always melded democracy and the rule of law together; from the perspective I have offered here, it might be said that it employs democracy *as a means* of achieving the rule of law. The president was not found guilty, but he did suffer at least short-term political consequences for his actions: not only in terms of weakened political capital, but in terms of the resources he was forced to devote to defending against impeachment rather than to other matters, and the political and fund-raising capital he deeded over to his enemies. At the same time, the political environment in which impeachment is embedded worked to minimize any catastrophic costs to the system as a whole, while still ensuring a measure of accountability for the president's misdeeds. The wounds to his presidency were absorbed, at least in part, by the sheer size of the American body politic, which comprises not only the president but Congress and a multitude of state and local governments besides, as well as the judiciary and nonstate actors such as the financial markets. Those wounds were cauterized by the existence of a regular turnover in executive office, which brought an election (albeit one that was itself deeply contested and, ultimately, juridified) to change the players and sweep the slate clean.

In short, democracy created the impeachment process itself, as a rule-of-law-oriented metarule governing the fuzzy outer boundaries of the political process. It created the conditions for the president's impeachment, and for his acquittal. And it created the metarule by which the subsequent presidential election served as a form of "controlled revolutionary activity" to replace the governing regime—and, in the longer run, its opponents as well, who may have been blamed for frittering away their time on partisan games. Just as we are all dead in the long run, so, in a properly functioning democracy, political oblivion ultimately dissolves all disputes, no matter how heated. Contrary to those who argued that the rule of law specifically demanded a legal resolution in the case of Clinton's impeachment, democracy in fact *was* the rule of law in that episode.

To summarize, it is false to view democracy and the rule of law as wholly separate goods. We must resist the urge to view the rule of law through either too idealized or too juridical a framework. The rule of law in its ideal state must be distinguished from the rule of law as implemented. On the level of implementation, the forms it takes can be political as well as legal, embracing all the varied means through which politics works. In short, democracy can be viewed as one of the many means by which the rule of law is implemented in a properly functioning democratic society.

Choosing among Implementation Mechanisms: Or, the Rule of Law and the Costs of Settlement

I have offered two implicit caveats so far, which may be found in the words "one of the many means" and "a properly functioning democratic society" in the previous sentence. That is, while democracy is one of the methods by which the rule of law is implemented, it is not the only one. The legal process itself, of course, is another, the one that is usually thought of when the rule of law is invoked. Furthermore, one of the necessary conditions for the use of democracy as an implementing mechanism for the rule of law is that it must occur in a properly functioning democracy. Exploring the nature of these conditions is the subject of this part of the discussion, and it may be illuminated by a consideration of the third broad concept I have raised in this paper: transitional justice.

Some of what is necessary for democracy to be a sound implementation vehicle for the rule of law should be evident from Hampton's description of democracy as "*controlled* revolutionary activity" (emphasis added). In order for the democratic process to serve as an effective means of advancing the kinds of values that are usually thought of as rule of law values, one needs a properly functioning political system, with a fairly open franchise, regularly frequent opportunities for elections, and so on. One almost certainly needs a variety of political rights, such as the right to organize freely and speak publicly. And one needs a mechanism—the constitutional amendment process contained in Article V of the Constitution is ours—by which the metarules can be changed, one that itself follows some form of democratic process.

These are all essential requirements. Beyond them, though, something more is needed, and it is not so much mechanical as social. For democracy to function as an effective implementing mechanism for the rule of law, one also needs a stable political culture. Political decisions must be viewed as settling important matters, more or less. What is settled by the political process must be *accepted* as settled, at least for the time being. Political disputes and their resolution cannot fester and break out into open violence, secession, or widespread rejection of the political process. Democracy's decisions may be treated as provisional, but they must be obeyed as far as they go, and that obedience must be a matter of general public consensus. Without that culture of consensus, it is unlikely that democracy will ensure that the people accept the legitimacy of society as a whole, let alone the legitimacy of the rule of law in that society. In those circumstances, the "control" drops out of "controlled revolutionary activity," society breaks into open and possibly violent conflict, and all bets are off.

Another way of putting this is that how to implement the rule of law—whether through democracy, legal process, or other means—depends on a variety of social facts. Despite the conventional conception of the rule of law as general and universal, it does not exist and cannot be examined usefully without being taken in the entire context of the system in which it operates—legal, political, and cultural. That most certainly includes the strength and stability of the political system that surrounds it. This is true for *any* rule-of-law implementing mechanism. The rule of law itself cannot function effectively, even if it is implemented through the juridical process that rule of law advocates usually have in mind, unless the force of the state and the fairness of its processes are widely acknowledged. Similarly, stability and consensus with respect to the democratic process are necessary if democracy is to be an effective rule of law implementing mechanism.

What is more, the rule of law is costly—as is its implementation. Whatever metaphysical status its more romantic champions may wish to claim for it, the rule of law, like any other practical and political good, is not an absolute good. And the rule of law is not the *only* good that must be weighed. It must be balanced against, among other things, such goods as democracy itself. Any good within a social system involves costs, benefits, and tradeoffs among them.

Those costs and benefits are not always clear. For example, some argue that there is necessarily a tradeoff between liberty and security,[35] while others argue that liberty, or other democratic goods, can actually enhance security.[36] I am thus not suggesting that we must always cut back on the rule of law for consequentialist reasons. Rather, I am suggesting that our consideration of the rule of law—what it requires, and how it is to be implemented—must include a sensitivity to its costs. Those costs will vary depending on the surrounding context. And so, too, the means by which we implement the rule of law may also vary depending on the surrounding context. How well one implementing mechanism works, and whether it is preferable to other implementing mechanisms, will depend on a host of factors, including the stability of the political system and the degree of public consensus that surrounds it.

To coin a phrase, or at least to repurpose it, we might think of the costs and benefits of various implementing mechanisms for the rule of law in terms of "the costs of settlement." I am not referring here to what are sometimes called "settlement costs" in litigation, although the concepts are related.[37] I mean instead the notion that how well the rule of law works, and how it is implemented, depends in part on the costs—social, political, and otherwise—of particular mechanisms for implementing it.

Thinking about the rule of law in terms of the costs of settlement may be a far cry from the usual rhapsodies over the rule of law that tend to surround and afflict this concept. But it is also a necessary and valuable step. It reveals something—not something unknown, perhaps, but something that can easily be neglected—about the rule of law and its implementation, whether through democracy or through other mechanisms. It suggests that different means of enforcing the rule of law will be more or less necessary, and more or less costly or viable, depending on particular variables.

I will focus on two. In assessing the value and viability of particular implementing mechanisms for the rule of law, we must weigh both the amount of prior social investment in the conditions under which the rule of law is viable (call these "past investments"), and the costs that a particular implementing mechanism will have downstream (call these "future costs"). A rule of law implementing mechanism for which there have been inadequate past investments is unlikely to succeed. A rule of law implementing mechanism whose future costs are too great is unlikely to be worth the expenditure of societal resources.

This is where our third general concept, transitional justice, can play a helpful role. Although, as we have seen, transitional justice too is a vague term, it has been defined roughly as "the processes of trials, purges and reparations that take place after the transition from one political regime to another."[38] We can already see at work in this definition, with the primacy of place it grants to trials, the juridical turn that is also apparent in discussions of the rule of law.[39] As David Gray observes, "Given that 'justice' is traditionally understood in terms of those well-worn coins 'responsibility,' 'crime,' and 'punishment,' it is no surprise that criminal trials and punishments are often the standard for justice in transitions."[40] As the reference to purges and reparations suggests, however, transitional justice is not limited to narrowly juridical remedies, but consists of a wide range of mechanisms by which societies address the shift to new political regimes. These mechanisms are both backward-looking and forward-looking. They address both the shift itself and the need to "rebuild . . . broken communities" in order for that shift to succeed.[41] More broadly, then, we might define transitional justice as *any* set of remedies, juridical or nonjuridical, that secure a lasting transition to a new political regime while addressing the wrongs worked by the old one.

Unsurprisingly, given the sheer diversity of forms of old and new regimes and the particular conditions—political, racial, and ethnic, cultural, historical, and so on—in which societies confront the injustices of the old regime and adjust to the new, transitional justice is a realm of the practical and the particularistic. As a judge in one transitional society has written, "[T]here is no one simple solution capable of addressing the complexities and subtleties inherent in a range of different factual situations. The peculiar history, politics, and social structure of a society will always inform the appropriate approach to [the] question [of transitional justice] in any given context."[42] Efforts at transitional justice thus reveal a host of mechanisms by which nations and international bodies have attempted to operationalize the rule of law and democracy in new regimes while addressing the wrongs of their predecessors.

The success and failure of these different mechanisms in different contexts may be viewed helpfully through the lens of the costs of settlement that I have described above. Whether a given mechanism will work at instituting transitional justice is, in large part, a function of the combination of the past investments in and the future costs to both democracy and the rule of law in a transitional society. Moreover, to the extent that regime transitions are not just legal but political, to the extent that they involve not only the implementation of the rule of law but of democracy also, the choice of implementation mechanism in transitional justice will also depend in part on the degree to which the "rule of law" makes "democracy" more or less costly or viable.

Some examples may help fill out this picture. Some regime transitions have been effected without any of what are now viewed as the conventional mechanisms of transitional justice. Spain, for example, appears to have effectively transitioned from a fascist to a democratic system because of, or in spite of, its decision to forgo any effort to redress the wrongs of the Franco regime.[43] In other regimes, by contrast, the decision has been made to aggressively pursue prosecution of the former regime leaders, even if those prosecutions threaten the stability of the new democratic regime. An interesting early example of this is the city-state of Athens, which, after the restoration of democracy in 411 B.C.E. following an oligarchic regime, "carried out harsh retribution" against the former oligarchs.[44] What is interesting here is that this decision proved unsuccessful. Following the restoration of democracy in 403 B.C.E. after another coup, the new regime responded differently. Rather than focus on punishment, it concentrated its efforts on enacting "constitutional changes to eliminate features that had brought democracy into disrepute," while treading lightly with respect to the leaders of the ancien regime; it preferred "the forward-looking goal of social reconciliation over the backward-looking goal of retribution."[45]

Still other regime changes have combined aggressive prosecution with dramatic political changes, although even here those prosecutions have often been limited in scope, and efforts to prosecute have quickly lost their vigor. One example of this is the progenitor of modern transitional justice: the treatment of Germany following World War II. The Nuremberg trials resulted in the immediate and massive prosecution of Nazi war criminals, accompanied by a process of purgation of civil servants. But the impracticability of a sustained prosecution and purgation of the German bureaucracy, combined with the pressure to maintain a workable German state as it became a key strategic region in the Cold War, took the wind out of the sails of denazification.[46] At the same time as they implemented a prosecutorial model of transitional justice, the Allied powers also pursued a democratic model: retributive postwar measures were combined with joint Allied and German efforts at constitutional reform, together with massive foreign aid, to form and strengthen a new democratic German state.[47]

Finally, other transitional regimes have combined political reform with alternative measures that break from a "binary approach to the matter of accountability that reduce[s] the choice to trials or no trials."[48] The most famous such model is that of the truth and reconciliation commission, as in South Africa.[49] Elsewhere, as in Central and Eastern Europe following the downfall of the Soviet regime, transitional justice was achieved largely administratively, through a process of "lustration" or purgation, under which former officials of or collaborators with the ancien regime were barred from positions of public power or influence in the new, democratic regimes.[50]

This is only a brief tour of some of the approaches to transitional justice that have been employed by different emerging democracies, and many emerging democracies have combined various elements of these approaches. What is important here is the recognition that the choice of particular transitional justice mechanisms, and their efficacy, depends in each case on the balance of past investments in, and the future costs of, democratization and the institution of the rule of law.

These factors can work in crosscutting directions. Consider first what I have labeled past investments in democracy and the rule of law. Where a prior regime has been thoroughly undemocratic and particularly cruel in its application of force to some segment of the population, some measure of retributive justice may be more necessary in order to establish either the rule of law *or* democracy in the emerging society. Without it, the new regime simply will not be able to command the respect of its citizens, many of whom have been victims of serious crimes. Or it may be that the emerging society is still too weak to provide a stable democratic or juridical process by which these wrongs can be addressed. We may see this, for example, in the establishment of international criminal tribunals to mete out justice in societies emerging from despotic and genocidal political regimes. At the same time, conditions on the ground will still determine the course that this prosecutorial approach takes. As the international status of the last example (or of the Nuremberg tribunal itself) suggests, a publicly acceptable domestic forum for trial and punishment may be unavailable where the existing judicial ranks are either nonexistent or are tainted by too close an association with the old regime.

In short, an important factor in evaluating the efficacy of various transitional justice measures based on past investments in democracy and the rule of law will be the extent to which the emerging society has an existing foundation of democratic and law-abiding institutions and officials to draw on.[51] Thus, democratization could be a more effective measure for ensuring the rule of law and a successful political transition in postwar countries such as Belgium, France, and the Netherlands, whose "[p]rewar [democratic] institutions and their personnel were shattered but not eliminated" by the war.[52] In each case, in evaluating the efficacy of various transitional justice measures in new regimes, the successor governments will have to assess whether the new institutional structure is built on solid foundations, whether the crimes it must judge are particularized enough to make successful prosecutions likely or whether those crimes are either so diffuse or so difficult to prove as to make successful trials unlikely, whether the judges in such a cause are likely to command popular consent with their rulings, whether the political institutions that might serve as an alternate forum for resolution of these issues are sufficiently hardy, and so on.[53]

Just as important as past investments, however, is the question of future costs. As Jon Elster writes, "The incoming forces often have two conflicting desires: for a peaceful transition and for transitional justice. When negotiating with the outgoing leaders to achieve the first goal, they may have to sacrifice the second."[54] Any selection of transitional justice mechanisms thus must weigh the future costs to stability that those mechanisms might impose. In some cases, the future costs to democracy and the rule of law will counsel *against* impunity. In political transitions in Central and South America, for example, some form of legal accountability was considered to be a necessary part of the transition in order to move the society out of an ongoing cycle of repression and conflict.[55]

In other cases, the incoming regime is aware that, for a variety of reasons, it cannot make "justice" complete without endangering the success of the transition to a democratic regime—and hence, in the longer run, reducing the prospect that the rule of law will flourish in that society. South Africa's decision to implement a truth and reconciliation process rather than a fully-fledged system of criminal trials is a leading modern example. In negotiating the transition to democracy, the African National Congress was well aware of the threat that the outgoing officials of the apartheid regime would not cede power quietly, and doubtless was thinking too of how to balance the need for black South Africans to feel that some measure of justice had been done with the need for white South Africans to honor the legitimacy of the new democratic process. The Truth and Reconciliation Commission thus "worked to provide a measure of justice sufficient to legitimate the new order, but which would not upset the military and economic status quo—a status quo understood to be vital to nonviolent transition. Justice and reconciliation were to be balanced as both [were] necessary to the stability of any new political order."[56]

Thus, the selection of transitional justice implementation mechanisms involves a trade-off between what might seem like the absolute claims of "justice" and the longer-term need for the successor regime to effectively institute a workable system of both democracy and the rule of law. These trade-offs reveal "the political and instrumental character of [transitional justice mechanisms] and their asserted relation to societal reconciliation and, relatedly, to the restoration of the rule of law."[57] Even in an age where international law and the prospect of international criminal tribunals loom large, "domestic political conditions" are still the prime mover in effecting the transition to a new democratic regime, and negotiating those conditions will help determine the choice and effectiveness of particular policy instruments to govern the transition.[58]

Transitional regimes must always weigh not only whether the past investments in democracy and the rule of law are sufficient to support a particular policy instrument, but also whether the future costs of that choice of instrument will outweigh its gains. "Efforts to address past wrongs should not be pursued at the expense of other transitional goals if the trade-off threatens the success of transition itself."[59] Building or rebuilding a robust rule-of-law system will not be worth it if that system ultimately endangers the democratic process, which in turn will put at risk the viability of the rule of law. Conversely, a new regime may need to provide at least a modicum of retributive justice if it is to command the assent of the people to the new democratic system. These choices will always be difficult and contingent.

Rule of Law Mechanisms in Stable Democracies

The discussion in the last section focused on emerging democratic regimes, whose transitional status may render them fragile and subject to a host of difficult considerations concerning the costs and benefits of different policy mechanisms. Now consider how the same questions play out in stable democratic regimes. Transitional justice studies normally focus exclusively on fledgling democracies. But if Hampton is right to call democracy a system of "controlled revolutionary activity," then some of the same questions are surely present with each change of government in a functioning and stable democracy. As Eric Posner and Adrian Vermeule have written, "[L]egal and political transitions lie on a continuum, of which regime transitions are merely an endpoint."[60] In stable democratic societies too, the processes of "ordinary lawmaking" must contend with shifts in political leadership, popular opinion, and other factors.[61]

Now, it should be evident that in stable and law-abiding democracies, the past investments in democracy and the rule of law have, *ex hypothesi*, been sufficient to provide for a functioning system. Regime changes through the established democratic process are accepted as legitimate; in turn, the rule of law commands wide public consensus and the use of prosecutions to secure rule-of-law values is accepted. This is true even when the juridical implementation of rule-of-law values has political aspects, provided again that the democratic system that underwrites those political aspects is stable. To reprise the examples I noted earlier, the fact that prosecutors in our society husband their prosecutorial resources and make decisions about how to allocate them has not seriously damaged widespread belief in the legitimacy of the criminal law, although sometimes prosecutors may be publicly questioned, condemned, and replaced through the political process based on how they allocate those resources. And despite all the grave talk of political and constitutional crisis that surrounded the Nixon and Clinton impeachments, neither incident was met with armed resistance, and both of them faded quite rapidly from public memory once the democratic process had secured a changeover in leadership. So we might say that there is every reason to believe that the prosecution of, say, a major official of the Bush Administration for alleged crimes committed in connection with the war on terror might proceed without raising any of the costs of settlement we have seen at work in less stable transitional societies.

That is only part of the story, however. Our weighing of the costs of settlement must include not only a consideration of past investments in democracy and the rule of law, but also the future costs to those values of any particular policy instrument for resolving alleged past misconduct. And on that side of the ledger, some future costs might weigh against choosing a juridical and retributive rather than a political and democratic means of addressing the past wrong.

First, we must consider the possibility that one of the reasons a functioning democracy is stable is precisely that it has proved itself capable of implementing the rule of law through the democratic process. That is, a functioning democracy may command sufficient popular respect that its citizens accept as settled disputes that might have been resolved through retributive juridical processes, but are instead dealt with through the regular political and electoral process. Its success in doing so—the fact that both the winners and the losers in those disputes accept the political settlement as just and worthy of respect—tends to reinforce and perpetuate popular accession to and participation in the political process. To the extent that we value such a functioning democracy, and recognize the ways in which its continued existence both represents and strengthens the rule of law, we might justifiably hesitate to upset that balance by pressing for the resolution of these disputes in a different, nonpolitical forum.

We might thus be concerned about the costs to the existing democratic system and the rule of law of proceeding by a prosecutorial rather than a political route in attempting to address particular instances of alleged wrong-doing by political officials. As we have just seen, one such cost might be the destabilizing of the existing democratic political structure. Where the incoming and outgoing political elites and their followers have agreed to abide by a compromise in which everyone accepts the results of the ongoing political process, pursuing prosecutorial rather than political remedies might upset that compromise.

But resolving a dispute through the justice system rather than the political process may have costs for the rule of law as well. Suppose that the party in power decided to pursue its political adversaries not only through the political process, but also, or primarily, through the legal process. Such a decision might introduce a virus into the body politic. The targets of such prosecutions would argue vigorously that the prosecutions were fundamentally political, thus weakening the public sense of the legitimacy of the rule of law. They would have every incentive to engage in retaliatory prosecution, using those levers available to them at the moment (which might be considerable in a system like ours, in which power is divided both horizontally and vertically), or biding their time until they reached a position of power and could turn the tables. In the meantime, the party in power would have an added incentive to insulate itself from future accountability, whether through lawful or unlawful means, and to entrench itself in power, perhaps by seeding the judiciary and the civil service with its allies. Both democracy *and* the rule of law would be the losers in such a system.

This is not a wholly chimerical concern. To some extent, it is, in fact, a description of the American political scene in the late 1790s and early 1800s, in which the orderly transition of power between political parties at the federal level was by no means guaranteed. A host of mechanisms, both legal and political, were employed as weapons in the partisan conflicts of the day, including prosecutions under the Alien and Sedition Acts, the attempt to entrench the outgoing party within the federal judiciary, and the retaliatory attempt to dislodge those appointees through impeachment. One of the resolutions of this conflict was the Supreme Court's famed decision in *Marbury v. Madison*,[62] which is commonly understood as entrenching the rule of law in the American legal and political landscape.[63] Equally important, however, was the fact of the transition of power itself—the fact that the results of the controversial election of 1800 were ultimately accepted and that politics, rather than violent revolution (with the obvious and glaring exception of the Civil War), came to be accepted as the conventional mechanism by which power would change hands in the United States. That the rule of law came under such a threat in the early Republic, and that the resolution of this threat was as much political as legal, should demonstrate the potential future costs to both democracy and the rule of law of the pursuit of legal and prosecutorial rather than political and democratic mechanisms for resolving politically divisive disputes.

All this suggests what might be a somewhat startling conclusion. Whatever the particular balance of considerations might recommend with respect to the choice of rule of law implementation mechanisms in emerging democracies, an examination of the costs of settlement suggests that implementing the rule of law through prosecutorial legal means rather than through the political process may be suboptimal in fully functioning and stable democratic systems—even though those are precisely the systems whose past investments in the rule of law make prosecutions both available and viable. In these systems, the past investments in the rule of law are matched by past investments in democracy; and the future costs to both democracy *and* the rule of law may counsel in favor of political resolutions of disputes, rather than juridical approaches that might unsettle the viability of those goods in the long run.

To be sure, that does not mean that redress for violations of law by political officials is always or necessarily best handled through the political process rather than a prosecutorial model. Nor does it mean more generally that political rather than legal resolutions of such matters are always preferable. Sometimes both the rule of law and democracy will best be vindicated in whole or in part through a retributive legal process. Nuremberg may offer such a model: it may be that vigorous prosecutions of former officials of the Nazi regime were required for both democracy and the rule of law to flourish in the new German state. Similarly, in other cases the need for retribution may be so strong, politically speaking, and the available resources for prosecution may be sufficiently stable while the political resources are not, that a legal model of redress is preferable to a political one. [64] As always, it will depend on the context. But in each case a careful weighing of the costs of settlement will be necessary in selecting an appropriate enforcement mechanism. And it may well be that in stable democratic societies, a political rather than a legal model of addressing past wrongs will be better and less destabilizing in the long run for both democracy and the rule of law. In some cases, "controlled revolutionary activity" will simply be better than, or at least the best available form of, "justice."

Revisiting Democracy as the Rule of Law: The Case of the Bush Administration

That brings us, finally, to the question confronted by this book: whether it is necessary to prosecute former members of the Bush Administration (or, potentially, current members of the Obama Administration) for wrongs committed in connection with the war on terror in order to vindicate the rule of law. What I hope the discussion thus far has demonstrated is that this is not a simple question, and that it certainly cannot be answered simply by invoking "the rule of law."

Whatever the rule of law may mean precisely, one must distinguish between the rule of law as such and its implementation. The rule of law may be implemented through a variety of devices, and the democratic process itself can be one of those implementing mechanisms. Thus, asking whether "prosecuting Bush" is necessary to vindicate the rule of law is the wrong question. We should ask instead whether democracy *and* the rule of law are best served by resolving any disputes over the Bush Administration's actions through a prosecutorial model, or through the mechanism of politics. And the answer to that question will turn on a weighing of the costs of settlement implicated in these competing mechanisms.

Without definitively resolving this question, I believe there are good reasons to conclude that the costs of settlement weigh against the prosecutorial model and in favor of the political model in this case. To be sure, as I have argued, the past investments in our society in democracy and the rule of law are such that resources would be available for pursuing a prosecution. But the future costs posed by the prosecutorial model for the stability of our system are potentially great. Even if the prosecutorial system has ample resources to pursue cases against former Bush Administration officials, allocating those resources would inevitably embroil the current administration in a controversy whose protracted and divisive nature would lock up its time and detract from its attention to more pressing policy concerns—including the very national security matters that gave rise to the controversy in the first place.[65] More generally, pursuing a prosecutorial model would risk destabilizing the compromise by which controlled revolutionary activity is pursued by common consensus through the political process, and risk a vicious circle of strategic retaliation and retrenchment among and between parties and administrations. The public would refight battles that had seemingly been settled politically, with resulting consequences for public faith in both democracy *and* the rule of law.

Against these costs—which are, admittedly, risks rather than certainties—we must weigh the sufficiency of the political process as a means of implementing the rule of law with respect to the former administration's actions in the war on terror. To concede that the political process cannot resolve all these issues decisively, and that leaving these issues to the political process rather than the legal process might itself have negative consequences for the rule of law, still leaves open the possibility that the political process can do an *adequate* job of vindicating the rule of law, and one that might have fewer negative consequences than a legal model would.

In fact, the political model seems to have done rather a good job of addressing and vindicating the rule of law concerns raised by the Bush Administration's actions (which, again, I assume to be valid concerns for purposes of this discussion). As with any presidential contest, the changeover of power represented by the election of 2008 was hardly a single-issue referendum, and we might ask whether the outcome would have been the same without the intervention of the economic crisis. But thanks to the Twenty-Second Amendment, the executive leadership would have changed no matter which party won. As it turned out, the then-party in power suffered significant electoral losses, in Congress as well as the executive branch. All the central decision makers who formulated and executed the Bush Administration's national security policy are gone from executive office. Most of them are out of public service entirely, and some of them, including some of the key players in the national security drama—John Yoo and Alberto Gonzales among them—have suffered no shortage of public and professional condemnation for their actions while in office.

Of course, just as transitional justice in practice generally involves not a binary choice between trials and nothing, but a hybrid of different implementation mechanisms, so a preference for a political rather than a legal process of dealing with the Bush Administration's assumed misdeeds does not imply amnesty or preclude *any* legal or quasi-administrative means of addressing those actions. Of course, political oblivion is itself a remedy of sorts, and one that a politician is likely to experience as having real weight. Beyond elections themselves, however, a host of legal remedies short of prosecution are still potentially available. For those Justice Department officials who were involved in dispensing legal advice that I assume here was both legally wrong and violative of the law or complicit in legal violations, there remains the possibility of ethical sanctions, both by the Justice Department itself and by the appropriate state bar authorities.[66] The possibility of civil redress for legal violations by those officials also remains,[67] although there may be cause for concern about such actions.[68] Finally, and following something like the truth and reconciliation model pursued by South Africa and other African nations, the political model does not rule out the possibility of investigation of the former administration's actions by appropriate political bodies within both Congress and the executive branch, just as internal and congressional investigations followed in the wake of the COINTELPRO revelations and the Iran-Contra affair.

That leaves the prospect of international justice—of some form of prosecutorial model pursued at the international level or by a single nation invoking universal jurisdiction.[69] Other contributors to this book address this possibility in greater detail, but a few words are in order. The latter model is somewhat limited by the narrow category of crimes for which universal jurisdiction is contemplated under international law.[70] Even so, leaving aside any reservations one may have about universal jurisdiction,[71] the argument I have pursued here certainly suggests that any nation contemplating the exercise of this power should keep in mind that the democratic process can itself be a form of domestic response to the violation of the rule of law by the defendant's home state. It should thus step lightly, lest it disturb the balance of democratic and rule of law goods in that state and impose settlement costs about which it lacks information and expertise.

As for the former model, the Statute of Rome establishing the International Criminal Court, to which the United States is not a party, precludes the exercise of jurisdiction where a case has been or is being investigated or prosecuted by the state with principal jurisdiction over that case, and that state has not been shown to be unwilling or genuinely unable to carry out that investigation or prosecution. Again, given the costs of settlement I have discussed here, how that provision is interpreted should at least take into account the possibility that the democratic process, as well as investigation by duly authorized political bodies such as Congress, can itself be a way of addressing potential international law violations.

In sum, given the costs of settlement I have described above and the relative efficacy of the political response to the Bush Administration, I am not convinced that pursuing a prosecutorial model rather than a political model in the case of the former Bush Administration is *necessary* in order to vindicate the rule of law. The rule of law is surely one good to be addressed, but it is not the only one; the costs to democratic stability must also be considered. In any event, it should not be assumed that a political model of addressing the Bush Administration's actions is contrary to the rule of law; rather, democracy can be seen as a *form* of implementation of the rule of law.

On that view, the Bush Administration's current state of political oblivion is itself a form of vindication of the rule of law—a "controlled revolution" that adequately addressed, if not redressed, any legal violations committed by that administration in the course of the war on terror. The question is not therefore one of trials or nothing, or of whether the rule of law will remain unvindicated unless the members of the administration are brought to trial; it is whether any further gains to the vindication of the rule of law realized by pursuing a legal remedy *in addition to* the political remedy that we have already experienced will be offset by the potential costs to both democracy and the rule of law if we proceed down that path. Seen from this perspective, the game may not be worth the candle.

Conclusion

This may seem, to some domestic and international critics of the Bush Administration's actions, both too little and too late. Forced political retirement, with nothing more, may seem like an insignificant response to the actions of the Bush Administration. On this view, to vindicate a grand value such as the rule of law, one that is generally seen as sounding in terms of legal process, nothing less than a fully-fledged trial will do.

But the point I have been pursuing here is that the rule of law, whatever it may be, cannot be evaluated at such an abstract level and should not be viewed in strictly juridical terms. What is needed to vindicate the rule of law cannot be judged without considering the context and weighing the costs of settlement involved in particular enforcement mechanisms. Nor, as the international experience with transitional justice suggests, can it be judged in splendid isolation and without counting the costs to both democracy *and* the rule of law of pursuing a purely or predominantly legal and prosecutorial vision of the rule of law. The rule of law and democracy are in fact closely related goods; each may affect the other, and each may be a method of *implementing* the other. What the peaceful transition from the Bush era to the Obama era teaches us is that democracy itself can be the rule of law, and that sometimes it may be the best available method of vindicating the rule of law. Whatever else it may be, the rule of law is not just the rule of legalism; it can be the rule of politics too.

1. I am grateful to my fellow participants in this project, to Shahar Dillbary, Lawrence Douglas, Kelly Horwitz, Dan Joyner, Jason Mazzone, Andrew Trask, Kelly Horwitz, and Andrea Worden for productive comments and conversations, and to Martha Rogers for research assistance.

2. *See* W. B. Gallie, "Essentially Contested Concepts," 56 *Proc. Aristotelian Soc'y* 167 (1956).

3. *See, e.g.,* John Ferejohn & Lawrence Sager, "Commitment and Constitutionalism," 81 TEX. L. REV. 1929, 1933 (2003) ("Democracy is an essentially contested concept"); *see generally* Arend Lijphart, *Patterns of Democracy: Government Forms and Performance in Thirty-Six Countries* (New Haven: Yale University Press, 1999) (noting widespread international disagreement over the meaning and implementation of democracy).

4. Allan C. Hutchinson & Patrick Monahan, "Preface," in *The Rule of Law: Ideal or Ideology,* eds. Allan C. Hutchinson & Patrick Monahan (New York: Transnational Publishers, 1987), iii- iv. For other examples, see, *e.g.,* Brian Z. Tamanaha, *On the Rule of Law: History, Politics, Theory* (Cambridge: Cambridge University Press 2004), 3. ("Notwithstanding its quick and remarkable ascendance as a global ideal, . . . the rule of law is an exceedingly elusive notion. Few government leaders who express support for the rule of law, few journalists who record or use the phrase, few dissidents who expose themselves to the risk of reprisal in its name, and few of the multitude of citizens throughout the world who believe in it, ever articulate precisely what it means. . . . The theory experts have it no better. Political and legal theorists also often hold vague or sharply contrasting understandings of the rule of law."); Richard H. Fallon, Jr., "'The Rule of Law' as a Concept in Constitutional Discourse," 97 COLUM. L. REV. 1 (1997) ("The Rule of Law is a much celebrated, historic ideal, the precise meaning of which may be less clear today than ever before."); Judith N. Shklar, "Political Theory and the Rule of Law," in *The Rule of Law: Ideal or Ideology,* at 1(noting the possibility that the phrase "rule of law" has "become meaningless thanks to ideological abuse and general over-use").

5. Jens David Ohlin, "On the Very Idea of Transitional Justice," 8 WHITEHEAD J. OF DIPLOMACY & INT'L RELATIONS 51, 51 (2007); *see also* Christine Bell, "Transitional Justice, Interdisciplinarity, and the State of the 'Field' or "Non-Field," 3 INT'L J. TRANSITIONAL JUSTICE 5, 27 (2009) (observing that the goals of transitional justice are themselves "often 'essentially contested concepts'").

6. Fallon, *supra* note 4, at 8 n.27 (summarizing Lon L. Fuller, *The Morality of Law* (New Haven: Yale University Press, 1964), 33–39).

7. *See id.* at 8–9.

8. Shklar, *supra* note 4, at 13.

9. Hutchinson & Monahan, *supra* note 4, at iv.

10. Tamanaha, *supra* note 4, at 114.

11. *See, e.g., Transitional Justice: How Emerging Democracies Reckon with Former Regimes Vol. 1,* ED. Neil J. Kritz (Washington D.C.: United States Institute of Peace Press, 1995), 68. (noting one Uruguayan judge's argument that "[d]emocracy isn't just freedom of opinion, the right to hold elections, and so forth. It's the rule of law. Without equal application of the law, democracy is dead.") (quoting from Lawrence Weschler, "The Great Exception I—Liberty," THE NEW YORKER, April 3, 1989, p. 84); *see also, e.g.,* Jane Stromseth, "Post-Conflict Rule of Law Building: The Need for a Multi-Layered, Synergistic Approach,"

49 WM. & MARY L. REV. 1443, 1443 (2008)("[T]he idea of the rule of law is often used as a handy shorthand way to describe the extremely complex bundle of cultural commitments and institutional structures that support peace, human rights, democracy, and prosperity."); Ruti Teitel, "The Law and Politics of Contemporary Transitional Justice," 38 CORNELL INT'L L.J. 837, 838 (2005)("Transitional justice evokes many aspirations: rule of law, legitimacy, liberalization, nation-building, reconciliation, and conflict resolution.").

12. See, e.g., Tamanaha, supra note 4, at 37 ("The relationship between the rule of law and democracy is asymmetrical: the rule of law can exist without democracy, but democracy needs the rule of law, for otherwise democratically established laws may be eviscerated at the stage of application by not being followed.").

13. Id.

14. José María Maravall, "The Rule of Law as a Political Weapon," in Democracy and the Rule of Law, ed. José María Maravall (Cambridge: Cambridge University Press, 2003), 275.

15. Id., citing Joseph Raz.

16. See William N. Eskridge, Jr. & John Ferejohn, "Politics, Interpretation, and the Rule of Law," in Nomos XXXVI: The Rule of Law, ed. Ian Shapiro (New York: NYU Press, 1994), 266.

17. Ian Shapiro, "Introduction," in Nomos XXXVI: The Rule of Law, supra note 16, at 1, 2.

18. See Hutchinson & Monahan, supra note 4, at 99.

19. A similar conclusion has been drawn about the third member of the trio of concepts I discuss here, transitional justice. See David Gray, "An Excuse-Centered Approach to Transitional Justice," 74 FORDHAM L. REV. 2621, 2623 (2006).

20. See, e.g., Paul Horwitz, "Three Faces of Deference," 83 NOTRE DAME L. REV. 1061, 1140–46 (2008) (discussing and collecting references to this literature).

21. See, e.g., José María Maravall & Adam Przeworski, "Introduction," in Democracy and the Rule of Law, supra note 14, at 15 ("The conflict between rule of majority and rule of law is just a conflict between actors who use votes and law as their instruments. Whether legislatures or courts prevail in particular situations is a matter of politics. Rule of law is just one possible outcome of situations in which political actors process their conflicts, using whatever resources they can muster. When law rules, it is not because it antecedes political actions. We wrote this book because we believe that law cannot be separated from politics.").

22. As always, there are exceptions. The most sophisticated treatment of the relationship between democracy and the rule of law that I have seen is the collection edited by Maravall & Przeworski, supra note 14. I also draw heavily in this section on Jean Hampton, "Democracy and the Rule of Law," in Nomos XXXVI: The Rule of Law, ed. Ian Shapiro, supra note 16, at 13–45.

23. Hampton, supra note 22, at 36.

24. Id.

25. Id. at 35.

26. Id. at 34.

27. Grant Gilmore, The Ages of American Law (New Haven: Yale University Press, 1977), 111.

28. Austin Sarat & Conor Clarke, "Beyond Discretion: Prosecution, the Logic of Sovereignty, and the Limits of Law," 33 L. & SOC. INQUIRY 387, 391 (2008).

29. Id. at 413.

30. *See* U.S. Constitution, Article II, sec. 4.

31. *See, e.g.,* Eric A. Posner, "Political Trials in Domestic and International Law," 55 DUKE L.J. 75, 76 (2005) (defining political trials); *see also id.* at 93 (discussing impeachments as a form of political trial).

32. *Id.*.

33. *See Nixon v. United States,* 506 U.S. 224 (1993).

34. *See, e.g.,* Richard A. Posner, *An Affair of State: The Investigation, Impeachment, and Trial of President Clinton* (Cambridge, Mass.: Harvard University Press, 1999).

35. *See, e.g.,* Richard A. Posner, *Not a Suicide Pact: The Constitution in a Time of National Emergency* (Oxford: Oxford University Press, 2006).

36. *See, e.g.,* Stephen Holmes, "In Case of Emergency: Misunderstanding Tradeoffs in the War on Terror," 97 CAL. L. REV. 301 (2009).

37. *See, e.g.,* William M. Landes, "An Economic Analysis of the Courts," 14 J.L. & ECON. 61 (1971); Richard A. Posner, "An Economic Approach to Legal Procedure and Judicial Administration," 21 J. LEGAL STUD. 399 (1973); George L. Priest & Benjamin Klein, "The Selection of Disputes for Litigation," 13 J. LEGAL STUD. 1 (1984).

38. Jon Elster, *Closing the Books: Transitional Justice in Historical Perspective* 1 (Cambridge: Cambridge University Press, 2004).

39. *See* Kieran McEvoy, "Beyond Legalism: Towards a Thicker Understanding of Transitional Justice," 34 J. L. & SOC'Y 411, 412 (2007) (noting the "dominance of legalism" as a key trend in transitional justice).

40. Gray, *supra* note 19, at 2621.

41. Jens David Ohlin, "On the Very Idea of Transitional Justice," 8 WHITEHEAD JOURNAL OF DIPLOMACY AND INTERNATIONAL RELATIONS 51 (2007).

42. Richard Goldstone, "Preface" to *Human Rights in Political Transitions: Gettysburg to Bosnia,* eds. Carla Hesse & Robert Post (Cambridge, Mass.: MIT Press, 1999).

43. *See, e.g.,* Eric A. Posner & Adrian Vermeule, "Transitional Justice as Ordinary Justice," 117 HARV. L. REV. 761, 768 (2004).

44. Elster, *supra* note 38, at 3.

45. *Id.*

46. *See, e.g., id.* at 54–55.

47. *See, e.g., id.* at 206.

48. Lisa J. Laplante, "Outlawing Amnesty: The Return of Criminal Justice in Transitional Justice Schemes," 49 VA. J. INT'L L. 915, 927(2009).

49. *See, e.g.,* Robert I. Rotberg & Dennis Thompson, eds., *Truth v. Justice* (Princeton, N.J.: Princeton University Press, 2000) (collected essays discussing the South African Truth and Reconciliation Commission and its proceedings).

50. *See, e.g.,* Roman Boed, "An Evaluation of the Legality and Efficacy of Lustration as a Tool of Transitional Justice," 37 COLUM. J. TRANSNAT'L L. 357 (1999).

51. *See also* Ruti Teitel, *Transitional Justice* (Oxford: Oxford University Press, 2000), 17–18 ("[T]he transitional justice precedents suggest that no one rule-of-law value is essential in the movement toward construction of a more liberal political system. Transcendent notions of rule-of-law values in transitional societies are highly contingent, depending, in part, on the states' distinctive political and legal legacies and, in particular, on the rule of law in the predecessor regime.").

52. Luc Huyse, "Justice after Transitions: On the Choices Successor Elites Make in Dealing with the Past," in *Transitional Justice, supra* note 11, at 104, 111.

53. *See also* Gray, *supra* note 19, at 2623 (transitional justice "must take positive account of the unique circumstances found in transitions and their predecessor regimes in constructing a transitional jurisprudence").

54. Elster, *supra* note 38, at 190.

55. Bell, *supra* note 5, at 13.

56. *Id.*

57. Teitel, *supra* note 51, at 54.

58. James Cavallaro & Stephanie Erin Brewer, "Never Again? The Legacy of the Argentine and Chilean Dictatorships for the Global Human Rights Regime," 39 *Journal of Interdisciplinary Study* 233, 234 (2008).

59. Gray, *supra* note 19, at 2626.

60. Posner & Vermeule, *supra* note 43, at 763.

61. *Id.* at 764.

62. 5 U.S. (1 Cranch.) 137 (1803).

63. *See, e.g.,* William E. Nelson, "*Marbury v. Madison*, Democracy, and the Rule of Law," 71 Tenn. L. Rev. 217 (2004).

64. *See, e.g.,* Thomas Humphrey, "Democracy and the Rule of Law: Founding Liberal Democracy in Post-Communist Europe," 2 Colum. J. E. Eur. L. 94, 105 (2008) ("[I]n contrast to Western consolidated democracies that generally exhibit a predisposition to liberal virtues, in transitional environments democratic elections alone tend to be insufficient" to vindicate liberal rights).

65. *See, e.g.,* Paul Horwitz, "Honor's Constitutional Moment: The Oath and Presidential Transitions," 103 Nw. U. L. Rev. 1067 (2009).

66. *See, e.g.,* Harold H. Bruff, *Bad Advice: Bush's Lawyers in the War on Terror* 294 (Lawrence, Kansas: University Press of Kansas, 2009), 294; Jose E. Alvarez, "Torturing the Law," 37 Case W. Res. J. Int'l L. 175, 215–21 (2006) (discussing the professional responsibility implications of the "torture memos" penned by Yoo and others in the Office of Legal Counsel).

67. *See Padilla v. Yoo*, -- F. Supp. 2d --, 2009 WL 1651273 (N.D. Cal. June 12, 2009) (denying motion to dismiss in civil suit brought by Jose Padilla against John Yoo alleging constitutional violations).

68. *See* Bruff, *supra* note 66 at 294 (arguing against both criminal and civil liability for executive branch lawyers based on the legal advice they provided in the course of the war on terror on the grounds that it might inhibit similarly situated lawyers in the future).

69. *See, e.g.,* Jordan J. Paust, "The Absolute Prohibition of Torture and Necessary and Appropriate Sanctions," 43 Val. U. L. Rev. 1535 (2009); Milan Markovic, "Can Lawyers Be War Criminals?" 20 Geo. J. Legal Ethics 347 (2007).

70. Kenneth C. Randall, "Universal Jurisdiction under International Law," 66 Tex. L. Rev. 785, 788 (1988).

71. *See generally* George P. Fletcher, "Against Universal Jurisdiction," 1 J. Int'l Crim. Just. 580 (2003); Chandra Lekha Sriram, "Revolutions in Accountability: New Approaches to Past Abuses," 19 Am. U. Int'l L. Rev. 301 (2003).

6

Justice Jackson, the Memory of Internment, and the Rule of Law after the Bush Administration

STEPHEN I. VLADECK[1]

Notwithstanding the force of the rhetoric employed on all sides, the contemporary debate over whether senior Bush Administration officials should be investigated (and potentially prosecuted) for their role in the U.S. government's torture of individuals detained as "enemy combatants" during the war on terrorism has been curiously indifferent to American history.[2] Even the most modest perusal of that history reveals—perhaps surprisingly— little precedent for holding personally to account those senior government officials most responsible for our gravest civil liberties and human rights abuses. Perhaps the most prominent example comes from one of the darkest civil liberties chapters in American history, the exclusion from the West Coast and internment of over 120,000 Japanese nationals and U.S. citizens of Japanese descent during World War II, and the implicit but unequivocal legal sanction given to these measures by the Supreme Court in a trio of rulings culminating with *Korematsu v. United States* in December 1944.[3]

More than just a temporal bookend, both *Korematsu*'s holding and its history provide illuminating lenses through which to situate these contemporary debates. In upholding Fred Korematsu's conviction for failing to comply with an exclusion order, Justice Hugo Black's opinion for the Court concluded that the government's claim of military necessity overrode (or at least justified) the latent racial discrimination:

> To cast this case into outlines of racial prejudice, without reference to the real military dangers which were presented, merely confuses the issue. Korematsu was not excluded from the Military Area because of hostility to him or his race. He *was* excluded because we are at war with the Japanese Empire, because the properly constituted military authorities feared an invasion of the West Coast and felt constrained to take proper security

measures, because they decided that the military urgency of the situation demanded that all citizens of Japanese ancestry be segregated from the West Coast temporarily, and finally, because Congress, reposing its confidence in this time of war in our military leaders—as inevitably it must—determined that they should have the power to do just this.[4]

Two of the Court's senior members—Justices Owen Roberts and Frank Murphy—challenged the majority on its own terms, dissenting, inter alia, because of their own conclusion that the evacuations from the West Coast were not necessary, and because mass, suspicionless internment was, in their view, plainly unconstitutional.[5] But Justice Robert H. Jackson took a different tack. Angered that the Court had crossed a substantive line he thought it had agreed to toe in the *Hirabayashi* case eighteen months earlier,[6] Jackson argued not that the exclusion orders violated the Constitution, but that the majority opinion, in concluding to the contrary, had done even worse—and had affirmatively undermined the rule of law. As he explained, "a commander in temporarily focusing the life of a community on defense is carrying out a military program; he is not making law in the sense the courts know the term. He issues orders, and they may have a certain authority as military commands, although they may be very bad as constitutional law."[7]

Put another way, for Jackson, who had previously served both as FDR's Solicitor General and Attorney General, the job of the executive branch was to do what it reasonably believed to be *necessary*, whereas the job of the courts was to pronounce, after the fact, upon whether such actions were *legal*. In his words, "the courts can exercise only the judicial power, can apply only law, and must abide by the Constitution, or they cease to be civil courts and become instruments of military policy."[8] Thus, as he warned in his dissent's most famous passage,

> Much is said of the danger to liberty from the Army program for deporting and detaining these citizens of Japanese extraction. But a judicial construction of the due process clause that will sustain this order is a far more subtle blow to liberty than the promulgation of the order itself. A military order, however unconstitutional, is not apt to last longer than the military emergency. Even during that period a succeeding commander may revoke it all. But once a judicial opinion rationalizes such an order to show that it conforms to the Constitution, or rather rationalizes the Constitution to show that the Constitution sanctions such an order, the Court for all time

has validated the principle of racial discrimination in criminal procedure and of transplanting American citizens. The principle then lies about like a loaded weapon ready for the hand of any authority that can bring forward a plausible claim of an urgent need. Every repetition imbeds that principle more deeply in our law and thinking and expands it to new purposes.[9]

In other words, according to Jackson, internment may have been a stain on America's moral conscience, but the majority opinion, by treating the government's claim of military necessity (which, in Jackson's view, the Court lacked the competence to assess) as being dispositive of the measure's legality, was a stain on the rule of law—and one that would be far more difficult to expurgate. The rule of law in Jackson's view was not jeopardized by government abuses; it was jeopardized by their legalization in the name of necessity. To Jackson, then, the rule of law was not simply the notion that the government was bound by the law, but rather that the law could not bend to accommodate government abuses under the guise of "necessity."

Jackson's dissent, as Dennis Hutchinson has written, "has always been a puzzle to both his admirers and his critics."[10] Peter Irons described it as "a curious kind of judicial schizophrenia";[11] writing shortly afterward, Eugene Rostow dubbed it "a fascinating and fantastic essay in nihilism."[12] After all, even while he castigated the majority, Jackson suggested that courts should not be in the business of reviewing claims such as those that the majority sustained. Indeed, for all the damage that the majority opinion did to the rule of law, Jackson was no less concerned about the potential impact of a decision that *rejected* the claim of military necessity, since the executive branch might very well ignore such judicial pronouncements—a possibility that, however remote, risked even greater damage to judicial legitimacy.[13]

Thus, the only way around the dilemma, in Jackson's view, was for the courts to stay out of the issue altogether; "a bet on the future," in Hutchinson's words, "that the excesses of the executive branch will be self-curing once the emergency expires, and as long as the judiciary withholds its formal approval of those excesses, the Constitution will remain intact."[14] As Jackson concluded his dissent,

> Of course the existence of a military power resting on force, so vagrant, so centralized, so necessarily heedless of the individual, is an inherent threat to liberty. But I would not lead people to rely on this Court for a review that seems to me wholly delusive. The military reasonableness of these orders can only be determined by military superiors. If the people ever

let command of the war power fall into irresponsible and unscrupulous hands, the courts wield no power equal to its restraint. The chief restraint upon those who command the physical forces of the country, in the future as in the past, must be their responsibility to the political judgments of their contemporaries and to the moral judgments of history.[15]

Ironically, perhaps because of his dissent (and the two others), the future against which Jackson railed never materialized, and the moral judgments to which he referred have been, at least over time, rather unkind. *Korematsu's* reasoning has been soundly discredited (and never again invoked as authoritative);[16] Fred Korematsu's conviction has been vacated;[17] and the internment camps in general are today almost universally condemned as one of the darkest civil liberties chapters in modern American history—so much so that Congress formally apologized for the camps in 1988, recognizing that "these actions were carried out without adequate security reasons . . . and were motivated largely by racial prejudice, wartime hysteria, and a failure of political leadership."[18] As the Civil Liberties Act of 1988 concluded, "a grave injustice was done to both citizens and permanent resident aliens of Japanese ancestry by the evacuation, relocation, and internment of civilians during World War II."[19] In the decades since, the federal government has appropriated over $1.6 billion in reparations to the internees and their heirs.[20]

Indeed, even after the terrorist attacks of September 11, when comparable hostility and suspicion were directed toward Muslim men of Middle Eastern national origin,[21] the need to avoid "another *Korematsu*" seemed to have at least some effect in shaping the government's legal response, especially as it related to the extracriminal detention of individuals legally within the United States.[22] To be sure, the government's record was hardly perfect in this regard, but it was, by any measure, a vast improvement over the internment example.[23]

All these developments suggest that whatever damage the *Korematsu* majority might have inflicted upon the rule of law has since been vitiated by the creation of a consensus historical narrative that the suspicionless exclusion from the West Coast and detention of Japanese Americans was neither necessary nor legal, and, as significantly, that the Supreme Court grievously erred by not saying so more decisively.[24] As Justice Ruth Bader Ginsburg has written, "[a] *Korematsu*-type classification . . . will never again survive scrutiny: Such a classification, history and precedent instruct, properly ranks as prohibited."[25]

Moreover, and critically, this consensus narrative discrediting internment in general and *Korematsu* in particular has emerged even though no one was ever held personally liable for the policies that led to the camps. No military or executive branch official was prosecuted or sued for violating the internees' rights; no government lawyer was disbarred—despite proof that the Justice Department affirmatively misled the courts as to the gravity of the military threat posed by Japan, especially in the second round of briefing before the Supreme Court in *Korematsu*.[26]

Indeed, one could even argue (unpopularly, I suspect) that internment was not clearly unconstitutional, at least based on then-extant Supreme Court jurisprudence; the Court would not formally apply modern equal protection analysis to the federal government until 1954.[27] It also bears remembering that thousands of German and Italian nationals were similarly detained during the war pursuant to the Alien Enemy Act of 1798,[28] a measure that has not been subject to nearly as much historical criticism as internment, and that would have provided comparable authority for the detention of the Issei (the first-generation Japanese Americans, many of whom were still Japanese nationals), but not their U.S. citizen offspring.[29] In short, we have come to accept the wrongfulness of internment, even without clarity as to the specific legal violation that internment represented or the personal liability of individual government officials for its commission. Somehow, the conclusion seems inescapable today that the rule of law in the United States eventually survived the damage wrought by *Korematsu*, notwithstanding (or perhaps thanks to) Justice Jackson's fear that it might not.

Contrast the internment experience with the contemporary debate over whether senior Bush Administration officials should be investigated (and potentially prosecuted) for their complicity in the torture of individuals detained as "enemy combatants" in the war against terrorism. Many of those who have advocated for such measures have argued that a failure to prosecute those who were responsible would promote impunity, and would thereby undermine the rule of law by weakening both formal and practical barriers to the commission of similar (if not more serious) abuses in the future.[30] On the other side, those who vehemently oppose what they have decried as the "criminalization of politics" have argued that first, it is not clear the specific interrogation methods used actually *were* unlawful; second, it is certainly not clear that senior government officials *knew* that the interrogation methods they were approving were unlawful; and third, in any event, use of these methods may nonetheless have been justified because they were "necessary" to gain actionable intelligence information and to thereby prevent future terrorist attacks.[31]

One can find any number of parallels between the debates over internment during World War II and torture after September 11, including the presence of prominent public intellectuals on both sides.[32] Even the majority opinion in *Korematsu*—which Jackson thought was the real problem—may have a modern counterpart in the various legal opinions prepared by the Office of Legal Counsel (OLC) that are at the heart of the current controversy, in which Justice Department lawyers adopted an incredibly narrow definition of "torture" and then separately concluded that a number of particular interrogation methods widely viewed as torturous fell outside that definition.[33] Perhaps not surprisingly, a number of scholars have argued that these opinions, rather than the underlying acts of torture documented by the International Committee of the Red Cross (among others),[34] represent the greatest threat to the rule of law resulting from the Bush Administration's counterterrorism policies, echoing (if not expressly invoking) the arguments marshaled by Jackson in his *Korematsu* dissent.[35]

The central question I want to explore in this essay is whether Jackson's understanding of the relationship between internment and the rule of law, and the subsequent creation of internment's historical memory, might help us to assess the stakes of today's debate. Put another way, if, like the majority opinion in *Korematsu*, the OLC opinions—and not the acts of torture themselves—pose the real danger to the rule of law going forward, are there lessons that we can learn from the creation of internment's historical narrative (at the expense of *Korematsu*) that will help us undo whatever damage the OLC opinions have caused?

My thesis is that the answer to this question is "yes," that is, the internment episode provides support in identifying both the true "rule of law" problem and at least one example for how such a problem can be cured. As significantly, this history suggests that such infringements upon the rule of law *can* properly be remedied without individual criminal liability, so long as adequate information about the abuses makes its way into the public record, allowing the populace—and history—to make its own judgments. One may nevertheless have one's own reasons for why the civil or criminal liability of individual government officers should be pursued; my point is simply that, whatever the circumstance-specific political merits of such endeavors, the rule of law can adequately be preserved without them.

To unpack this argument, I begin in Part I with Justice Jackson's *Korematsu* dissent, and its articulation of the relationship between internment, the courts, and the rule of law. As Part I explains, Jackson's complicated views as to the relationship between the courts and the military during wartime, which he called "the Achilles Heel of the Constitution,"[36] are best understood in light of his writings in each of the war powers cases to come before the World War II Court—including unpublished opinions he prepared in the case of the Nazi saboteurs and in two other internment cases.[37] By the time *Korematsu* was back before the Court in the fall of 1944, Jackson finally was ready to put into words not just the inherent uselessness of holding measures based upon military necessity to any kind of legal yardstick, but the perilous danger to the rule of law of doing so. There is a hard question to be asked about Jackson's conclusion, that is, whether the rule of law really does *not* require some form of legal accountability for military abuses of the war power, but Part I concludes that Jackson himself had a response to that concern.

Part II then shifts gears to a retracing of the creation of internment's memory—a movement that was already underway by the time the camps were officially closed, but that did not really reach fruition until well into the 1980s. As is clear in retrospect, although there were many barriers in the way of collective repudiation of the camps, the absence of individual criminal responsibility was never one of them. To be sure, the creation of internment's historical memory was neither easy nor painless, and took the better part of four decades to complete. But it happened nonetheless, and without any serious movement to investigate the government officials most directly responsible. And today, we understand that internment was a mistake, one we have quite publicly vowed never to repeat again. Although the government has made any number of missteps in its response to September 11, Part II concludes by demonstrating how it carefully avoided repeating the substantive error at the heart of internment, to wit: mass, race-based, suspicionless detention.

In Part III, I turn to the parallels between the creation of internment's memory and the emerging narrative concerning the mistreatment and torture of individuals detained as "enemy combatants" during the war on terrorism. Beginning with the parallels between the majority opinion in *Korematsu* and the "torture memos" prepared by the Bush Administration's OLC, Part III demonstrates how similar considerations are present in today's context. Thus, the resulting inference is that a similar narrative can be created with regard to the torture debate, and without individual criminal or civil liability for the responsible officials—but only with a full accounting of the means by which the government's misconduct received official sanction. Without such a full historical record, as Part III concludes, it is quite possible that the same Justice Jackson might have been closer to the mark in his closing statement as lead prosecutor at Nuremberg, where, invoking the specter of Shakespeare's *Richard III*, he concluded with a siren call for criminal liability—that, "[i]f you were to say of these men that they are not guilty, it would be as true to say that there has been no war, there are no slain, there has been no crime."[38]

I. Justice Jackson, Internment, and the Rule of Law

The analytical and rhetorical underpinnings of Jackson's *Korematsu* dissent are easily traced to opinions he drafted (but did not file) in two earlier war powers cases—*Ex parte Quirin*, in which the Court unanimously upheld President Roosevelt's use of a military commission to try eight Nazi saboteurs captured inside the territorial United States;[39] and *Hirabayashi v. United States*, in which the Court unanimously upheld the legality of the military's imposition of a curfew for individuals of Japanese descent along the West Coast.[40] As both Dennis Hutchinson and Jack Goldsmith have demonstrated, Jackson's draft opinions in these two cases—more than the opinion he actually filed in *Korematsu*—show a Justice caught between the horns of a dilemma that had military necessity on one side and the rule of law on the other.[41]

In *Quirin*, Chief Justice Stone's opinion for the Court relied on a strained reading of the Articles of War (precursor to today's Uniform Code of Military Justice) to find congressional authorization for the military commission, thereby avoiding more difficult questions about the scope of the president's unilateral authority during wartime.[42] Although the Court's attempt to distinguish its 1866 decision in *Ex parte Milligan* rejecting a similar assertion of military jurisdiction[43] may have been somewhat disingenuous, Jackson wholeheartedly agreed on the merits that the eight saboteurs could be tried by a military commission.[44] He nevertheless drafted a separate opinion to explain why he thought the Court's foray into statutory interpretation was, in his words, "unauthorized and possibly mischievous."[45] Specifically, Jackson's opinion raised two objections: first, that the Court's construction of the Articles might also wrongly apply to cases where the defendants were far more clearly entitled to constitutional protections, for example, servicemembers or U.S. civilians in occupied territory; and second, that the Court was trampling on the president's inherent (and possibly even *exclusive*) power to subject enemy belligerents to trial by military commission during wartime by relying on ambiguous statutory approval.[46]

Instead, "[o]nce it appears that one is a legitimate prisoner of war, no court should question or review any Order the President may consider will serve the interests of this nation, whatever its effect on the life or liberty of those individuals whose service of our enemies forfeits claim to our judicial consideration."[47] As he concluded, "[I]n the long run it seems to me that we have no more important duty than to keep clear and separate the lines of responsibility and duty of the judicial and of the executive-military arms of government. Merger of the two is the end of liberty as we in this country have known it."[48]

Perhaps because Chief Justice Stone added a passage to his opinion for the Court flagging the division among the justices over the role of congressional authorization,[49] or perhaps because the draft had been meant more for his own convincing than for the public, Jackson declined to publish his concurrence. But it would be fewer than six months before another case came to the Court implicating his concern over the separation of the military and judicial spheres during wartime—and far more prominently, at that.

In *Hirabayashi* (along with its companion case, *Yasui v. United States*),[50] the Court was asked for the first time to rule on the legality of various measures undertaken by Lieutenant General John L. DeWitt in carrying out President Roosevelt's Executive Order 9066,[51] which authorized the secretary of war or his designee "to prescribe military areas in such places and of such extent as he or the appropriate Military Commander may determine, from which any or all persons may be excluded, and with respect to which, the right of any person to enter, remain in, or leave shall be subject to whatever restrictions the Secretary of War or the appropriate Military Commander may impose in his discretion."[52]

Gordon Hirabayashi challenged his conviction for two offenses: first, for violating a "curfew order" that DeWitt had imposed upon all persons of Japanese ancestry living in particular areas along the West Coast; and second, for failing to report to a "civil control station" for processing—and all-but-guaranteed relocation to an internment camp.[53] Although Hirabayashi's case thus appeared to raise the constitutionality of the entire internment scheme, a procedural fortuity (that the trial judge had ordered Hirabayashi to serve his sentences concurrently rather than consecutively) allowed the Supreme Court to sidestep the constitutionality of his pending relocation in favor of his narrower challenge to the curfew.[54]

Jackson nonetheless agonized over the merits, and penned a draft concurrence that, though left unfiled (he withdrew the draft once the Court had settled on the narrower ground for decision), would subsequently form the basis for most of his dissent in *Korematsu*. As he framed the issue, the question for the Court "is whether we should sustain as an exercise of the war power a discrimination we would probably strike down as an exercise of legislative power."[55] But, he continued, "[w]e must also make a choice between two ways of reaching such a result. One is to uphold the order, as the Court does, because such discrimination is constitutional when there is a rational basis for it; the other is to let the order stand because it is beyond our power to review."[56]

In his *Hirabayashi* draft, more than in his published *Korematsu* dissent, Jackson suggested that part of the reason for adopting the latter position was the lack of clarity on the merits, for "[i]t is worse than idle to profess that legal standards determine the present result if they are not so settled and firm that we would stand by them should they hereafter lead to a decision against the government." Instead, "[i]f we cannot set out fairly definable legal standards to guide us, it would be better in my opinion both for the war and for the law that we refrain altogether from considering the validity of these military orders. To substitute the mere personal opinion of judges for the personal will of the Executive only substitutes a theorizing absolutism for a practical one."[57]

Specifically invoking several of President Lincoln's more notorious civil liberties abuses during the Civil War, Jackson agreed that the country had endured "temporary excesses of executive power, but they have proved to be incidents in the larger policy of preserving and perpetuating our free institutions."[58] Indeed, as Jackson concluded, "I do not know that the ultimate cause of liberty has suffered, and it may have been saved, by [Lincoln's] questionable arrests. I am sure the cause would have suffered if this Court had rationalized them, as Constitutional."[59]

Thanks to his *Hirabayashi* draft, Jackson was ready when internment returned to the Court the following year in a pair of cases—those of Fred Korematsu, convicted of violating an exclusion order,[60] and Mitsuye Endo, who, having voluntarily complied with a relocation order, petitioned for a writ of habeas corpus to release her from the custody of the War Relocation Authority.[61] With a majority of the Court poised to uphold the constitutionality of Korematsu's conviction based largely on the military's "Final Report" on the West Coast security situation (the Report raised serious concerns about the effects of possible espionage and sabotage and emphasized the difficulties of screening for individual suspicion),[62] Jackson prepared to dissent. And although Jackson's first draft highlighted the extent to which the majority's analysis simply did not follow from *Hirabayashi* (and thereby crossed a line he thought the Court had agreed to observe), the draft otherwise largely reflected—and borrowed liberally from—his final draft from *Hirabayashi*.

One important addition from the *Hirabayashi* draft contained an illuminating reflection on the Civil War: Citing the Supreme Court's rejection of President Lincoln's use of military tribunals in *Ex parte Milligan*[63] and Chief Justice Taney's rejection of Lincoln's unilateral suspension of habeas corpus in *Ex parte Merryman*,[64] Jackson finally identified a class of war powers cases that clearly *were* meant for the courts:

> If the general war power should be invoked as a mere pretext for arbitrary government or, once properly invoked, should be continued after all need for it had passed, or were perverted to the overturning of civil government, this Court in a proper case would be duty-bound to declare such abuse of the power illegitimate. Even if it lacked physical force to end the abuse, its declaration at least would absolve loyal people from the legal or moral duty of obedience to its decree.[65]

Korematsu's case was different, though, because "the question here is whether the courts may be required to enforce an extraordinary and dubious order upon becoming satisfied that the military authority had reasonable grounds to adopt it as useful to military ends. This involves some inquiry into the nature and functions of the military *as well as* the judicial power,"[66] an inquiry that was beyond the Court's competence. Jackson thus appeared to believe that the risk that the executive branch would ignore the courts' invalidation of a military measure *would* be worth taking in some cases—just not this one.

Jackson's final draft, as Hutchinson has noted, left out much of the important analysis in his earlier efforts, including his various examples of prior wartime clashes between the executive branch and the courts; his intriguing discussions of the Civil War cases; and a long footnote that noted with approval some of the central arguments Roberts and Murphy would use in rebutting the military necessity claim.[67] Instead, Jackson devoted his last, published version to the rhetorical core of his rule-of-law argument, and to the proposition that the Court and the country would have been far better off had the government never taken to the civilian courts in Korematsu's case, had the Court not granted certiorari to review the Ninth Circuit, or had the majority found some way to get rid of the case without a decision on the merits. Gone from the draft were the caveats and distinctions that had allowed Jackson to explain why *Korematsu* was different from other cases where judicial intervention would be appropriate. Whereas his earlier draft invoked *Merryman* (where President Lincoln had ignored Chief Justice Taney) as a positive example, the final draft showed that he was in fact "haunted by *Merryman*,"[68] and was convinced that the rule of law could not abide history repeating itself.

Of course, the same day that the Court decided *Korematsu*, it also decided *Endo*, in which the majority (including Jackson) had no trouble distinguishing *Korematsu* and holding that the government lacked the power to detain "loyal" U.S. citizens of Japanese descent who, unlike Hirabayashi and Korematsu, had not committed a "crime" by violating a curfew or exclusion order.[69] In other words, *Endo* held that internment *itself* was unlawful, at least for the vast majority of internees who voluntarily submitted themselves to the relocation program. Again, Jackson penned a draft opinion (concurring), emphasizing that Endo's was an "easy" case because she was not in "military custody for security reasons." As such, "[t]he whole idea that our American citizens' right to be at large may be conditioned or denied by community prejudice or disapproval should be rejected by this Court the first time it is heard within these walls. To fail is to betray."[70]

For reasons that remain unclear, Jackson never filed his *Endo* opinion either. But by that point it did not matter; the day before the decisions in *Korematsu* and *Endo* were publicly handed down, the Roosevelt Administration announced that the camps were to be closed. As Patrick Gudridge has explained, *Endo* was supposed to have been the more significant decision, whereas "Justice Black seems to have thought, or wanted his readers to think, that *Korematsu* addressed only an already-past short term."[71] Justice Jackson, at least, was not buying it.

Seven years later, in a celebrated address delivered at Buffalo Law School, Jackson conceded the danger of his *Korematsu* dissent: "[M]y view, if followed, would come close to a suspension of the writ of habeas corpus or recognition of a state of martial law at the time and place found proper for military control."[72] His dissent also predated the Court's emphatic assertion of its own supremacy vis-à-vis federal law in *Cooper* v. *Aaron* in 1958,[73] a holding that may have mitigated, at least to some degree, the possibility of executive branch disobedience. As such, there are reasons to look skeptically today upon his view that the courts would be the better off in crisis times for doing nothing; one could just as easily argue that there is not much point in having courts if they do not intervene when it counts. But this otherwise important debate may be beside the point here, for it is a choice between two alternatives to the approach taken by the *Korematsu* majority, rather than a justification for what the majority held. At least on that point, Jackson's thesis seems indisputable, and history would bear him out.

II. Internment, Redress, and the Politics of Memory

Justice Black's efforts to the contrary notwithstanding, *Korematsu* was destined to become the more significant case. Withering and sustained academic criticisms of the decision surfaced with surprising speed, the most important of which was, by far, the thorough and powerful denunciation by Eugene Rostow, later the Dean of Yale Law School, in the June 1945 issue of the *Yale Law Journal*. Rostow expressly followed Jackson's cue, placing the final responsibility for the internment program (which he called "hasty, unnecessary, and mistaken") not on the executive branch or the military, but on the *Korematsu* majority, concluding that their opinion "converts a piece of war-time folly into political doctrine, and a permanent part of the law."[74]

Rostow was hardly alone. Other contemporary commentators also laid the blame primarily (if not exclusively) at the feet of the *Korematsu* majority rather than the Roosevelt Administration, including Nanette Dembitz, a niece of Justice Brandeis and a Justice Department lawyer during much of the internment litigation, whose article in the March 1945 *Columbia Law Review* was similarly critical of the Court.[75] Even the Court itself was far more circumspect in 1946, when it was called upon to consider the constitutionality of provost courts convened to try civilians for nonmilitary offenses in Hawaii during World War II. Striking down the practice in *Duncan* v. *Kahanamoku*, the Court seemed willing to accept that the entire government—including, perhaps, the judiciary—had gone a bit too far during the war.[76] Although the majority rested on its interpretation of the Hawaii Organic Act, Justice Murphy wrote separately to insist that the Court assert the primacy of the Constitution: "[The government's position] is a rank appeal to abandon the fate of all our liberties to the reasonableness of the judgment of those who are trained primarily for war. It seeks to justify military usurpation of civilian authority to punish crime without regard to the potency of the Bill of Rights. It deserves repudiation."[77]

Nonetheless, early attempts by the internees (and others affected by the curfew and exclusion orders) to obtain appropriate reparations ran headlong into the legal precedent set by *Korematsu*—and the federal government's unwillingness to concede that any aspect of the exclusion and relocation process had been unjustified in law or in fact. Congress *did* enact the Evacuation Claims Act in 1948, which was ostensibly designed to provide reparations for economic losses incurred as a result of the relocation, but without any concession of wrongdoing.[78] Moreover, the Act only provided restitution for "tangible" losses to real or personal property that were a foreseeable consequence of relocation, and that could be proven (a requirement that often barred recovery where records failed to survive the war). Even then, no interest could be awarded. Thus, "Although 26,568 claims were filed for an amount totaling $148 million, the government paid only $37 million in compensation. Only a small percentage of people actually received compensation for their losses. The government paid about ten cents for every dollar of property lost."[79] Indeed, the Act only authorized the Attorney General to approve claims up to $2,500; higher values presumably had to be resubmitted to Congress for approval.

For a host of reasons, the next two decades witnessed little in the way of a concerted movement for any kind of reparations from the federal government. Instead, most of the Issei (first-generation Japanese Americans) and Nisei (second-generation Japanese Americans) living along the West Coast tried to put their lives back together while leaving the past unmentioned. That trend began to change only in the late 1960s, when the Sansei (third-generation Japanese Americans) actively began to investigate the facts behind—and background to—their parents' and grandparents' plight.[80] Soon thereafter, "redress" became an increasingly prominent goal for Japanese American civic groups.[81]

For starters, Japanese American interest groups played a central role in advocating for the 1971 repeal of the Emergency Detention Act,[82] a Cold War-era statute that had authorized the detention of U.S. citizens without charges in certain "internal security emergencies" as declared by the Attorney General.[83] Although the EDA had never been used, its continuing existence had become a source of concern among civil liberties groups, especially as antigovernment protests escalated during the Vietnam War.[84] As a result, and with members of Congress invoking *Korematsu*'s legacy, the bill to repeal the EDA also included an affirmative prohibition on extralegislative detention, writing into federal law the proviso that "[n]o citizen shall be imprisoned or otherwise detained by the United States except pursuant to an Act of Congress."[85] Even though Korematsu himself *was* technically detained pursuant to an Act of Congress (specifically, the March 21, 1942 statute that made it a crime to violate DeWitt's exclusion order), the internees who complied with DeWitt's orders were held pursuant to no comparable authority.

Five years later, in 1976, around the time that the Japanese American Citizens League established a National Committee for Redress, President Ford took another important—albeit entirely symbolic—step, issuing a proclamation that confirmed that Executive Order 9066 had formally expired with the end of World War II, and noting that "[w]e now know what we should have known then—not only was that evacuation wrong, but Japanese-Americans were and are loyal Americans."[86] Vowing that "this kind of action shall never again be repeated,"[87] the proclamation stopped short of formally apologizing for internment.

Finally, in 1980 the redress movement culminated with the creation by Congress of the Commission on Wartime Relocation and Internment of Civilians (CWRIC). Tasked with a statutory mandate to review the facts and circumstances leading to the internment camps and to "recommend appropriate remedies," the CWRIC held more than twenty days of hearings, took oral testimony from over 750 witnesses, and amassed a remarkable historical record documenting the true costs—economic and noneconomic—borne by the internees.

The Commission's final report, "Personal Justice Denied," reached a number of damning conclusions about the curfew, exclusion, and relocation orders, concluding that none of the measures actually were necessary—and that adequate, alternative remedies existed for the government to protect against sabotage and espionage on the West Coast.[88] The CWRIC thus recommended a host of additional measures to remedy the government's missteps, including a formal apology from the U.S. government, a one-time per capita payment of $20,000 to each surviving internee to compensate them for their losses, and the creation of a fund to educate future generations about the injustices of the internment camps.[89] Congress eventually adopted the recommendations in the Civil Liberties Act of 1988,[90] and President George H. W. Bush formally apologized on behalf of the U.S. government early in 1989.[91]

The work of the CWRIC was thus instrumental in (and a substantial contributor to) the creation of a narrative in which internment was discredited as a measure justified by military necessity. And such a narrative therefore served to undermine the factual foundation upon which the legal analysis of both *Hirabayashi* and *Korematsu* rested. But the Commission's work indirectly contributed to the evisceration of the key judicial precedents, as well. In early 1981, Aiko Yoshinaga-Herzig (a CWRIC researcher) and Peter Irons uncovered incontrovertible evidence of government misconduct in the litigation of the exclusion and internment cases during the 1940s. For starters, the pair uncovered an original copy of General DeWitt's "Final Report," which (unlike the version publicly disclosed and cited by the government in *Korematsu*) made clear that individualized determinations of suspicion *were* logistically feasible in 1942; the military had simply concluded that they were unlikely to be fruitful.[92]

Second, Yoshinaga-Herzig and Irons uncovered various contemporaneous memoranda from intelligence agencies discounting any genuine threat of espionage or sabotage from Japanese nationals and their descendants living along the West Coast, memoranda that were in the possession of the Justice Department long before the briefs were filed in *Korematsu*.[93] Third, and related to both of the first two discoveries, the pair uncovered an earlier version of the government's merits brief to the Supreme Court in *Korematsu*, which included language affirmatively casting doubt on the accuracy of various claims in the "Final Report" that were central to the military's assertion of military necessity (including the espionage and sabotage concerns). After intervention by the War Department, the footnote was rewritten prior to filing so as to obfuscate the Justice Department's well-founded concerns,[94] and to give the Report an authoritativeness that the Justice Department had itself disputed. Moreover, Eric Muller has since uncovered additional archival evidence suggesting that similar misrepresentations were made to the Court in the *Hirabayashi* litigation as well.[95]

The evidence discovered by Yoshinaga-Herzig and Irons provided the foundation for petitions for writs of error *coram nobis* (a common law remedy allowing for the correction of fundamental errors at trial when no other avenues of relief remain available)[96] filed in the same trial courts that convicted Hirabayashi, Yasui, and Korematsu. Korematsu won a sweeping victory in a landmark opinion by the U.S. District Court for the Northern District of California;[97] Yasui's conviction was vacated by the U.S. District Court for the District of Oregon at the government's request, and without any real investigation into the circumstances of his trial;[98] and Hirabayashi, after a mixed bag in the Seattle district court,[99] eventually prevailed across the board on appeal to the Ninth Circuit.[100] At bottom, the *coram nobis* cases helped to cement the narrative that the redress movement had been attempting to create and that the CWRIC had adopted, that is, that the internment camps were a terrible injustice; that the government's defense thereof was not just legally unconvincing, but was actually in bad faith; and that, for one reason or another, the Supreme Court's legal rationalization of the policies could not withstand historical scrutiny.

And although it took the better part of four decades for the redress narrative to prevail, two points bear emphasis: first, the movement to create such a narrative did not really get off the ground until the mid-1970s. From that point, it took just over ten years for the full story to emerge—a relatively short period of time, in historiographical terms.

Second, notwithstanding the increasing evidence that individual officials (especially government lawyers) may have been particularly to blame in influencing the Court's legal rationalization of the exclusion and relocation policies, the redress movement never included calls for individual liability as part of its agenda. Part of that, of course, can certainly be traced to the fact that many of the most significant players had passed away well before the mid-1970s, including President Roosevelt, General DeWitt, Secretary of War Stimson, and so on. But a critical mass of key figures survived—and were called to testify before the CWRIC—including John McCloy (who, as assistant secretary of war, was centrally involved in both the implementation of the internment policies and their legal defense before the Supreme Court), Colonel Karl Bendetsen (one of the architects of internment), Philip Glick (the solicitor for the War Relocation Authority), and others. If individual liability was believed to be an instrumental component to the creation of the redress narrative (leaving aside the obvious but perhaps not fatal statute-of-limitations problems), one *could* have identified living individuals against whom such measures might plausibly have been pursued.

In a provocative 2004 article, Jerry Kang suggested that the record is still somewhat incomplete. Specifically, Kang argued that the *coram nobis* decisions, though noble to the extent that they corrected some aspects of the historical record, also allowed the Supreme Court of the 1940s to evade responsibility for its role in internment, since the central premise of the *coram nobis* cases is that the government withheld material information from the Court (and that the Court would have ruled differently, and presumably correctly, if it had known then what we know now).[101] Whether the *Korematsu* majority's deference to the military's claim of necessity constituted willful blindness or not, though, the central point for present purposes is that the redress movement created a historical narrative that unequivocally undermined the factual and legal justifications for the exclusion and internment policies—and based on information that existed at the time, rather than becoming clear only retrospectively.

In the process, the redress movement thereby undermined the reasoning behind internment in general and *Korematsu* in particular, and vitiated the injury that, according to Justice Jackson, the majority opinion in the latter had inflicted upon the rule of law. If anything, *Korematsu* stands today as the exception that proves the rule, that is, that racial classifications are inherently pernicious and should be subjected to the most searching judicial scrutiny.[102] As much as anything else, it was the work of the CWRIC that was responsible for this contemporary reality.

Thus, Justice Jackson may have been correct that the *Korematsu* majority's conflation of military necessity with legality jeopardized the rule of law, but the redress movement established as a matter of historical certainty that the measures simply *were not* necessary on the record to which the government was privy at the time, and so could not have been legal even on Justice Black's morally problematic terms. Put another way, although internment would have been wrong even without *Korematsu*, *Korematsu* itself needed repudiating on both its facts and its principle: the former with regard to its conclusion that internment was necessary; the latter with regard to its conclusion that such necessity controlled internment's legality.

Finally, perhaps the strongest proof of *Korematsu*'s repudiation comes neither from the work of the CWRIC nor the *coram nobis* decisions, but from the aftermath of the September 11 attacks. Although the U.S. government was under enormous pressure to take immediate and decisive action to protect the country from further episodes of terrorism,[103] *Korematsu* nevertheless seems to have played a role in shaping the government's counterterrorism policy vis-à-vis detention. Thus, although the government *did* temporarily detain hundreds of Muslim men of Middle Eastern descent in the days and weeks after September 11,[104] such detention rested on specific—and *statutory*—authorities, including, inter alia, the power to detain noncitizens facing deportation[105] and the power to detain individuals suspected of being material witnesses to pending criminal prosecutions.[106] And when two individuals within the United States were detained as "enemy combatants," the courts considering their habeas petitions focused on whether the statutory authority relied upon by the government satisfied the 1971 Non-Detention Act.[107]

Given the government's documented overreliance on these authorities,[108] and the separate but related concern that *Korematsu*-like racism nevertheless surfaced in other contexts,[109] these developments are not entirely satisfying. Nevertheless, the length to which the government went to avoid mass, suspicionless detention within the United States after September 11 suggests that the memory of *Korematsu* and its repudiation did in fact have something to say in the formation (and judicial review) of counterterrorism policy. As then-Chief Judge Michael Mukasey wrote early in Jose Padilla's habeas litigation,

> The [government] is none too subtle in cautioning this court against going too far in the protection of this detainee's rights, suggesting at one point that permitting Padilla to consult with a lawyer "risks that plans for future attacks will go undetected." More than a match for that are passages in the *amicus curiae* submissions in this case, where lawyers raise the specter of

Korematsu v. United States, and call Padilla's detention "a repudiation of the Magna Carta," thereby suggesting that if Padilla does not receive the full panoply of protections afforded defendants in criminal cases, a dictatorship will be upon us, the tanks will have rolled. Those to whom images of catastrophe come that easily might take comfort in recalling that it is a year and a half since September 11, 2001, and Padilla's is not only the first, but also the only case of its kind. There is every reason not only to hope, but also to expect that this case will be just another of the isolated cases, like *Quirin*, that deal with isolated events and have limited application.[110]

Whether or not Mukasey was convincing in suggesting that Padilla's case was unique, it is difficult to discount the influence that *Korematsu* had in emphasizing the need for individualized and judicially reviewable determinations in detention cases. That influence was perhaps best captured by Justice Kennedy in his opinion for the Court in *Boumediene v. Bush*, holding that the Suspension Clause guarantees noncitizens detained at Guantánamo Bay a right to habeas corpus. As he emphasized, "[F]ew exercises of judicial power are as legitimate or as necessary as the responsibility to hear challenges to the authority of the Executive to imprison a person. . . . Their access to the writ is a necessity to determine the lawfulness of their status, even if, in the end, they do not obtain the relief they seek."[111] As a lesson on the wrongfulness of wartime detention based upon suspicionless (and race-based) stereotypes and the concomitant importance of *meaningful* judicial review, these holdings suggest that *Korematsu's* repudiation is complete. Where history has left its work unfinished, though, is as to the more generalized danger posed by legal opinions that justify government abuses through the mantle of thinly reasoned and hypertechnical legality.

III. Torture and the Rule of Law after the Bush Administration

An enormous amount has already been written about the documented and alleged civil liberties and human rights abuses committed by U.S. government officials during the presidential administration of George W. Bush.[112] Even the particular role of the Justice Department has spawned its own cottage industry as to the appropriate moral, ethical, and legal obligations of government lawyers.[113] And although the discussions have run the gamut of substantive topics, no other issue has galvanized public opinion and discourse to the same degree as the torture debate, and the related question of whether there is any set of circumstances under which senior government officials should be investigated (and potentially held to account) for acts of torture and other abuses committed against terrorism suspects detained as "enemy combatants" by U.S. servicemembers, intelligence personnel, or government contractors.[114]

Complicating the torture debate are a series of legal opinions prepared by the OLC in which the Justice Department adopted an incredibly narrow interpretation of the federal statute prohibiting torture, and separately concluded that a number of individual techniques largely considered to be torturous do not in fact violate federal (or international) law.[115] Although the central opinion (the August 1, 2002 "Bybee" or "torture" memo) was leaked to the *Washington Post* in the summer of 2004, the bulk of the other relevant memoranda did not become public until their disclosure by the Obama Administration early in 2009.[116]

Rather than a debate on the merits about whether particular acts of mistreatment do or do not constitute torture, the crux of the torture debate today has devolved into a fight over the substantive validity and the ethical propriety of these OLC opinions, on the theory that the opinions themselves may vitiate the liability of those who claim that they acted in good faith by relying upon the memos.[117] As a result, the August 2002 memos and their successors have become the focus of an inordinate amount of attention and analysis. Although by no means providing the consensus view, David Cole's summary is emblematic of perhaps the most widely shared position among legal scholars:

> [O]n many of the specific questions the memos address, there is undoubtedly a range of plausible interpretations. What is most telling in the end, however, is that at every juncture, the memos choose the interpretation most likely to foreclose any possibility of criminal responsibility for the CIA interrogators—regardless of how strained the interpretation is. It is this consistent pattern of result-oriented reasoning, insistently maintained in secret over several years and by several lawyers—even as both the statutory law and the administration's own public statements seemed to become more restrictive—that is ultimately the most compelling evidence of bad-faith lawyering.[118]

The claim that the August 2002 memos in particular were result-oriented, orchestrated to provide a "golden shield" to CIA interrogators,[119] is perhaps the most damning and troubling charge of the larger episode, one that finds support, inter alia, in the speed with which the Justice Department distanced itself from the "Bybee" memo when it became public in 2004.[120] And yet, although some of the specific analysis in the 2002 memos has been "withdrawn," the bottom line remains that every aspect of the CIA interrogation program that is public as of today rested at least in part on a legal opinion that officially provided for its legality. Put another way,

> [N]o matter how much the law changed on the surface, the Justice Department's secret bottom line never changed. Despite the very public repudiation of the August 2002 Torture Memo, despite the passage of the "McCain amendment," and despite repeated assurances that the U.S. "does not torture," official U.S. policy, as reflected in the secret memos, continued to authorize the CIA to strip suspects naked, deprive them of sleep for seven to eleven days straight, slam them into walls, slap them, douse them with cold water, force them into painful stress positions and cramped boxes for hours, and waterboard them repeatedly.[121]

For many, this reality helps to explain why the memos themselves have posed such a threat to the rule of law. In at least a somewhat comparable manner to judicial decisions, OLC opinions do not formally have the force of law, but they do bind the executive branch.[122] As such, OLC opinions that provide legal rationalization for particular government actions based on misrepresentations of the factual or legal justifications for that conduct raise the same specter as Supreme Court opinions that provide legal rationalizations based upon unfounded claims of military necessity.[123] In other words, even though OLC opinions are not binding outside the executive branch (and may, as was the case for the torture memos, be withheld from public scrutiny), and even though, as such, their legal analysis can easily be superseded by the courts, they implicate comparable rule-of-law interests so long as they remain in force. This reality helps to explain why so many in the current conversation appear more troubled by the actions of the OLC than by the actions of the CIA; to return to Jackson's *Korematsu* dissent, "A military commander may overstep the bounds of constitutionality, and it is an incident. But if we review and approve, that passing incident becomes the doctrine of the Constitution."[124]

The comparisons to Jackson's reaction in *Korematsu* may also help to explain the significance of the secrecy surrounding the key OLC opinions, most of which were kept classified for years; without transparency, there would be no opportunity to discredit the legal and factual predicates on which the opinions are based.[125] And yet, accepting that the OLC opinions raise rule-of-law concerns that are at least superficially analogous to those implicated by the majority opinion in *Korematsu* is only the beginning of the inquiry; it remains to ascertain whether the same process that ameliorated the rule-of-law injury in the case of internment, that is, the redress movement, might be used to comparable effect vis-à-vis the torture debate.

As was always possible with regard to the Supreme Court and *Korematsu*, there is the chance that OLC's legal analysis will be specifically and authoritatively repudiated by the OLC itself. To a limited extent, this has already happened; in addition to withdrawing the August 1, 2002 "Bybee" memo, the OLC also filed a memorandum on January 15, 2009 (released a few weeks later) disclaiming some of the analytical underpinnings of the Bybee memo and others. As Stephen Bradbury explained in the January 15 memo, "The purpose of this memorandum is to confirm that certain propositions stated in several opinions issued by the Office of Legal Counsel in 2001–2003 respecting the allocation of authorities between the President and Congress in matters of war and national security do not reflect the current views of this Office."[126] Nonetheless, Bradbury was at pains in the same memorandum to emphasize that "[t]he opinions addressed herein were issued in the wake of the atrocities of 9/11, when policy makers, fearing that additional catastrophic terrorist attacks were imminent, [strove] to employ all lawful means to protect the Nation," explaining that OLC was faced with "novel and complex legal questions in a time of great danger and under extraordinary time pressure."[127]

And yet, although the Bradbury memo repudiated the theory of constitutional power that undergirded the torture memos, it did not say anything more about the specific conduct that the memos sanctioned. It is possible, of course, that a future OLC opinion might more specifically conclude that the torture memos were based on fundamentally flawed factual and legal premises, but such a result seems unlikely, especially in light of the smaller steps that the Justice Department has taken to distance itself from the earlier opinions. For many, though, such measures have simply not been enough, since they have not included any formal concession of government wrongdoing.

Another possibility is that the OLC's legal conclusions could be overridden by the federal courts in an appropriate lawsuit. Indeed, Jose Padilla's civil suit against John Yoo, which maintains that Padilla was mistreated while detained as an "enemy combatant," and that Yoo, as author of the relevant OLC memos, is responsible for the foreseeable consequences of his work product, is perhaps the best current candidate for furnishing the courts with an opportunity to establish, as a matter of law, that the conclusions reached in various OLC memos, which may have been substantially responsible for

Padilla's mistreatment, were incorrect.[128] Indeed, under qualified immunity doctrine, Padilla's suit could establish his claim even while absolving Yoo himself of individual monetary liability, so long as the court concludes that it was not "clearly established" at the time of Yoo's conduct that the actions he sanctioned were actually unlawful.

As of this writing (in spring 2010), the district court had denied Yoo's motion to dismiss, but Yoo's appeal to the U.S. Court of Appeals for the Ninth Circuit was pending. Although Padilla's suit therefore *could* provide the means for revisiting the torture memos, the odds that the courts will take up the invitation are, in the end, quite long.[129] Indeed, whereas Padilla's suit is the first to be brought against one of the OLC lawyers, civil suits brought by post–9/11 detainees against individuals more directly related to their mistreatment have been categorically unsuccessful.[130]

Even so, the notion that the courts stand well-suited to disclaim the OLC's legal conclusions may also be an animating impetus behind calls for investigations of individual *criminal* liability. Just as a civil suit might provide the opportunity to establish that the OLC's conclusions were clearly unjustified, any criminal prosecution of senior government officials would presumably turn on evidence that the relevant officials did not just cross the line, but should have known that the actions that they were facilitating (through the legal justification provided in the OLC opinions) were illegal. Such evidence, if it existed, could go a long way toward undermining the factual and legal predicates to the OLC opinions in much the same way that the CWRIC's work and the research of Aiko Yoshinaga-Herzig and Peter Irons undermined the predicates to *Hirabayashi* and *Korematsu*.

But the critical lesson from the internment experience is that such evidence can just as easily (if not more easily) be ascertained *without* pursuing individual liability. After all, the question for purposes of individual civil or criminal liability inevitably reduces to the mens rea of individual officials, as opposed to government institutions. Thus, depending upon what actually transpired, different individuals could conceivably face individual accountability for the same actions by the institution—imagine two distinct scenarios: one in which the OLC memos were prepared under direct orders to reach a predetermined result; a second where they were prepared in "good faith," representing the best answer that their authors could provide under the circumstances. The memos might be just as "wrong" in either case, even though the individual responsibility might vary substantially.

Apart from these concerns, attempts to establish individual liability could also backfire. If the goal is to establish that the legal opinions were based on fundamentally flawed legal or factual assumptions, the prosecution's inability to establish any single element of the crime may actually serve to vindicate the conduct at issue (a possibility that is also present in civil litigation). And in any event, as the current debate demonstrates, there will be any number of defenders of the targeted individuals who dismiss the pursuit of individual liability, no matter its merits, as a political witch-hunt and the worst kind of victor's justice.

What we should learn from the internment experience, I submit, is that we as a society can avoid some of these pitfalls while still attempting to establish a narrative that, where appropriate, discredits the contested government conduct. Thus, I think David Cole has it exactly right when he concludes that "[t]he first step . . . should be appointment of an independent, nonpartisan, high-caliber commission, . . . to investigate and assess responsibility for the United States' adoption of coercive interrogation policies. Only such a commission has the possibility of rising above the partisan wrangling that any attempt to hold accountable high-level officials of the prior administration is certain to trigger."[131] Like Cole, I agree that any such body must have the subpoena power, security clearances, access to all the relevant information, and adequate funding. For Cole, such an investigation is merely the beginning, and he remains quite open to the possibility that, in light of such a commission's findings, "disbarment proceedings, civil damages actions, or criminal prosecution may also be warranted."[132] Here, though, he and I part company. There may well be political or other policy-based reasons to pursue such measures in individual cases, but if the internment experience is a guide, such proceedings are *not* necessary to create a narrative that discredits the government conduct and the legal reasoning behind it. It is certainly possible that prosecutions *could*, if successful, help to create such a narrative, but prosecutions are not the only (or even the optimal) way of doing so, and would raise their own unique challenges as well.

Instead, the goal for preserving the rule of law, and not just a means to some distinct end, should be the creation of a comprehensive and unassailable historical record that documents both the nature and origins of the relevant government abuses, and that also allows for a reevaluation of the legal analysis concluding that such abuses were in fact "lawful." It may not be ideal in any number of respects, but it is a candid admission that Justice Jackson was at least partially correct in *Korematsu*—that the rule of law is not invariably jeopardized when our government crosses the line; it is threatened especially when the relevant actors manufacture unconvincing legal justifications to excuse rather than accept the illicit consequences, depriving history, in Jackson's words, of the chance to form its own moral judgments.

Finally, one last lesson from the internment experience should also be heeded today: when redress efforts finally gained momentum in the 1970s, it was the narrative of the victims, as retold by the Sansei, that helped to catalyze the movement. Any effort toward the creation of a comparable narrative with regard to the torture debate should similarly aspire to incorporate the perspective of the victims, a task that will be all the more complicated owing to the reality that these individuals, as noncitizens residing outside the United States, generally lack any kind of meaningful political constituency. The burden will rest only that much more squarely on NGOs and other similarly situated groups to speak for the victims, and on the public to ensure that such voices are heard.

To briefly recap, there are striking parallels between the OLC memos and their legal rationalization of torture on the one hand, and the *Korematsu* majority's legal rationalization of internment on the other. And although any attempt to reach a consensus definition of the "rule of law" is inevitably fraught with peril, I think it is safe to agree with Justice Jackson that the *Korematsu* Court damaged the rule of law perhaps more gravely than anyone directly associated with internment itself, and to further conclude that history, as traced in Part II, has largely—if slowly and painfully—repaired that damage.

The fundamental paradox of this kind of historical collective (rather than individual) accountability, though, is the impossibility of handicapping its likelihood in the immediate aftermath of the abuses. The best we can do, then, is help to speed up the process. And while prosecutions may contribute to the formation of such a narrative, the internment experience and the redress movement suggest that other (and better) means exist for achieving the same end.

Conclusion

For most (albeit not all) of the period since the end of World War II, the United States has been one of the driving forces behind the movement for individual criminal accountability at the international level. And perhaps the central normative justification for international criminal law as a field is the belief that impunity begets violence to the rule of law, removing law as both a formal and practical barrier to future atrocities. Thus, where a country is either unable or unwilling to investigate its own officials for certain particularly serious offenses, the response has been the creation of an independent transnational institution that is empowered to do so, including the *ad hoc* criminal tribunals for the former Yugoslavia and Rwanda, and, later, the permanent International Criminal Court. The United States was instrumental in the creation of the former, and remains decisively, if enigmatically, opposed to the latter.

This distinction embodies the United States' oft-perplexing position vis-à-vis the project of international criminal justice: as one of its champions when other countries' officials are involved, and as one of its fiercest opponents when it comes to the potential liability of U.S. personnel—an opposition that has been codified in the American Service-Members' Protection Act of 2002, which commands the use of the military to retrieve by force any U.S. service-member subjected to the ICC's jurisdiction.[133] Is it hypocrisy, or is it justified by a belief, however difficult to prove, that the relationship between individual criminal accountability and the rule of law might be more attenuated in the United States than elsewhere?

In the preceding pages, I have attempted to suggest that, using the internment experience as a foil, the rule of law in the United States may best be vindicated by the historical (and moral) acceptance of legal justifications for government conduct rather than by the individual liability of particular government officers for specific abuses. If true, such a conclusion not only bolsters the context-specific argument that criminal investigations of the Bush Administration are unnecessary in order to preserve the rule of law (whether or not they are politically desirable, a question that will surely divide reasonable readers), but it might also provide the basis for rethinking our broader understanding of the relationship between impunity, the role of courts in our legal system, and the rule of law.

In a constitutional system in which judicial independence is the linchpin, we have an almost blind faith that those who issue legal pronouncements do so in the best tradition of the legal profession, even when they get the answer terribly wrong. When that faith is tested, the rule of law is jeopardized,[134] if for no other reason than because their judgments, unlike those of our elected officials, are not easily overturned. We should still struggle against Justice Jackson's suggestion in his *Korematsu* dissent that, as a result, the better move for the courts will often be to stay on the sidelines of our most significant disputes during times of crisis. But if one thing is clear, it is that Jackson was unequivocally correct that the courts—and any official who has the power to say what the law is in any meaningful respect—have an incredibly awesome and delicate responsibility should they choose to intervene.

1. My thanks to Mike Allen, Steve Burbank, Barry Friedman, Craig Green, Stefanie Lindquist, Chad Oldfather, Caprice Roberts, Ted Ruger, Andy Siegel, my junior colleagues at the Washington College of Law, and students in my spring 2009 Separation of Powers class for a number of helpful conversations, to Maureen Roach for exemplary research assistance, and to Nasser Hussain and Austin Sarat for inviting me to participate in the conference for which this essay was prepared. This paper also benefited from a faculty workshop at Marquette University's School of Law, and from an informal workshop at American University Washington College of Law on "Judges and Judging," for my participation in which I owe thanks to Mary Clark, Lynda Dodd, and Amanda Frost.

2. For a lucid summary of the debate, see David Cole, *The Torture Memos: Rationalizing the Unthinkable* (New York: New Press, 2009), 1–40.

3. *Korematsu v. United States*, 323 U.S. 214 (1944). The earlier cases were *Yasui v. United States*, 320 U.S. 115 (1943), and *Hirabayashi v. United States*, 320 U.S. 81 (1943).

4. *Korematsu*, 323 U.S. at 223.

5. *Ibid.* at 225–33 (Rutledge, J., dissenting); *ibid.* at 233–42 (Murphy, J., dissenting).

6. *Hirabayashi v. United States*, 320 U.S. 81 (1943). For Jackson's anger over the broken deal, see Dennis J. Hutchinson, "'The Achilles Heel' of the Constitution: Justice Jackson and the Japanese Exclusion Cases," *Supreme Court Review* 2002 (2003): 480–82.

7. *Korematsu*, 323 U.S. at 244 (Jackson, J., dissenting).

8. *Ibid.* at 247.

9. *Ibid.* at 245–46.

10. Hutchinson, "Achilles Heel," at 455.

11. Peter Irons, *Justice at War: The Story of the Japanese-American Internment Cases* (Berkeley: University of California Press, 1983), 332.

12. Eugene V. Rostow, "The Japanese-American Cases—A Disaster," *Yale Law Journal* 54 (June 1945): 511.

13. Hutchinson, "Achilles Heel," at 485, 489.

14. *Ibid.* at 493.

15. *Korematsu*, 323 U.S. at 248 (Jackson, J., dissenting).

16. The only aspect of *Korematsu* that survives in contemporary constitutional law is the principle, first hinted at six years earlier in the *Carolene Products* case, that race-based classifications should be subjected to the "most rigid" (or "strict") judicial scrutiny. *Ibid.* at 216 (majority opinion). Even that principle, though, is almost never cited to *Korematsu*. Hutchinson, "Achilles Heel," at 485 n.99.

17. *Korematsu v. United States*, 584 F. Supp. 1406 (N.D. Cal. 1984).

18. Civil Liberties Act of 1988, 50 U.S.C. app. § 1989a(a) (2000).

19. *Ibid.*

20. Jerry Kang, "Denying Prejudice: Internment, Redress, and Denial," *UCLA Law Review* 51 (April 2004): 975–76; Peter Irons, *Justice Delayed: The Record of the Japanese American Internment Cases* (Middletown: Wesleyan University Press, 1989), 3–46.

21. Aya Gruber, "Raising the Red Flag: The Continued Relevance of the Japanese Internment in the Post-*Hamdi* World," *University of Kansas Law Review* 54 (January 2006): 309–11.

22. As explained in more detail below, the government only detained three individuals within the United States under authority unrelated to either criminal or immigration law—U.S. citizens Yaser Hamdi and Jose Padilla, and foreign national Ali al-Marri. None of the three remain in military detention; Hamdi was released late in 2004, and Padilla and al-Marri were both transferred to the civilian criminal justice system, where Padilla was convicted and al-Marri pleaded guilty to terrorism-related crimes.

23. Eric L. Muller, "Inference or Impact? Racial Profiling and the Internment's True Legacy," *Ohio State Journal of Criminal Law* 1 (Fall 2003): 104–09.

24. *Korematsu's* companion case, *Ex parte Endo*, 323 U.S. 283 (1944), actually *did* conclude that internment was unlawful in those cases where (1) the government conceded that the internee was "loyal"; and (2) the internee had not violated a curfew or exclusion order. But the tragic irony of both decisions is that the Roosevelt Administration had announced, the day before the two opinions were released, that the camps were to be closed. For the entire story, see Patrick O. Gudridge, "Remember *Endo*?" *Harvard Law Review* 116 (May 2003): 1933–39.

25. *Adarand Constructors, Inc. v. Pena*, 515 U.S. 200, 275 (1995) (Ginsburg, J., dissenting).

26. Irons, *Justice Delayed*, at 4–5.

27. *Bolling v. Sharpe*, 347 U.S. 497 (1954). In *Bolling*, the Court extended the logic of *Brown v. Board of Ed.*—that racially segregated public schools violated the Equal Protection Clause of the Fourteenth Amendment—to public schools in the District of Columbia, to which the Fifth Amendment (which does not have its own Equal Protection Clause), and not the Fourteenth, applied.

28. 50 U.S.C. §§ 21–24 (2000). The Supreme Court upheld the constitutionality of the Act, even as applied to detention subsequent to the cessation of hostilities, in *Ludecke v. Watkins*, 335 U.S. 160 (1948). For criticism, see Stephen I. Vladeck, "*Ludecke's* Lengthening Shadow: The Disturbing Prospect of War without End," *Journal of National Security Law & Policy* 2 (2006): 53.

29. William H. Rehnquist, *All the Laws but One: Civil Liberties in Wartime* (New York: Knopf, 1998), 209–11.

30. Cole, *The Torture Memos*, at 36–37.

31. Stuart Taylor, "Torture: Stop Harassing the Lawyers," *National Journal* (Sept. 12, 2009); Michael Hayden & Michael B. Mukasey, "The President Ties His Own Hands on Terror," *Wall Street Journal* (Apr. 17, 2009): A13; Jack Goldsmith, "No New Torture Probes," *Washington Post* (Nov. 26, 2008): A13.

32. The acclaimed constitutional historian Charles Fairman famously defended the internment camps, albeit to his eventual discredit. Harry N. Scheiber & Jane L. Scheiber, "Bayonets in Paradise: A Half-Century Retrospect on Martial Law in Hawai'i, 1941–1946," *University of Hawaii Law Review* 19 (Fall 1997), 533–34. For Fairman's original work, see Charles Fairman, "The Law of Martial Rule and the National Emergency," *Harvard Law Review* 55 (June 1942): 1299–1302.

33. Memorandum from Jay S. Bybee, Assistant Att'y Gen., Office of Legal Counsel, to Alberto R. Gonzales, Counsel to the President, Regarding Standards of Conduct for Interrogation Under 18 U.S.C. §§ 2340-2340A (Aug. 1, 2002) [hereinafter "Bybee Memo"]; Memorandum from Jay S. Bybee, Assistant Att'y Gen., Office of Legal Counsel, to John Rizzo, Acting General Counsel, CIA, Regarding Interrogation of al Qaeda Operative (Aug. 1, 2002) [hereinafter "Rizzo Memo"].

34. Mark Danner, "U.S. Torture: Voices from the Black Sites," *New York Review of Books* (Apr. 9, 2009).

35. Daniel Kanstroom, "On 'Waterboarding': Legal Interpretation and the Continuing Struggle for Human Rights," *Boston College International & Comparative Law Review* 32 (Spring 2009): 215–16.

36. Hutchinson, "Achilles Heel," at 467–68.

37. The case of the Nazi saboteurs is *Ex parte Quirin*, 317 U.S. 1 (1942). The other two internment cases in which Jackson prepared—but did not file—opinions were *Hirabayashi* and *Ex parte Endo*.

38. *Trial of the Major War Criminals before the International Military Tribunal* 19 (Nuremberg: International Military Tribunal, 1948), 432.

39. 317 U.S. 1 (1942).

40. 320 U.S. 81 (1943).

41. Hutchinson, "Achilles Heel," at 457–76; Jack L. Goldsmith, "Justice Jackson's Unpublished Opinion in *Ex parte Quirin*," *Green Bag* (2d series) 9 (Spring 2006): 226–30.

42. *Quirin*, 317 U.S. at 27–29. For a full accounting of why the decision in *Quirin* was (and remains) controversial, see Carlos M. Vázquez, "'Not a Happy Precedent': The Story of *Ex parte Quirin*," in *Federal Courts Stories*, eds. Vicki Jackson & Judith Resnik (New York: Foundation Press, 2009), 219.

43. *Ex parte Milligan*, 71 U.S. (4 Wall.) 2 (1866).

44. Goldsmith, "Jackson's Unpublished Opinion," at 226–30.

45. *Ibid.* at 233.

46. *Ibid.* at 233–38.

47. *Ibid.* at 238.

48. *Ibid.* at 241.

49. *Quirin*, 317 U.S. at 47–48 ("[A] majority of the full Court are not agreed on the appropriate grounds for decision. Some members of the Court are of opinion that Congress did not intend the Articles of War to govern a Presidential military commission convened for the determination of questions relating to admitted enemy invaders and that the context of the Articles makes clear that they should not be construed to apply in that class of cases. Others are of the view that—even though this trial is subject to whatever provisions of the Articles of War Congress has in terms made applicable to 'commissions'—the particular Articles in question, rightly construed, do not foreclose the procedure prescribed by the President or that shown to have been employed by the Commission in a trial of offenses against the law of war and the 81st and 82nd Articles of War, by a military commission appointed by the President.").

50. 320 U.S. 115 (1943).

51. Exec. Order 9066, 7 Fed. Reg. 1407 (Feb. 19, 1942).

52. *Ibid.*

53. *Hirabayashi v. United States*, 320 U.S. 81, 83–85 (1943).

54. Under the then-extant "concurrent sentence doctrine," a valid conviction on any one count would vitiate the need to consider the validity of the other counts, since the single valid conviction justified the entire sentence. *Benton v. Maryland*, 395 U.S. 784, 787–90 (1969).

55. Hutchinson, "Achilles Heel," at 469.

56. *Ibid.*

57. *Ibid.* at 471.

58. *Ibid.* at 473–74 (footnote omitted).

59. *Ibid.* at 474 n.9.

60. *Korematsu v. United States*, 140 F.2d 289 (9th Cir. 1943).

61. *Ex parte Endo*, 323 U.S. 283, 285 (1944).

62. *Korematsu v. United States*, 323 U.S. 214, 218–19 & n.1 (1944) (citing the Final Report).

63. 71 U.S. (4 Wall.) 2 (1866).

64. 17 F. Cas. 144 (C.C.D. Md. 1861) (No. 9487).

65. Draft Opinion of Justice Jackson, *Korematsu v. United States*, No. 22, at 5 (Nov. 13, 1944). It is possible that *Merryman* was not as clear-cut as Jackson believed. For an alternative theory that would have vindicated both Taney and Lincoln, see Stephen I. Vladeck, "The *Field* Theory: Martial Law, the Suspension Power, and the Insurrection Act," *Temple Law Review* 80 (Summer 2007): 391–439.

66. Draft Opinion of Justice Jackson, *Korematsu*, at 6 (emphasis added).

67. Hutchinson, "Achilles Heel," at 480.

68. *Ibid.* at 490.

69. Gudridge, "Remember *Endo*?" at 1933–34.

70. Hutchinson, "Achilles Heel," at 484.

71. Gudridge, "Remember *Endo*?" at 1934.

72. Robert H. Jackson, "Wartime Security and Liberty under Law," *Buffalo Law Review* 55 (January 2008), 1105.

73. *Cooper v. Aaron*, 358 U.S. 1 (1958).

74. Rostow, "The Japanese-American Cases," at 491.

75. Nanette Dembitz, "Racial Discrimination and the Military Judgment: The Supreme Court's *Korematsu* and *Endo* Decisions," *Columbia Law Review* 45 (1945): 175.

76. *Duncan v. Kahanamoku*, 327 U.S. 304 (1946). The Court was less circumspect about line-crossing where the treatment of enemy soldiers was concerned, as embodied in the *Yamashita* decision earlier in 1946, upholding a conviction by an American military commission in the Philippines despite numerous procedural and substantive shortcomings that provoked angry dissents from Justices Murphy and Rutledge. *In re Yamashita*, 327 U.S. 1 (1946).

77. *Duncan*, 327 U.S. at 329 (Murphy, J., concurring).

78. American-Japanese Evacuation Claims Act, 50 U.S.C. app. §§ 1981–87 (2000).

79. Wendy Ng, *Japanese American Internment during World War II: A History and Reference Guide* (Westport: Greenwood Press, 2002), 100.

80. *Ibid.* at 105–06.

81. *Ibid.* at 106–07.

82. Emergency Detention Act of 1950, Pub. L. No. 81-31, ch. 1024, tit. II, 64 Stat. 987, 1019–31 (1950) (repealed 1971).

83. Stephen I. Vladeck, "The Detention Power," *Yale Law and Policy Review* 22 (Winter 2004): 176–80.

84. *Ibid.*

85. 18 U.S.C. § 4001(a) (2000). Ironically, this provision would be at the heart of the post-September 11 lawsuits brought by the two U.S. citizens detained as "enemy combatants." *Hamdi v. Rumsfeld*, 542 U.S. 507 (2004); *Padilla v. Rumsfeld*, 352 F.3d 695 (2d Cir. 2003).

86. Proclamation No. 4417 (Feb. 19, 1976), 41 FED. REG. 7741 (Feb. 20, 1976).

87. *Ibid.*

88. *Personal Justice Denied: Report of the Commission on Wartime Relocation and Internment of Civilians* (Washington: CWRIC, 1982). The report is also accessible online at http://www.nps.gov/history/history/online_books/personal_justice_denied/index.htm.

89. *Ibid.*

90. 50 U.S.C. app. §§ 1989–1989d (2000).

91. Ng, *Japanese American Internment during World War II*, at 109.

92. Kang, "Denying Prejudice," at 976–77.

93. *Ibid.* at 977–78.

94. *Ibid.* at 978–79.

95. Eric L. Muller, "*Hirabayashi*: The Biggest Lie of the Greatest Generation," unpublished working paper, Aug. 18, 2008, http://papers.ssrn.com/sol3/papers. cfm?abstract_id=1233682.

96. For a recent discussion, see *United States* v. *Denedo*, 129 S. Ct. 2213, 2220–21 (2009).

97. *Korematsu* v. *United States*, 584 F. Supp. 1406 (N.D. Cal. 1984).

98. *Yasui* v. *United States*, 772 F.2d 1496 (9th Cir. 1985) (discussing the district court's unpublished order).

99. *Hirabayashi* v. *United States*, 627 F. Supp. 1445 (W.D. Wash. 1986).

100. *Hirabayashi* v. *United States*, 828 F.2d 591 (9th Cir. 1987).

101. Kang, "Denying Prejudice," at 985–95.

102. For proof, consider the varying opinions penned in *Adarand Constructors, Inc.* v. *Pena*, 515 U.S. 200 (1995), in which virtually all the justices criticized *Korematsu*, and the majority applied strict scrutiny even to a federal statute that created a benefit for historically disadvantaged racial minorities.

103. Apparently, the Bush Administration even floated the idea of formally suspending habeas corpus, only to be rebuffed by Rep. James Sensenbrenner, then the Republican chair of the House Judiciary Committee. For more, see Amanda Tyler, "Suspension as a Political Question," *Stanford Law Review* 59 (November 2006): 347 & n.80.

104. For a summary of the roundup, see *Ashcroft* v. *Iqbal*, 129 S. Ct. 1937, 1943 (2009).

105. *Ibid.*

106. 18 U.S.C. § 3144 (2000). The Second Circuit upheld this practice in *Awadallah* v. *United States*, 349 F.3d 42 (2d Cir. 2003).

107. *Padilla* v. *Rumsfeld*, 352 F.3d 695 (2d Cir. 2003); *al-Marri* v. *Pucciarelli*, 534 F.3d 213 (4th Cir. 2008) (en banc). The government also detained U.S. citizen Yaser Hamdi within the United States, even though he was initially detained in Afghanistan. In his case too, the Non-Detention Act played a central role. *Hamdi* v. *Rumsfeld*, 542 U.S. 507, 517–24 (2004) (plurality).

108. *al-Kidd* v. *Ashcroft*, 580 F.3d 949, 954–55 & n.5 (9th Cir. 2009).

109. Elbert Lin, "*Korematsu* Continued . . .," *Yale Law Journal* 112 (May 2003): 1911–18.

110. *Padilla ex rel. Newman* v. *Rumsfeld*, 243 F. Supp. 2d 42, 57 (S.D.N.Y. 2003) (citations omitted).

111. *Boumediene* v. *Bush*, 128 S. Ct. 2229, 2277 (2008).

112. On the torture issue alone, three important examples include Mark Danner, *Torture and Truth: America, Abu Ghraib, and the War on Terror* (New York: New York Review of Books, 2004); Philippe Sands, *Torture Team: Rumsfeld's Memo and the Betrayal of American*

Values (New York: Palgrave Macmillan, 2008); and Jane Mayer, *The Dark Side: The Inside Story of How the War on Terror Turned into a War on American Ideals* (New York: Doubleday, 2008). For an insider's perspective, consider Jack Goldsmith, *The Terror Presidency: Law and Judgment inside the Bush Administration* (New York: W. W. Norton, 2007).

113. For exemplar works, see Harold H. Bruff, *Bad Advice: Bush's Lawyers in the War on Terror* (Lawrence: University Press of Kansas, 2009); David Luban, "The Torture Lawyers of Washington," in *Legal Ethics and Human Dignity* (New York: Cambridge University Press, 2007), 162–205; Peter Margulies, "True Believers at Law: National Security Agendas, the Regulation of Lawyers, and the Separation of Powers," *University of Maryland Law Review* 68 (2008): 1–88; and Kathleen Clark, "Ethical Issues Raised by the OLC Torture Memorandum," *Journal of National Security Law & Policy* 1 (Winter 2005): 455–72.

114. Cole, *The Torture Memos*, at 38–40.

115. The two memos filed on August 1, 2002, are cited in full in note 33, and are reprinted in Cole, *The Torture Memos*, at 41–127.

116. The full timeline is recounted in a narrative prepared by Senator John D. Rockefeller IV, Chairman of the Select Committee on Intelligence, and reprinted in Cole, *The Torture Memos*, at 277–91.

117. Cole, *The Torture Memos*, at 37–38 & n.67.

118. *Ibid.* at 20.

119. Bruff, *Bad Advice*, at 239–47.

120. *Ibid.*

121. Cole, *The Torture Memos*, at 11.

122. Randolph D. Moss, "Executive Branch Legal Interpretation: A Perspective from the Office of Legal Counsel," *Administrative Law Review* 52 (Fall 2000): 1308–09.

123. For more on this argument, see George C. Harris, "The Rule of Law and the War on Terror: The Professional Responsibilities of Executive Branch Lawyers in the Wake of 9/11," *Journal of National Security Law & Policy* 1 (Winter 2005): 450–53.

124. *Korematsu* v. *United States*, 323 U.S. 214, 246 (1944) (Jackson, J., dissenting).

125. Thus, for example, some in Congress have introduced legislation to require that OLC at least report to certain congressional committees when it adopts an opinion concluding that the executive branch is not bound by particular acts of Congress. See, for example, the OLC Reporting Act of 2009, H.R. 278, 111th Cong. (2009).

126. Memorandum from Stephen G. Bradbury to Files Re: Status of Certain OLC Opinions Issued in the Aftermath of the Terrorist Attacks of September 11, 2001 (Jan. 15, 2009), at 1.

127. *Ibid.*

128. *Padilla* v. *Yoo*, 633 F. Supp. 2d 1005 (N.D. Cal. 2009) (denying, in relevant part, Yoo's motion to dismiss).

129. In light of the Supreme Court's decision in *Ashcroft* v. *Iqbal*, 129 S. Ct. 1937 (2009), it seems unlikely that Padilla's claims will survive summary judgment absent the production of evidence that far more directly links Yoo's memo to Padilla's alleged mistreatment. And in any event, the Court's decision in *Pearson* v. *Callahan*, 129 S. Ct. 808 (2009), would allow the district court to dismiss on the basis of qualified immunity *without* first holding that Yoo was in fact responsible for the violation of Padilla's rights.

130. For three important examples (among many others), consider *Arar* v. *Ashcroft*, 585 F.3d 559 (2d Cir.2009) (en banc) (affirming the dismissal of a lawsuit brought by an

innocent victim of the government's "extraordinary rendition" program); *Rasul* v. *Myers*, 563 F.3d 527 (D.C. Cir. 2009) (affirming the dismissal of a lawsuit brought by former Guantánamo detainees claiming that they were tortured); *El-Masri* v. *United States*, 479 F.3d 296 (4th Cir. 2007) (holding that the "State Secrets privilege" bars consideration of a lawsuit brought by an innocent victim of "extraordinary rendition"). As this essay went to print, a federal district judge in Washington also threw out a civil suit arising out of the suspicious deaths of several inmates at Guantánamo. *Al-Zahrani* v. *Rumsfeld*, 684 F. Supp. 2d 103 (D.D.C. 2010).

131. Cole, *The Torture Memos*, at 39.

132. *Ibid.* at 40.

133. 22 U.S.C. §§ 7421–7433 (2006). In particular, § 7427 provides "authority to free members of the armed forces of the United States . . . detained or imprisoned by or on behalf of the International Criminal Court."

134. Thus, in 2009 the Supreme Court held that the Due Process Clause required an elected state judge to recuse himself from a lawsuit in which one of the parties had been a major donor to that judge's recent campaign culminating in his election. *Caperton* v. *A.T. Massey Coal Co.*, 129 S. Ct. 2252 (2009). Noting that codes of ethical conduct "serve to maintain the integrity of the judiciary and the rule of law," *ibid.* at 2266, Justice Kennedy went on to explain that "[c]ourts, in our system, elaborate principles of law in the course of resolving disputes. The power and the prerogative of a court to perform this function rest, in the end, upon the respect accorded to its judgments. The citizen's respect for judgments depends in turn upon the issuing court's absolute probity. Judicial integrity is, in consequence, a state interest of the highest order." *Ibid.* at 2266–67 (internal quotation marks omitted).

About the Contributors

CLAIRE FINKELSTEIN is the Algernon Biddle Professor of Law and Professor of Philosophy at the University of Pennsylvania.

LISA HAJJAR is Associate Professor in the Law and Society Program at the University of California, Santa Barbara.

DANIEL HERWITZ is Director of the Institute for the Humanities and Mary Fair Croushore Professor of Humanities at the University of Michigan.

STEPHEN HOLMES is Walter E. Meyer Professor of Law at NYU School of Law.

PAUL HORWITZ is Associate Professor at the University of Alabama School of Law.

NASSER HUSSAIN is Associate Professor of Law, Jurisprudence, and Social Thought at Amherst College.

AUSTIN SARAT is William Nelson Cromwell Professor of Jurisprudence and Political Science at Amherst College.

STEPHEN I. VLADECK is Professor of Law, American University Washington College of Law.

Index

prosecution for abuse of detainees, 143; interrogation abuses by, investigation of, 4; Iraqi nuclear program, 8; Italian UJ prosecutions of CIA operators, 106–107, 112; OLC liability for encouraging interrogators to commit torture, 40–41, 49–51, 55, 62; OLC torture memo (August 1, 2002) ("Bybee memorandum"), 102, 131–132, 202–203

Cisneros, Henry, 2

Civil Liberties Act (1988), 186, 197

Clinton, Bill, 96, 161–162, 163, 171

Clinton, Hillary, 9

cobwebs, 121

CODESA (Coalition for a Democratic South Africa), 72–73

cognizable lawbreaking, 124

Cohen, William, 2

Cole, David, 202, 206

Comey, James B., 7

Commission on Wartime Relocation and Internment of Civilians (CWRIC), 197, 199

"common knowledge of rationality," 46

conspiracy law, 62–63

Constitutional Dictatorship (Rossiter), 14–15

Convention against Torture. *See* CAT

Convention on the Elimination of Racial Discrimination (1965), 93

Cooper v. Aaron, 194

Corn, David, 8

costs of settlement associated with: prosecution of Bush Administration officials, 171, 174, 177; rule of law, 164–165, 173; transitional justice, 166–167, 171

Council of Europe, 106

Council of the European Union, 100

"Counter Resistance Techniques" (Haynes), 10–11

Cox, Larry, 31n23

crimes against humanity: Guantánamo and, 69; universal jurisdiction and, 91–92

"criminalization of politics," 187–188

Crocker, Chester, 79

CWRIC (Commission on Wartime Relocation and Internment of Civilians), 197, 199

De Klerk, W. F., 72

De Souza, Sabrina, 106

Defiance Campaign, 79

Dembitz, Nanette, 195

democracy, 159–164, 170–173; as "controlled revolutionary activity," 159–160, 163–164, 170, 173; executive power and, 48; as a form of rule of law, 155, 156–164; meaning, 157; as a means of achieving rule of law, 162, 163–164, 171; need for a stable political culture, 164; as nonideal theory, 157; rule of law in stable democracies, 28, 155, 170–173; violations of publicity condition in, 47

Democratic Republic of Congo v. Belgium, 99–100

Dershowitz, Alan, 140–141

detention cases: following 9/11, 200–201, 210n22; individualized and judicial determinations in, 201

DeWitt, John L., 191, 196, 197, 199

Dicey, Albert Venn, 13

disbarment, 142

DOD. *See* U. S. Department of Defense

Dodge, Simon, 8

DOJ. *See* U. S. Justice Department

domestic surveillance: emergency surveillance without a warrant, 7; by NSA, 5–7; President's Surveillance Program (PSP), 6; retroactive immunization from liability for unwarranted domestic surveillance, 7; Terrorist Surveillance Program (TSP), 5–6; unauthorized, 5–7; warrants, need for, 5

Dunant, Henry, 90

Duncan v. Kahanamoku, 195

Edwards, John, 9

Eisenhower Administration, 110

EITs. *See* enhanced interrogation techniques

El-Masri, Khaled, 106–107

Elster, Jon, 169

Emerson, Ralph Waldo, 80–81

Endo, Mitsuye, 192

England, Lynndie, 126

international law: American courts as interpreters and enforcers of, 110–111, 208; American exceptionalism, 18–19; American liberalism and, 18; American public's attitudes about, 111–112; domestic law and, 18; *Filartiga v. Péna,* 101; rule of law and, 17–19; supremacy of domestic over, 48; torture as peremptory norm, 95; universal jurisdiction and, 91–92; willingness of foreign courts to seek accountability, 19

International Military Tribunal, 38

international tribunals and courts, 96, 97

interrogations/interrogators: after-the-fact get-out-of-jail-free cards for CIA interrogators, 132; culpability of, denial of, 42, 43, 49–51, 58; deaths during detention, 127; designers of Bush administration interrogation policy, 127–128; as illegal but nevertheless justified practices, 58–60; immunization from prosecution for abuse of detainees, 143; secrecy about interrogation policies, 55–57; techniques used, 50; torture memo (August 1, 2002) ("Bybee memorandum"), 43–45, 48, 49–51, 58, 66n18, 102, 131–133, 202–203; Yoo's torture memo (March 14, 2003), 11

Introduction to the Study of the Law of the Constitution (Dicey), 13

Iran, 70

Iraq War: authorization for, 136–137; falsification of case for, 7–9; humanitarianism, damage to, 70; Iraqi nuclear program, 8–9; settler culture and, 82–83; yellowcake uranium, 9

Irons, Peter, 185, 197–198, 205

Isikoff, Michael, 8

Italy, 106–107, 112

Jackson, Robert H.: *Endo* decision, 194; in *Hirabayashi v. United States,* 191–193; *Korematsu v. United States,* dissent in, 28, 29, 184–186, 188–189, 191–194, 200, 203, 208; legalization of abuses in the name of necessity, 185; at Nuremburg trials, 29, 31n23, 91–92; on prosecutorial discretion, 13; rule of law and government

abuses, 185, 206; tripartite scheme of presidential powers, 15–16

Japanese internment camps: ascertaining evidence without pursuing individual liability, 105; closing of, 194; defender of, 210n32; *Ex parte Endo,* 194, 210n24; Executive Order 9066, 196–197; individual liability for, lack of calls for, 199; Justice Department and, 187, 198; lessons from, 206–207; memory of, creation of, 189, 195–201; military necessity as justification for, 197; redress movement, 196–197; reparations for, 195–196; rule of law and, 188, 190–194; Supreme Court decisions, 183–184; writes of error *coram nobis,* 198; wrongfulness of, acceptance of, 187. See also *Korematsu v. United States*

Jeppesen Dataplan, 105

Joint Personal Recovery Agency (JPRA), 10

Kabila, Laurent, 99

Kaleck, Wolfgang, 87, 105

Kang, Jerry, 199

Keck, Margaret, 90

Kennedy, Anthony, 201, 215n134

Kerry, John, 9

Khmer Rouge, 65n5

King, Martin Luther, Jr., 79

Kissinger, Henry, 107

Kitchener, Horatio Herbert, 82

Koh, Harold, 15

Korematsu, Fred, 183, 192, 196, 198

Korematsu v. United States: Black's opinion, Hugo, 183–184; companion case, 210n24; constitutionality of Japanese internment camps, 28–29; damage inflicted on rule of law, 186–187, 200, 207; discrediting/condemnation of, 186–187; factual basis, undermining of, 197; influence of, 201; Jackson's dissent, Robert, 28, 29, 184–186, 188–189, 191–194, 200, 203, 208; majority opinion, 188, 199–200, 207; memory of, 200–201; military necessity argument, 199–201; Murphy and, Frank, 184; Roberts and, Owen, 184; Rostow on, Eugene, 195; surviving aspect of, 209n16

Rumsfeld, Donald: "gloves off" approach to intelligence gathering, 10; impunity for lawbreaking by, 138; indictment of, 87, 107–108; interrogation policy designed by, 127; NATO headquarters, threat to relocate, 100; political activism against, 149; retirement life, 153

Rutledge, Wiley Blount, Jr., 193, 212n76

Saddam Hussein: 9/11 attacks and, 137; al-Qaida and, 7, 8, 137; bin Laden and, Osama, 144; weapons of mass destruction, 7, 137

Salah v. Titan/CCI, 118n63

Sands, Phillipe, 11

Savage, Beth, 75–76

Scalia, Antonin, 12

Scarry, Elaine, 2–3, 10, 20

Schumer, Chuck, 9

Second Treatise (Locke), 14

Senate Armed Services Committee, 10, 69, 111–112

Senate Intelligence Committee, 8

Sensenbrenner, James, 213n103

SERE (Survival Evasion Resistance and Escape), 10

Shapiro, Ian, 156

Sharon, Ariel, 100

Shklar, Judith, 155–156

Sikkink, Kathryn, 90

Silberman, Lawrence, 142

Sissulu, Walter, 79

South Africa: Boer War (1899-1902), 82; Interim Constitution (1994), 72–73; United States compared to, 78–80. See also Truth and Reconciliation Commission

sovereign immunity, 129

Spain, 100, 108–109, 119n75, 167

Spanish Supreme Court, 108–109

state secrets doctrine: immunity from prosecution and, 148; Obama Administration and, 139, 143–144

Stimson, Henry L., 199

Stofberg, Koos, 80

Stone, Harlan Fiske, 190

subsidiarity principle, 108, 109

Swift, Jonathan, 128, 133

Taft, William, 133

Taguba, Antonio, 87

Taliban: Geneva Conventions and, 129–130; as "unlawful enemy combatants," 53, 56, 61–62

Tamanaha, Brian, 156

Taney, Roger, 15, 194

Teitel, Ruti, 19

Tenet, George, 138

Terror Presidency, The (Goldsmith), 133–134, 145–146

Terrorist Surveillance Program (TSP), 5–7

Theory of Justice, A (Rawls), 45–46

Tocqueville, Alexis de, 1

torture: 18 U.S.C. §§ 2340-2340A (U.S. torture statute), 49, 52, 128, 132; in 2008 presidential primaries, 103–104; at Abu Ghraib, 58; al-Qaida claims of, 134; by America compared to less powerful nations, 103; CAT on, 10; criminal liability for, 93–94, 101; custodial relationship between parties, 94; definition, 94, 188; in exceptional circumstances, 10; Filartiga v. Péna, 101; gaps in chain of custody, 148; grievousness of, 94; as just deserts for terror, 112; Justice Department complicity in, 135; lawyers as accomplices to crime of, 49–51; legal professionals and, 105, 119n65; nonderogability of, 94–95; Obama and, Barack, 54, 104; OLC liability for encouraging interrogators to commit torture, 40–41, 49–51, 55, 62; OLC torture memo (August 1, 2002) ("Bybee memorandum"), 11, 38, 43–45, 48, 49–51, 58, 66n18, 102, 131–133, 202–203; OLC torture memo (March 14, 2003), 11; as peremptory norm of international law, 95; popular perception that it works, 112; prosecution of Bush Administration officials for use of, 9–12; public opinion about justifiability of, 144; public rather than personal harm, 94; rule of law and, 201–202; Salah v. Titan/CCI, 118n63; universal jurisdiction and, 88, 93–95; witnesses, disappearance of, 148

Torture Convention. See CAT